The early Spenser, 1554–80

Manchester University Press

The Manchester Spenser

The Manchester Spenser is a monograph and text series devoted to historical and textual approaches to Edmund Spenser – to his life, times, places, works and contemporaries.

A growing body of work in Spenser and Renaissance studies, fresh with confidence and curiosity and based on solid historical research, is being written in response to a general sense that our ability to interpret texts is becoming limited without the excavation of further knowledge. So the importance of research in nearby disciplines is quickly being recognised, and interest renewed: history, archaeology, religious or theological history, book history, translation, lexicography, commentary and glossary – these require treatment for and by students of Spenser.

The Manchester Spenser, to feed, foster and build on these refreshed attitudes, aims to publish reference tools, critical, historical, biographical and archaeological monographs on or related to Spenser, from several disciplines, and to publish editions of primary sources and classroom texts of a more wide-ranging scope.

The Manchester Spenser consists of work with stamina, high standards of scholarship and research, adroit handling of evidence, rigour of argument, exposition and documentation.

The series will encourage and assist research into, and develop the readership of, one of the richest and most complex writers of the early modern period.

General Editors Joshua Reid, Kathryn Walls and Tamsin Badcoe
Editorial Board Sukanta Chaudhuri, Helen Cooper, Thomas Herron, J.B. Lethbridge, James Nohrnberg and Brian Vickers

Also available
Literary and visual Ralegh Christopher M. Armitage (ed.)
The art of The Faerie Queene Richard Danson Brown
A concordance to the rhymes of The Faerie Queene Richard Danson Brown and J.B. Lethbridge
A Supplement of the Faery Queene: By Ralph Knevet Christopher Burlinson and Andrew Zurcher (eds)
A Companion to Pastoral Poetry of the English Renaissance Sukanta Chaudhuri
Pastoral poetry of the English Renaissance: An anthology Sukanta Chaudhuri (ed.)
Spenserian allegory and Elizabethan biblical exegesis: A context for The Faerie Queene Margaret Christian
Monsters and the poetic imagination in The Faerie Queene: 'Most ugly shapes and horrible aspects' Maik Goth
Celebrating Mutabilitie: Essays on Edmund Spenser's Mutabilitie Cantos Jane Grogan (ed.)
Spenserian satire: A tradition of indirection Rachel E. Hile
Castles and colonists: An archaeology of Elizabethan Ireland Eric Klingelhofer
Shakespeare and Spenser: Attractive opposites J.B. Lethbridge (ed.)
Dublin: Renaissance city of literature Kathleen Miller and Crawford Gribben (eds)
A Fig for Fortune by Anthony Copley: A Catholic response to The Faerie Queene Susannah Brietz Monta
Spenser and Virgil: The pastoral poems Syrithe Pugh
The Burley manuscript Peter Redford (ed.)
Renaissance psychologies: Spenser and Shakespeare Robert Lanier Reid
European erotic romance: Philhellene Protestantism, Renaissance translation and English literary politics Victor Skretkowicz
Rereading Chaucer and Spenser: Dan Geffrey with the New Poete Rachel Stenner, Tamsin Badcoe and Gareth Griffith (eds)
God's only daughter: Spenser's Una as the invisible Church Kathryn Walls
William Shakespeare and John Donne: Stages of the soul in early modern English poetry Angelika Zirker

The early Spenser, 1554–80
'Minde on honour fixed'

JEAN R. BRINK

Manchester University Press

Copyright © Jean R. Brink 2019

The right of Jean R. Brink to be identified as the author of this work has been asserted by her in accordance with the Copyright, Designs and Patents Act 1988.

Published by Manchester University Press
Altrincham Street, Manchester M1 7JA
www.manchesteruniversitypress.co.uk

British Library Cataloguing-in-Publication Data
A catalogue record for this book is available from the British Library

ISBN 978 1 5261 4258 0 hardback
ISBN 978 1 5261 5178 0 paperback

First published 2019

The publisher has no responsibility for the persistence or accuracy of URLs for any external or third-party internet websites referred to in this book, and does not guarantee that any content on such websites is, or will remain, accurate or appropriate.

Typeset
by Toppan Best-set Premedia Limited

In memory of Daniel Theodore Brink
26 May 1940 – 17 October 1997

Contents

	Acknowledgements	*page* viii
	Abbreviations and textual explanations	xi
	Introduction	1
1	Lineage and the 'Nowell Account Book'	7
2	Spenser's education and Merchant Taylors' School	31
3	Pembroke College (1569–74)	49
4	'Southerne shepheardes boye' (1574–79)	70
5	Gabriel Harvey and Immerito (1569–78)	88
6	'Minde on honour fixed': Spenser, Sidney, and the early modern chivalric code	110
7	*Aprill* and *November*	133
8	Puzzling identities: From E.K. to Roffy's 'boye' to Rosalind	153
9	*Familiar Letters* (1580)	170
10	Ireland and the preferment of Edmund Spenser (1580)	198
	Conclusion	208
	Bibliography of works cited	215
	Index	231

Acknowledgements

When I first began to consider the need for a life of Spenser, I thought that the project should be undertaken by a historian and tried to recruit Norman Jones. Norm told me that I had to do it and promised his assistance. I studied the secretary hand with Anthony G. Petti, and Norm has patiently answered my questions over where to look for things and how archives are organized. He also very graciously read the very first draft of this manuscript. I also owe much to my colleague and friend Andrew Hadfield because his 2012 biography has replaced Judson (1945) as the standard life of Spenser and has made it possible for me to focus more narrowly on Spenser's early life and try to make sense of the facts we have – while pointing out the gaps in our knowledge. My thanks also to Richard McCabe, whose dependable and painstaking edition of Spenser's shorter poems made my work much, much easier. For Robert and Peter Brink, thanks for computer tips and for functioning as my non-specialist, but educated, general readers.

Resident scholars at the Huntington are fortunate in having administrators who understand scholarship and create an atmosphere that it is humbling to experience: Thanks to Alan Jutzi, Sue Hodson, Mary Robertson, Laura Stalker, David Zeidberg. To Stephen Tabor, I owe special thanks for his assistance in sorting out numerous bibliographical problems and my gratitude to these and other Huntington staff for their friendship. Let me conclude by expressing my appreciation for the financial support received at crucial times from the National Endowment for the Humanities, Arizona State University, and the American Philosophical Society.

Acknowledgements

I am fortunate in having experienced extraordinary collegiality from those in my field. I go way back with Steven May, whom I met at the Huntington. He and Bill Ringler put me in touch with Peter Beal. Peter has taught me a great deal. It was embarrassing to me when my university asked Barbara Lewalski to act as my outside reviewer for tenure and promotion and offered her no honorarium. How many senior scholars would be generous enough to read, not just articles in print, but an unpublished manuscript, for no honorarium? Barbara Lewalski, who did not even know me at the time, did that. Early on, I was encouraged by William Barker who shared with me his computerized transcription of *Familiar Letters*. In the field of Neo-Latin my debts are legion because, even if I can parse the words, my translations from Latin are tentative and uninspired. Dana Sutton has been immensely cordial. If there is anyone who is unfamiliar with the Philological Museum, google it immediately and browse the many Neo-Latin translations available thanks to Dana. John Mulryan was helpful to me by adding verve to my pedestrian translations in Chapter 5. My thanks as well to Thomas Herron for his conviviality and consistent encouragement.

As for the Spenserians who have been teaching me, charming me, and unmercifully teasing me for years, I could never list them all. Just as an example, when I questioned Spenser's authorship of the *View of the Present State of Ireland*, my apostasy led to a Porlock session at Kalamazoo where it was agreed that no one should ever accept a printed version of my curriculum vitae because only a holograph could be considered authentic. At another session, I received a pin saying, 'Somewhere your high-school guidance counsellor is laughing'. I have always envied George Chapman his ability to channel those who have gone before us: Homer and Marlowe both spoke to Chapman. I would like to channel Spenser, Thomas Nashe, and Gabriel Harvey, and have them all on my team when I face whatever next awaits me from my Spenserian colleagues.

I cannot list you all and so I will concentrate on those whom I know best: my helpful critic, Judith Anderson; my perceptive reader, Roger Kuin; my dear comrade, Anne Prescott; my source on intellectual history, Rob Stillman. I also want to mention the late Victor Stretkowicz, who shared my passion for bibliography. I am still thinking about Tom Roche's comment to me: isn't anyone who reads a literary text a literary critic? Among those critics and friends who have been especially helpful in completing this project are Wayne Erickson, Norman Jones, Mary Ellen Lamb, Julian Lethbridge, William Oram, and Josh Reid. I can assure all and sundry that anything incorrect, unclear, or just plain wrong is not the fault of Bill Oram. His detailed commentary has only made this book better.

Last, but not least, I acknowledge my best critic and strongest supporter, Dan Brink, to whom this book is dedicated.

Abbreviations and textual explanations

Harvey

There is no modern edition that contains all of Harvey's works.

Harvey, *Works*, ed. Grosart
 Works of Gabriel Harvey, ed. Alexander Grosart, 3 vols, Huth Library (London; Hazell, Watson & Viney, Ltd, 1884–85). This poorly annotated edition only selectively discusses the Latin works, but at present is the most comprehensive edition.

Familiar Letters
 Three Proper and wittie, familiar Letters: lately passed betwene two Universitie men: touching the Earthquake in Aprill last, and our English refourmed Versifying. With the Preface of a wellwiller to them both. Two Other very commendable Letters of the same mens writing: both touching the foresaid Artificiall Versifying, and certain other Particulars: More lately delivered unto the Printer (London: H. Bynnneman, 1580). RB 69544. The Huntington Library, San Marino, CA. EEBO reproduces this text. This copy is missing F2–F3.

Foure Letters
 Foure Letters, and certaine sonnets; especially touching Robert Greene, and other parties by him abused (London: John Wolfe, 1592). RB 61305. The Huntington Library, San Marino, CA.

Gratulationes Valdinenses
 Gabrielis Harueij Gratulationum Valdinensium Libri Quatuor (Londini: Henrici Binnemani, 1578). RB 59268. The Huntington Library, San Marino, CA.

Letter-Book
  The Letter-Book of Gabriel Harvey, A.D. 1573–1580, edited from the original ms. Sloane 93 in the British Library, ed. Edward John Long Scott, Camden Society New Series, 33 (Westminster: Nichols and Sons, 1884). Text cited throughout this study. Scott's edition is a worthy transcription of Sloane 93, but he does simplify cross-outs and cross-overs.

Marginalia
  Gabriel Harvey's Marginalia, collected and edited by G.C. Moore Smith (Stratford-upon-Avon: Shakespeare Head Press, 1913).

Progresses
  This new edition of John Nichols's *The Progresses and Public Processions of Queen Elizabeth I: A New Edition of the Early Modern Sources*, ed. Elizabeth Goldring, Faith Eales, Elizabeth Clarke, and Jayne Elisabeth Archer, 5 vols (Oxford: Oxford University Press, 2014) includes a complete translation as well as annotated text of *Gratulationes Valdinenses*. The Latin text is reprinted from RB 59268 at the Huntington Library, San Marino, CA, which was used in preparing this study. I continue to use my translations, but, for the reader's convenience, I cite the pagination of *Progresses* for *Gratulationes Valdinenses*.

Smithus
  Gabrielis Harueii Valdinatis: Smithus; vel Musarum Lachrymae. (Londini: Henrici Binnemani, 1578). RB 35263. The Huntington Library, San Marino, CA.

Stern, *Harvey*
  Stern, Virginia, *Gabriel Harvey: His Life, Marginalia, and Library* (Oxford: Clarendon Press, 1979).

Nashe

Nashe, *Works*
  The Works of Thomas Nashe, ed. Ronald B. McKerrow and corrected and supplemented by F.P. Wilson (Oxford: Blackwell, 1958). All citations are from this edition.

ODNB

Oxford Dictionary of National Biography, ed. H.C.G. Matthew and Brian Harrison, 60 vols (Oxford, 2004). I have updated my citations from the 2004 printed edition to the 2008 version cited online as per September 2018.

Sidney

Sidney, *Correspondence*
Sidney, Sir Philip. *The Correspondence of Sir Philip Sidney*, ed. Roger Kuin, 2 vols (Oxford: Oxford University Press, 2012).
Sidney, *Life*
Duncan-Jones, Katherine, *Sir Philip Sidney, Courtier Poet* (New Haven: Yale University Press, 1991).
Sidney, *Miscellaneous Prose*
Miscellaneous Prose of Sir Philip Sidney, ed. Katherine Duncan-Jones and Jan Van Dorsten (Oxford: Clarendon Press, 1973).

Spenser

Grosart, *Life*
The Complete Works of Verse and Prose of Edmund Spenser, edited with a New Life, ed. Rev. Alexander Grosart, 9 vols (London and Aylesbury: Hazell, Watson, and Viney, Ltd, 1882–84). Volume 1 contains Grosart's biography.
Hadfield, *Life*
Hadfield, Andrew, *Edmund Spenser, A Life* (Oxford: Oxford University Press, 2012). Replaces Judson as the standard biography for Spenser's life.
Judson, *Life*
Judson, Alexander Corbin. *The Life of Edmund Spenser* (Baltimore: Johns Hopkins University Press, 1945).
Knowles, *HMC*
Fourth Report of the Royal Commission of Historical Manuscripts, ed. R.B. Knowles, (London: George Edward Eyre and William Spottiswoode, 1874).
Nowell Account Book
Manchester, Chetham's Library, MS A.6.50. 'Accounts of the Executors of Robert Nowell', Attorney of the Queen's Court of Wards.
Spenser Encyclopedia
Spenser Encyclopedia, ed. A.C. Hamilton. General Editor; Donald Cheney, Senior Co-Editor; W.F. Blissett, Co-Editor; David A. Richardson, Managing Editor; William W. Barker, Research Editor (Toronto: Toronto University Press, 1990).
Spenser, *Faerie Queene*
The Faerie Queene, ed. A.C. Hamilton. Text edited by Hiroshi Yamashita and Toshiyuki Suzuki (London: Longman, 2001).

Spenser, *Shorter Poems*, ed. McCabe
 The Shorter Poems, ed. Richard A. McCabe (London: Penguin Books, 1999). This excellent and painstaking edition is used throughout to cite Spenser's shorter works.

Spenser, *View*
 W.L. Renwick, *A View of the Present State of Ireland* (1934; Oxford: Clarendon Press, 1979). This widely available text is used for citations, but I also reference the *Spenser Variorum* edition. There is no authoritative edition of the *View* because five new manuscripts were discovered after the preparation of *Spenser's Prose Works*, vol. 10, ed. Rudolf Gottfried, in *Works of Edmund Spenser: A Variorum Edition*, ed. Edwin Greenlaw, Charles Grosvenor Osgood, Frederick Morgan Padelford, Ray Heffner, 11 vols (Baltimore: Johns Hopkins University Press, 1932–45).

Townley Hall MSS, ed. Grosart
 The Townley Hall MSS. The Spending of the Money of Robert Nowell of Reade Hall, Lancashire: Brother of Dean Alexander Nowell. 1568–1580, ed. Alexander Grosart (Manchester: Charles E. Simms, 1877). A transcription of 'Accounts of the Executors of Robert Nowell' Manchester, Chetham's Library, MS A.6.50.

Introduction

Edmund Spenser (1554–99) and Sir Philip Sidney (1554–86) are regarded as the two most important sixteenth-century non-dramatic writers. Among English Renaissance writers, there is a remarkable symmetry of birth dates; Spenser and Sidney were born exactly ten years before Shakespeare and Marlowe (1564) and eighteen years before Donne and Jonson (1572).[1] Except for Sidney, who died in his early thirties, all of these writers might well have met each other in sixteenth-century London, a city estimated to have a population of two hundred thousand. In writing Spenser's epitaph, William Camden, the principal chronicler of Elizabeth's reign, said that he had surpassed Chaucer and that he was the greatest poet of his age, *anglicorum poetarum nostri seculi facile princeps*.[2] Since his death in 1599, Spenser's popularity has waxed and waned with the taste for narrative poetry or allegory, but the judgement of his contemporaries has endured: Spenser has earned a place in the literary canon.[3]

In *Edmund Spenser, A Life* (2012), Andrew Hadfield perceptively comments that Spenser is 'regarded as less familiar and knowable than his contemporaries, even when their life records are as sketchy as his'.[4] Hadfield concludes: 'We are presented with a fundamental dilemma: either take what appears in the literary works as evidence of the poet's life or abandon any quest for that life and declare that it is unwritable' (12). Like many who have patiently awaited an archival discovery, the veritable smoking gun that will make all clear about a sixteenth-century figure, I have grappled with the challenge implicit in Andrew Hadfield's statement and come to recognize its good sense. Among the many virtues of

Hadfield's own biographical contribution, *Edmund Spenser, A Life* (2012), is his success in establishing the broad contexts in which Spenser's life was lived. I view my work as complementary to Hadfield's because I have focused more narrowly on Spenser's early life in a study that, I hope, will raise almost as many questions as it answers.

Once it is agreed that Spenser's works are a source of biographical information, then we face the questions: when, where, and to what degree? To address these questions, let us re-examine three seminal examples of autobiographical allusions in Spenserian texts, only one of which has influenced Spenser's received biography. Differentiating fact from fiction when it comes to an author's autobiographical references is always challenging – but particularly so when we reconstruct the lives of early modern figures. When Irenius says that he witnessed an Irish woman drinking blood at the execution of Murrough O'Brien, can we then place Spenser in Ireland as early as 1577 or is the 'I' Irenius uses entirely a fictional construct?

> And so have I seen some of the Irish do but not their enemies' but friends' blood, as namely at the execution of a notable traitor at Limerick called Murrogh O'Brien, I saw an old woman which was his foster mother took up his head while he was quartered and sucked up all the blood running there out, saying that the earth was not worthy to drink it, and therewith also steeped her face and breast, and tore her hair, crying and shrieking out most terribly. (Renwick, 62; *Spenser Variorum*, pp. 112–13, ll. 1935–42)[5]

If Spenser witnessed this execution, then he was in Munster on 1 July 1577 when O'Brien was beheaded by the order of Sir William Drury, President of Munster. To place Spenser in Ireland in 1577 would make the issue of acquaintanceship with the Sidneys relatively moot.

If this autobiographical reference, occurring in a number of manuscripts, were to be confirmed, it would have a stunning impact on our understanding of Spenser's early life and might reshape the narrative leading Spenser to Ireland. It would then be logical to consider the possibility that Spenser accompanied Philip to Ireland when he visited his father in 1576. It would seem likely that he, like Lodowick Bryskett, became Sir Henry's servant and would fully explain Irenius's description of witnessing O'Brien's execution in 1577. In late 1579, when Sir Henry realized that he would not be appointed Lord Lieutenant of Ireland with Philip as his Deputy, it would be plausible that he recommended Spenser to Grey. This scenario may not have enough external evidence to be entirely persuasive, but it is not implausible. Some biographical issues can be clarified if we recognize that we are dealing not with a dichotomy between fact and fiction but with a continuum extending from the 'possible' to the 'probable' to the 'likely' to the 'certain'. Perhaps there is insufficient evidence to make a certain, or even a likely, case that Spenser was in Ireland in 1576, when Philip visited his father, or in 1577, when O'Brien was executed, but neither of these supposed visits is improbable.

Two other seemingly autobiographical allusions concern Spenser's visits to the court and meetings with the Queen. In my reading of *Aprill* and *November* in Chapter 7, I raise only in passing the issue of when Spenser first met the Queen. In the *November* eclogue of the *Shepheardes Calender*, however, there is the suggestion that Spenser was introduced to the court, presumably by Philip Sidney, prior to going to Ireland in 1579–80. We are told that Dido-Elissa, whom, following John Watkins, and others, I understand to figure as Queen Elizabeth, did not disdain Colin Clout:[6]

> So well she couth the shepherds entertayne,
> With cakes and cracknells and such country chere.
> Ne would she scorne the simple shepheards swaine,
>   For she would cal hem often heme
> And giue hem curds and clouted Creame.
>   O heauie herse,
> Als *Colin cloute* she would not once disdayne.
>   O carefull verse.
>
>   (95–102)[7]

There is at least the suggestion that Colin Clout had encountered the Queen in line 101 above.

According to the received biography, Spenser was introduced to the Queen and court in 1590 by Sir Walter Ralegh and, on this occasion, Spenser read his works to the court. The evidence is found in the following lines from *Colin Clouts Come Home Againe*:

> The shepheard of the Ocean (quoth he)
> Vnto that Goddesse grace me first enhanced,
> And to mine oaten pipe enclin'd her eare,
> That she thenceforth therein gan take delight,
> And it desir'd at timely houres to heare
>
>   (358–62)

We cannot document that Spenser *ever* met Queen Elizabeth except for autobiographical passages in his poetry. Why is one autobiographical allusion treated as fact and the other ignored? One explanation may be that it has become an accepted tenet in Spenserian criticism that Spenser and Sidney never met. It seems consistent, as well as reasonable, to keep both autobiographical allusions, one from the *November* eclogue and the other from *Colin Clouts Come Home Againe*, in mind when we try to place Spenser in 1579–80 and in 1589–90.

When Spenser entered Pembroke College in 1569, it is likely that his benefactors expected him to take holy orders. It cannot be proved that Spenser seriously considered a career in the church, but in the sixteenth century a young man without property and family connections had few options other than the church or the army. That Spenser considered a career in the church is also suggested by his staying on at Pembroke to obtain the M.A. degree. J.A. Venn, who compiled the biographical records on Cambridge graduates, stated that the 'odds are almost ten to one that a man who had proceeded to the M.A. degree either had taken, or eventually did take, holy orders'.[8] Spenser completed the B.A. in the spring of 1573, but decided to stay on for the M.A. References to Spenser in the Pembroke College Account Books conclude in 1574. We do not know where he went or what happened next, but I will make the case in Chapter 4, 'Southerne shepheardes boye', that from 1574 to 1578 Spenser was probably in London working for John Young, Master of Pembroke and then Bishop of Rochester in 1578.

There is no solid evidence of why or how Spenser moved from service under Bishop Young to the patronage of Arthur Lord Grey of Wilton. At some point between 1578 and 1579, Spenser exchanged the role of shepherd-priest for that of shepherd-poet.[9] The *Shepheardes Calender* records this vocational shift as well as functioning as a landmark work of English literature.[10] In Chapter 6, 'Minde on honour fixed', I marshal whatever circumstantial evidence exists to suggest that Spenser knew and was influenced by the Sidneys, who introduced him to the early modern chivalric code. Under their influence, he came to perceive himself as the bard who would sing the epic story of Elizabethan England. Like Philip Sidney, Spenser preferred the knightly service of fighting for Dutch independence or the chivalric adventure of Ireland to the Elizabethan court.

Although I agree with Hadfield's surmise that Spenser's 'real desire was for a literary career' rather than a career in the church (111), it seems probable that Spenser thought that he could combine the two, much as John Hall, George Herbert, and Robert Herrick did. In terms of documentary records, we know very little, but the little we do know points to his connections with London clergymen. Spenser's name, for example, does not appear in the admission records of Merchant Taylors' School.

As I discuss in Chapter 1, 'Lineage and the "Nowell Account Book"', we know that he attended this school only because he was the recipient of grants from the estate of Robert Nowell, Attorney of the Queen's Court of Wards. Once we acknowledge that gaps such as these exist, further research on Spenser's lineage may assist us in more fully understanding the formative years of Edmund Spenser.[11]

One of the principal contributions of this study of the early Spenser is that I distinguish Edmund Spenser from Gabriel Harvey. In *Familiar Letters*, Spenser is portrayed as Harvey's admiring disciple, but this portrait of Spenser was Harvey's invention.[12] Harvey's magisterial tone has fuelled speculation that he was Spenser's tutor, but he cannot have been. Spenser matriculated at Pembroke in 1569 and graduated in 1573. Fellows did not instruct undergraduates until after they had earned the M.A. and become regents. As I discuss in Chapter 3, 'Pembroke College', Harvey's M.A. was not awarded until 1573, the very year that Spenser graduated with the B.A.

To differentiate Harvey from Spenser, in Chapter 5, 'Gabriel Harvey and Immerito (1569–78)', I supply the first close reading of Harvey's *Gratulationes Valdinenses* (1578), a work which Harvey intended to serve as his *Shepheardes Calender*. In Chapter 9, '*Familiar Letters* (1580)', I show that Spenser had already received preferment prior to the publication of *Familiar Letters* and suggest that Harvey orchestrated this academic publication to obtain the position of University Orator. Spenser's whereabouts at the time are uncertain, but he was probably already in Ireland by the time that the letters were printed. In response to *Familiar Letters*, the Latin play *Pedantius* (1581) was produced at Cambridge, and its authors pick up phrases from Harvey's published works, such as *Gratulationes Valdinenses*, and so anticipate Nashe's satiric thrusts at Harvey.

In any biography, particularly of a figure about whom as little is known as Spenser, unproved assumptions are made that shape how evidence is presented. These assumptions derive from circumstantial evidence, not facts. This study is no exception, and it may be useful to make these hypotheses very clear. I question that Spenser aspired to be what Karl Marx described as 'Elizabeth's arse-kissing poet'. That does not mean that I think he lacked ambition; far from it. Spenser took seriously the prospect of writing the Renaissance epic; I, however, assume that Spenser, much like Philip Sidney, was ambivalent about the court. In this regard, he was unlike Gabriel Harvey, Lodowick Bryskett, and Sir Walter Ralegh. The early Spenser had literary aspirations, but it is far from clear that he harboured the ambition to figure as a court poet.

Notes

1 Christopher Marlowe (1564–93) and William Shakespeare (1564–1616) and eighteen years before John Donne (1572–1631) and Ben Jonson (1572–1637).
2 William Camden, *Tomus alter idem: or, The historie of the life and reigne of that famous princess, Elizabeth* ... Trans. Thomas Browne, fourth part of Camden's *Annales rerum ... covering the years 1589–1603* (London: Printed by Tho. Harper for William Web, 1629). RB 600237. The Huntington Library, San Marino, CA.
3 One of the best bibliographical sources is the on-line Edmund Spenser World Bibliography supervised by Donald Stump, St Louis University; it includes everything relevant in *Spenser Newsletter*, *Spenser Review*, and the *MLA International Bibliography* from 1972 to 2009 (http://bibs.slu.edu/Spenser). See, also, Thomas Herron, 'Complex Spenser: New Directions in Recent Research', *Renaissance Quarterly*, 68, No. 3 (Fall 2015), 957–69; Willy Maley, 'Bibliography: Spenser and Ireland', *Spenser Studies* 9 (1991), 227–42; J.B. Lethbridge, ed., *Edmund Spenser: New and Renewed Directions* (Madison and Teaneck: Fairleigh Dickinson University Press, 2006). For a database on Spenser's influence, see Spenser and the Tradition: English Poetry, 1579–1830, ed. David Hill Radcliffe (http://Spenserians.cath.vt.edu).
4 Hadfield, *Life*, 12.
5 Spenser, ed. W.L. Renwick, *A View of the Present State of Ireland* (1934, Scholartis Press; Oxford: Clarendon Press, 1979), 62. Most manuscripts contain blank spaces immediately following this section. See, also, Spenser, *View*, pp. 112–13, ll. 1935–42; *Spenser's Prose works*, vol. 10, ed. Rudolf Gottfried in *Works of Edmund Spenser: A Variorum Edition*, ed. Edwin Greenlaw, Charles Grosvenor Osgood, Frederick Morgan Padelford, Ray Heffner, 11 vols (Baltimore: Johns Hopkins University Press, 1932–45).
6 John Watkins, *The Specter of Dido: Spenser and Virgilian Epic* (New Haven: Yale University Press, 1995), 79–82.
7 Spenser, *Shorter Poems*, ed. McCabe, November, 95–103.
8 *Alumni Cantabrigienses: A Biographical List of All Known Students, Graduates and Holders of Office at the University of Cambridge from the Earliest Times to 1900*, compiled by John Venn and J.A. Venn (Cambridge: Cambridge University Press, 1922), 1: xiv.
9 For Spenser's attitude toward the church, see Jeffrey Knapp, 'Spenser the Priest', *Representations*, 81 (2003), 61–78. On the political and religious context, see David Norbrook, *Poetry and Politics in the English Renaissance* (1984; rev. ed. Oxford: Oxford University Press, 2002).
10 On vocation, see seminal studies by David L. Miller, 'Spenser's Vocation, Spenser's Career', *English Literary History*, 50 (1983), 197–231; Richard Helgerson, *Self-Crowned Laureates: Spenser, Jonson, Milton, and the Literary System* (Berkeley: Universityof California Press, 1983); Patrick Cheney, *Spenser's Famous Flight: A Renaissance Idea of a Literary Career* (Toronto: University of Toronto Press, 1993).
11 For what is needed, see Mark Eccles, 'Elizabethan Edmund Spensers', *Modern Language Quarterly*, 5 (1944), 413–27.
12 The short title, *Familiar Letters*, refers to the Harvey–Spenser correspondence. Both John Lyly and Thomas Nashe describe this correspondence as 'Familiar Epistles'. For the bibliographical rationale, see Chapter 5, note 5.

1

Lineage and the 'Nowell Account Book'

Edmund Spenser's contemporaries celebrated him as the greatest non-dramatic poet of his age. His schoolmasters identified him as a brilliant student, and it was this intellectual distinction that financed his education. If he had chosen a career in the church, he could have aspired to, and perhaps achieved, the status of an Elizabethan bishop, as did several of his academic peers at Merchant Taylors' School and Cambridge. Spenser's lineage is not identified in documentary records, and his family is not mentioned in the literary tributes offered by his fellow poets. This silence suggests that his parentage was undistinguished and possibly unknown. Although, late in his career, he advertised kinship ties with the wealthy Spencers of Althorp, the relationship, if it existed, was so remote that Spenser had to make his own way. He was a 'new' man in an age that was suspicious of 'self-made' men.

It is not surprising that Spenser would be self-conscious about his humble origins. William Cecil, Lord Burghley, the most powerful political official in England, was so troubled by charges that he was an upstart that he worked and reworked his family tree. Edmund Spenser, however, was one of the few early modern cultural figures – perhaps the only one – who advertised the insignificance of his social background. When Spenser introduced himself to the literary world in the *Shepheardes Calender* (1579), he signed himself 'Immerito' and described himself as 'unkent', an unknown, in contrast to Sir Philip Sidney, the dedicatee, who is identified as the 'president / [o]f noblesse and chevalree':

> Goe little booke: thy selfe present
> As child whose parent is unkent:
> To him that is the president
> Of noblesse and chevalree.
> ('To His Booke', 1–4)[1]

Spenser also calls himself 'Colin Clout', a literary identity he was to retain throughout his career. The name 'Colin Clout' is borrowed from a poem by John Skelton, but Spenser's contemporaries would have associated the surname 'Clout' with the soil, e.g., as in 'clod' of dirt. Clout was memorably used by John Foxe in his *Book of Martyrs* to describe a collection of rags. Spenser's lowly 'Colin Clout' with hints of dirt and rags contrasts to the pseudonym 'Astrophil', or star lover, the neo-Platonic literary name adopted by Philip Sidney. Philip's godfather was Philip of Spain, and at the time of Philip Sidney's birth King Philip was the husband of the Queen of England, Mary Tudor. Sidney's mother was descended from the powerful Dudley family. Spenser, though now linked to Sidney in literary assessments of the age, did not in the sixteenth century belong to his social class.

Spenser's society valued gentility and lineage and revered those who came from old families whose rank and property spanned generations. Sumptuary laws ensured that people of the lower classes would not dress above their station; they were forbidden by law to wear the fine cloth reserved for the gentry. Social status, however, was not a prerequisite for literary achievement. William Shakespeare was not an exception among Elizabethan writers. Few aspiring poets could claim the status of a Sidney or belonged to the elite. Samuel Daniel and Michael Drayton, both non-dramatic poets who had laureate ambitions, offer useful comparisons and contrasts with Sidney and Spenser. Samuel Daniel, though not by birth a member of the political and social elite, was educated as though he were. Daniel, the son of a music teacher, was educated at Magdalen Hall, Oxford. He was employed by the English ambassador in Paris before visiting Italy. After his return, he was employed as tutor to the son of the Countess of Pembroke, Mary Sidney Herbert. Daniel's pupil, William Herbert, the future Earl of Pembroke, was himself a poet and was one of the dedicatees of Shakespeare's First Folio. Daniel also tutored Lady Anne Clifford at Skipton Castle in Yorkshire; Lady Anne concluded her life as the Dowager Countess of Dorset, Pembroke, and Montgomery. Daniel is notable because he was the only Elizabethan poet who received a court appointment, a position awarded after James I came to the throne.

Michael Drayton, who, like Spenser and Daniel, aspired to laureate status, was less socially respectable than Samuel Daniel. Drayton started his life as a servant in the household of Thomas Goodere, the younger brother of Sir Henry Goodere of Polesworth.[2] Drayton fictionalizes a genteel youth at Polesworth where he enjoyed the attention of a tutor, but at best he was a visitor to Polesworth. He later joined the household of Sir Walter Aston as a servant. Yet, far from emphasizing his humble background, Drayton selected as his literary pen-name, 'Rowland' or 'Roland', the name of the hero of Ariosto's *Orlando Furioso* and an epithet suggesting the old French *chanson de geste*. Drayton's Rowland celebrates his neo-Platonic mistress, 'Idea', echoing Samuel Daniel's praise of 'Delia', an anagram for Ideal. Both Daniel and Drayton began their careers by imitating Sidney's neo-Platonism. They celebrate 'Delia' and 'Idea' just as Sidney immortalized Astrophil's dark-eyed 'Stella' (star lover's star). In contrast to Sidney, Daniel and Drayton, Spenser selects the humble name Colin Clout for his literary persona. This selection, when contextualized, is more than a conventional gesture of self-deprecation; it is telling evidence that, whatever feelings he may have had about his social origins, Spenser will feature, not disguise, his lowly status.

Less is known about Edmund Spenser than about William Shakespeare; we know the names of Shakespeare's parents and his father's occupation. From references in Spenser's poems, we can infer that he grew up in London and that Elizabeth was his mother's first name. In *Amoretti* 74 he alludes to his three 'Elizabeths' and identifies them as his wife-to-be, Elizabeth Boyle; his mother; and his queen. Spenser's name does not appear in the admission records of the Merchant Taylors' School. His father's name was not recorded when he enrolled at Pembroke College, Cambridge. We have no concrete evidence of his social class. It is possible that he was illegitimate; in this period to be born outside of wedlock did not carry the same stigma that it was to have in the nineteenth-century villages of Thomas Hardy. In sixteenth-century England, it was possible to be illegitimate and still achieve elite status. Thomas Egerton, later Lord Ellesmere and finally the Earl of Bridgewater, was the illegitimate son of a country squire. Spenser, like Ben Jonson, may have had a complex family background. Jonson was the son of a university-educated clergyman, but his mother's second husband was a bricklayer. Spenser was a sizar at Cambridge, and so he did not derive from an affluent family. Because of uncertainty about Spenser's family background and the absence of a likely documentary record, his birth date has remained conjectural.

Birth date and matriculation at Cambridge

Spenser's date of birth has been estimated to have been '1552 (?)'.[3] However, there is evidence that Spenser, like two of his illustrious contemporaries, Philip Sidney and Walter Ralegh, was born in 1554.[4] Spenser matriculated at Pembroke College, Cambridge, on 20 May 1569. In using his matriculation date to calculate his age, we need to take account of the latest estimates of the age of university matriculation. Recent scholarship has revised early twentieth-century estimates of when young men entered a university. We also need to take account of Spenser's exceptional academic promise, which will be discussed at length below. Early scholarship on Spenser seems to have assumed that sixteenth-century students, like their modern counterparts, matriculated at age seventeen or eighteen. W.L. Renwick, for example, estimated the 'normal age' of matriculation as seventeen. He said: 'If he was of the normal age when he matriculated in May, 1569, then he was born about 1552–3'.[5] By the time that Ruth Mohl wrote the article on Spenser's life for the *Spenser Encyclopedia* (1990), the traditional age of matriculation had been revised to sixteen: 'He may have been born in 1552 or 1553 if he was the usual age of sixteen when he matriculated at Cambridge on 20 May 1569'.[6] Studies of the university now generalize that students matriculated at age fifteen, with more precocious students entering as early as fourteen.[7]

Philip Sidney, acknowledged by his contemporaries as exceptional, matriculated at fourteen at Christ Church, Oxford. In 1569, Richard Hooker matriculated at Corpus Christi, Oxford, at age fifteen. Thomas Lodge, who entered Merchant Taylors' School in 1571, after Spenser had left for Cambridge, spent only a couple of years there. He matriculated at Trinity College, Oxford, at age fifteen. George Peele and Thomas Nashe, whose birth dates are less certain, seem also to have entered their respective universities at age fifteen. William Camden was born in 1551, and, in spite of a bout with the plague, he matriculated at Oxford in 1566 at age fifteen. Comparison with these contemporaries, supplemented by recent research on the universities, suggests that Spenser would have been fifteen years old when he entered Pembroke College in 1569. His birth date would then be 1554.

Spenser's fortieth birthday and *Amoretti* 60

The notion that Spenser was born in 1552 seems to have developed out of reconstructions of how old he may have been when he composed certain sonnets in his sonnet sequence, the *Amoretti*, which was published with the *Epithalamion* but not until 1595. In *Amoretti* 60, the poet twice describes himself as 'fourty'. He would then have been born in 1554, as Spenser's age of matriculation at Cambridge suggests:

> So since the winged God his planet cleare
> began in me to moue, one yeare is spent:
> the which doth longer vnto me appeare,
> then al those fourty which my life outwent.
> Then by that count, which louers books inuent,
> the spheare of Cupid fourty yeares containes:
> which I haue wasted in long languishment,
> that seemd the longer for my greater paines.
> But let my loues fayre Planet short her wayes
> this yeare ensuing, or else short my dayes.
>
> (p. 417: 5–14)

Most reference works have been influenced by the inferences of Alexander Judson, who somewhat confusingly, concludes that Spenser was forty-two when he wrote that he was forty:

> In his *Amoretti* Spenser remarks that the one year he has been courting his mistress seems longer than all the forty of his previous life. The manuscript of *Amoretti* was dispatched to the publisher in the autumn of 1594, and sonnet LX, in which occurs the reference to his tedious year of courting, was very likely written late in 1593. If the round number forty is to be taken literally, then Spenser was probably born in 1552. But we cannot be certain.[8]

Judson's conclusions were drawn fifteen years prior to the seminal numerological work of A. Kent Hieatt (1960) and thirty-three years before Carol Kaske's important numerological and liturgical analysis of the structure of the *Amoretti* and *Epithalamion* (1978).[9] These and other studies show that numerology and time are central to the meaning of these poems, and underscore the importance of the precise date of Spenser's marriage on 11 June 1594, St Barnabas's day (*Epithalamion*, l. 266). Given what we know to be the importance of numerology to his wedding date, the 'fourty' of *Amoretti* 60 should be reckoned from the date 1594 – not from a hypothetical date of composition.[10]

Biographers of Spenser: Judson (1945), Grosart (1882–84), Hadfield (2012)

We have no documentary evidence concerning Spenser's parentage. No records identify his father's name, and so we do not know what occupation he had. From the 'Nowell Account Book' discussed below, we know that Spenser attended Merchant Taylors' School, but his name does not appear in the admission records. On the basis of his having attended Merchant Taylors' School, the Reverend Alexander Grosart guessed that his father was a merchant tailor, and so constructs Spenser as the son of a middle-class tradesman. Alexander Judson takes literally Spenser's allusions to his Spencer patrons and elaborates his kinship ties with the wealthy Spencers of Althorp. Andrew Hadfield records and reconciles both of these hypotheses concerning Spenser's lineage: Grosart's middle-class tradesman background and the aristocratic connections emphasized by Judson.[11]

The biographies of Grosart and Judson remain the foundation for the accounts of Spenser included in all standard reference works, ranging from school books, such as the Norton and Oxford Anthologies, to the Oxford Dictionary of National Biography, Spenser Encyclopedia, and Oxford Handbook of Edmund Spenser. Neither Judson nor Grosart offers an entirely accurate account of his birth and life records, and, even when the facts are presented, they are inaccurately contextualized. Printed in a limited edition, Grosart's biography is available only in research libraries with strong Renaissance collections, and so the factual bases for his various claims about Spenser have not been critically evaluated.[12] Because it was published with the Spenser Variorum (1932–57), Judson's biography is far more accessible and so, until Hadfield (2012), functioned as the standard life of Spenser.

Judson's methodology is deliberately impressionistic because his aim is to create an atmosphere for experiencing Spenser's verse. Instead of directly addressing his predecessor, Grosart's, work, he fails to list Grosart's biography in his bibliography. A professor at Indiana University, Judson wrote his biography while in residence at the Henry E. Huntington Library, San Marino, CA, and so had easy access to Grosart's biography. His omission of Grosart was a deliberate choice.[13] Even when Judson is faced with a very important biographical assertion, e.g., that Spenser's father was a journeyman tailor, Judson neither repeats the argument nor sifts the evidence: 'It is sometimes conjectured that he was the son of a certain John Spenser, a 'free journeyman' in the 'art of mystery of cloth-working' known to have been connected with the Merchant Taylors' Company of London in 1566' (8).[14] Judson correctly cites R.B. Knowles as the source for this conjecture but fails to indicate that he later retracted this identification.

Both Judson and Grosart dwell on narrative fictions in Spenser's poetry and interpret these fictions as historical fact. If Colin Clout had an unrequited love affair, then Spenser, too, was disappointed in love. Grosart and Judson illustrate varying ways in which personality and contemporary conventions may lead a biographer or critic to put a particular spin on Spenser's life, but they are identical in one respect. Both of these influential biographies fill in blank spaces in the narrative, and it is this persistent 'filling in' that has kept us from recognizing important empty spaces, such as Spenser's actual parentage. By underscoring this blank space and other such blank spaces, it is hoped that this biography will be suggestive for future scholarship and prompt the discovery of an entry that will solve the mystery of Spenser's birth and parentage.

The aristocratic Spenser

Judson begins his account of Spenser's life with a description of the very affluent Spencers of Althorp. His first sentence states that 'on June 29, 1552, there was born to Sir John and Lady Katherine Spencer, of Wormleighton and Althorp, their third daughter, whom they named Elizabeth' (1). Judson repeats Spenser's literary allusion to kinship with the Spencers of Althorp, treats it as fact, and then devotes his entire first chapter to a description of this wealthy sixteenth-century family.[15] We, however, are not told that Ed. Spencer might refer to the Edward Spencer born into this very family.

Elizabethan kinship claims, however, need to be carefully contextualized. Spenser had the same surname as the Spencers of Althorp. Sharing a common surname might be understood to indicate kinship, and so Spenser's kinship claim could be a gesture politely offered by an author seeking patronage and accepted by his patrons in the same spirit. On far fewer grounds than a surname, King James acknowledged a kinship tie with the antiquary Sir Robert Cotton. This kinship claim was based on Cotton's first and middle names, Robert Bruce. These names were understood to be a reference to James's ancestor, the Scottish hero Robert Bruce, and so the king recognized the antiquary as his kinsman.

Because Judson's 'well-connected' Spenser derives from allusions in Spenser's dedications and verse, we need to consider in detail the timing and precise wording of these references. It is significant that we hear nothing about kinship ties to the Spencers of Althorp when Spenser entered the university and was trying to finance his education at Cambridge. We hear of the aristocratic connection only after the publication of the *Faerie Queene* (1590). In the *Complaints* (1591) he first alludes to his kinship connections with the Spencers, the sisters who also function as dedicatees to this volume. He reiterates these kinship claims in *Colin Clouts Come Home Again* (1595), where he also deprecates his own status:

> Ne lesse praisworthie are the sisters three,
> The honor of the noble familie:
> Of which I meanest boast my selfe to be,
> And most that vnto them I am so nie.
>
> (536–9)

In *Prothalamion*, published the following year, he identifies London as his 'natiue sourse' and says that his name derives from a 'house of ancient fame'.

> At length they all to mery *London* came,
> To mery London, my most kyndly Nurse,
> That to me gaue this Lifes first natiue sourse:
> Though from another place I take my name,
> An house of aunciant fame.
>
> (127–31)

He alludes to London as his 'kyndly Nurse', and ambiguously comments that another 'place' is the source of his name but does not state that his blood as well as his name derives from the house of Spencer.

As Spenser and his readers were aware, the Spencers of Althorp were not a 'house of aunciant fame'; they were wealthy sheep farmers, who belonged to the gentry, not to the nobility. Nevertheless, the Spenser family was extremely prosperous, so richly endowed that in 1595 the College of Arms obligingly invented a pedigree for them. Their descent was traced to the Despencers, Earls of Gloucester and Winchester. King James included the head of the house in his broad distribution of honours, creating Sir Robert Spencer, Baron Spencer of Wormleighton in 1603. In 1596 the Spencer family had fortune but no title. Even the title awarded in the seventeenth century did not satisfy the old nobility that the Spencers of Althorp were 'a house of aunciant fame'. When the title was almost a generation old, during a 1621 debate in the House of Lords, Lord Arundel sneered at Spencer that his ancestors were herding sheep when the Arundels were serving king and country.[16] Contemporary gossip has it that Lord Spencer replied with a pointed allusion to the Arundels' repeated attainders for treason.

Ironically, in the 1590s, when Edmund Spenser was enhancing his pedigree by claiming kinship with the Spencers, the Spencers were working hard to enhance their own merely genteel status by arranging upwardly mobile marriages for their daughters. The one contemporary who takes special notice of the kinship claim between the poet and the Spencers very slyly pokes fun at the social aspirations of the Althorp Spencers. In his *Apologie* (1596), Sir John Harington observes that Sir John Spencer has not followed the court. This was a sore point among the elite because fortunes were lost at court but made by those who stayed in the country. Harington describes the Spencer sisters as 'well favored, well featured, well statured, for plaine country wenches' and scoffs at the vast sums spent to provide them with handsome dowries.[17]

Each of Spenser's 'sisters three, / The honor of the noble familie' (*Colin Clouts Come Home Againe*, 536–7) married above her station. Elizabeth Spencer (the only female dedicatee to the *Faerie Queene* other than the Countess of Pembroke) first married Sir George Carey, Elizabeth's kinsman, who succeeded as second Lord Hunsdon in July 1596, and then Ralph, third Lord Eure. Anne Spencer married three times: William Stanley, Lord Monteagle; Henry, Lord Compton; and finally, Robert Sackville, heir to Lord Buckhurst and later second Earl of Dorset. Alice Spencer made the most brilliant match of all, marrying Ferdinando Stanley, Lord Strange, heir to the Earl of Derby. Alice is Amaryllis and Derby is the dead Amyntas in Spenser's *Colin Clouts Come Home Againe* (1595). Alice's spouse, a Protestant, was by lineage a native-born Derby, and he could boast a claim to the throne of England. Ferdinando's death on 16 April 1594 was a great blow to those who supported a Stanley claimant as a possible successor to Elizabeth. Alice Spencer Stanley next married Sir Thomas Egerton, a gifted lawyer (and illegitimate) who became Lord Chancellor. This marriage had the side benefit of allowing her to press suits regarding the disposition of the Derby estate without undo expense; Alice, however, continued to use the title 'Countess of Derby' even after her marriage to Egerton.

Harington's comments are laden with irony. This is not a straightforward confirmation that Edmund Spenser was related to the Spencers of Althorp. An important conclusion to be drawn from Harington's comments is that he is intent on disparaging the Spencers. Since he describes the Spencer sisters as 'plaine country wenches' (229), his reference to the honour of the Spencer name is ironic. He appears to suggest that Spenser brings more honour to the name Spenser than the Althorp Spencers: 'you have a learned writer of your name, make much of him, for it is not the least honour of your honorable familie' (230). We should note in passing that Harington does not precisely echo Spenser's claim of kinship; he says, 'you have a learned writer of your name' – not house or blood. He compliments the poet, not the patrons.

In addition to promoting an aristocratic Spenser, Judson assumes that Spenser's verse is autobiographical. He is comfortable with this assumption because he is intent on supplying his readers with a romantic sense of Spenser's time and place. After summarizing the seventeenth-century tradition that Spenser was born in East Smithfield, he comments: 'It is pleasant to turn from these conjectures to the more certain evidence of Spenser's own verse. His boyhood seems to have been free, happy, zestful' (9).[18] Judson finds evidence that Spenser had an 'unrepressed, joyous youth' in the *December* eclogue of the *Shepheardes Calender*:

> Of course, we need not assume that we have in this fearless, madcap boy racing through the woods, gathering nuts for Christmas, hunting the young buck and the hare, or climbing an oak to drive a raven from her nest a literal picture of the young Spenser, but the spirit, the temper of his boyhood, as here depicted we need not question. Liberty, enthusiasm, joy, these must all have characterized his early years. (10)

Judson's fanciful picture depicts the youthful Spenser as a character in one of Wordsworth's poems even though the tone of the *December* eclogue of the *Shepheardes Calender* is unreservedly mournful and bleak.

Middle-class Spenser

The genteel Spenser with his aristocratic connections is ignored in late twentieth-century and early twenty-first-century reference works. Post-Second World War critics have favoured the middle-class Spenser constructed by the Reverend Alexander Grosart.[19] Grosart should be credited with many of the factual discoveries regarding Spenser's life, but we need to recognize that he has an unsettling way of supplying exquisitely detailed arguments to support questionable assumptions. For example, he uses the spelling of the family name 'Spenser' (as opposed to Spencer) to argue that Spenser's family originated in Lancashire. Grosart was an experienced archivist, and, unquestionably, would have known that precise distinctions in spelling, such as the differentiation of 's' and 'c' in Spencer, do not occur in sixteenth-century documents. Spelling was not standardized, and the poet's name is spelled with a 'c' as well as an 's' in virtually all contemporary records.[20]

In addition to using the spelling of Spenser's name to make this case, Grosart also points to a reference to 'your shier' in a letter in his friend Gabriel Harvey's *Letter-Book* as geographical evidence that Spenser had relatives in the Pendle Hill district of Lancashire (xii–xiii). As Grosart tells the tale, Spenser was allowed to attend Merchant Taylors' School 'among the first of its pupils' because his father was associated with the City Company of the Merchant Taylors (xxxiii). Though Hadfield is sceptical about Grosart's identification of Spenser's father as a specific tradesman and thinks that his literary identity was 'rooted in both the city and the country', he comments: 'a key element was undoubtedly an identity established at a school in London for the "middling sort"' (Hadfield, *Life*, 24–5).

Grosart's argument regarding Spenser's lineage is based on R.B. Knowles's identification of John Spencer, journeyman tailor, as Edmund's father. Knowles later changed his mind and rescinded what he himself describes as at best a 'conjecture':

> Since writing my report I have gone through the whole of Colonel Towneley's Spenser Manuscript ['Nowell Account Book', discussed below], and I have found reason to doubt the conjecture that John Spenser the 'free jorneyman' of Merchant Taylors', was the father of Edmund Spenser. That conjecture is subject to the drawback that John Spenser, afterwards President of Corpus Christi College, Oxford, ... was at Merchant Taylors' at the same time as Edmund. His Christian name would give him a stronger claim to be the son of the 'free jorneyman' than the poet's.[21]

Knowles is correct. Since we do not know Spenser's father's first name, any identification of a putative father rests only on conjecture.

Grosart bolsters his identification of a particular John Spencer as Edmund's father by ruling out another John Spencer. He argues that, if Edmund's father were rich and related to the Lord Mayor (another John Spencer), then the poet would not have received scholarship support. Having settled on the journeyman John Spencer as Edmund's father, Grosart merely dismisses the problem that there was a contemporary John Spencer, also a student at Merchant Taylors' School and more likely to have been the son of the journeyman John Spencer. To make his identification work, Grosart speculates that Knowles's John Spencer was also the journeyman's son and so putatively Edmund's younger brother (xxxviii). No one seems to have accepted this part of the claim, but Grosart's argument concerning Spenser's lineage has been repeated so frequently in major reference works that it is now almost accepted as fact.

Immerito's 'unkent' lineage

After the publication of Judson's standard biography, the assumption seems to have been made that everything that could be known about Spenser's early life had been reported, but, now that we are computerizing our archives, there is every likelihood that new records will be discovered. There is no reason to salvage either an aristocratic or a middle-class Spenser. Some puzzles, such as Spenser's precise lineage, are best left unresolved until we are sure that we have sufficient evidence to draw satisfactory conclusions. In 1944, shortly after tentatively identifying one of the few life records that we have for Edmund Spenser, Mark Eccles published his compilation of data identifying the various Elizabethan Edmund Spensers and Spencers.[22] Eccles's lists are by no means complete: we need to add to his data and finish the task of tracing the likely lineage of the poet.

Even Spenser's place of birth is uncertain because, when Spenser tells us that London was his 'kyndly Nurse', that may mean only that London is where he grew up. Spenser could have been brought to London as a very young child or merely decided that it was his spiritual home. Filling in these blanks by reiterating antiquarian speculation may be reassuring in the short run, but in the long run it may discourage further research on Spensers or Spencers born in London, or Northamptonshire, or elsewhere in the year 1554.

'Nowell Account Book'

Since Spenser's name does not appear in the extant admission records of Merchant Taylors' School, we know that he was a student at Merchant Taylors' School only because of entries in a sixteenth-century account book now entitled 'Accounts of the Executors of Robert Nowell' (Manchester, Chetham's Library, MS A.6.50; hereafter, 'Nowell Account Book').[23] This manuscript account book records disbursements of funds to students, teachers, and even university professors financed by the estate of Robert Nowell, Attorney of the Queen's Court of Wards, and brother of Alexander Nowell, Dean of St Paul's.[24] While still in the possession of the descendants of John Towneley, half-brother to Robert Nowell, the manuscript was loaned to Alexander Grosart, who transcribed and printed it in an edition of only 100 copies under the title *The Towneley Hall MSS. The Spending of the Money of Robert Nowell of Reade Hall, Lancashire: Brother of Dean Alexander Nowell, 1568–1580.* (Hereafter, Grosart, *Towneley Hall MSS*).[25] This manuscript is the most important documentary source for Spenser's early life, and a physical description of the manuscript is useful for its interpretation.

The 'Nowell Account Book' is a paper manuscript now made up of 118 leaves in addition to two fly sheets on modern paper.[26] The manuscript has been paged and foliated and contains blank leaves and pages; it is not at present chronological. For example, on 30 January 1578, Peter Barrow, Lady Margaret Professor of Divinity, received 10s (Grosart, *Towneley Hall MSS*, 62); an earlier grant to Barrow of 20s, dated 10 January 1575 appears later in the manuscript (106). Not every entry is dated, and Grosart seems to have transcribed the manuscript as it was without trying to reconstruct a logical chronology. The work is foliated in ink (pre-1850); the blank leaves are also foliated. Grosart does not include these blank pages in his foliation, even though they are numbered in his pagination.[27] It is useful to note that, in the Appendix to the *Fourth Report* of the Historical Manuscript Commission, R.B. Knowles has the following comments on the 'Nowell Account Book':

> An interesting manuscript on 177 leaves of paper, folio, some missing at the beginning, middle, and end, in the handwriting of the 16th century and containing the payments of executors of Robert Nowell of Gray's Inn for his funeral expenses, payment of debts and legacies, gifts to the poor, &c.[28]

Knowles's description indicates that approximately 59 leaves, over a third of the account book, may have been separated from the original manuscript at some point before or during the transfer from the Towneley collection to Chetham's Library. These leaves may well be extant under another title and may cast more light on Spenser and other beneficiaries of Nowell's estate.

The 'Nowell Account Book' demonstrates that there was a network of clergymen and teachers who promoted the academic careers of promising students and that Edmund Spenser was one of the beneficiaries of their patronage. We have substantive evidence that Spenser's most important early patrons were the clergymen who, like Alexander Nowell and Edmund Grindal, held examinations for London schoolboys in regularly scheduled visitations. These ecclesiastical authorities took a keen interest in grammar schools and used their visitations to examine pupils, assess the quality of instruction, and identify gifted pupils, such as Edmund Spenser.

Surviving records illustrate both the examination process and the potential for establishing connections between churchmen and promising students. We have the record of a visitation on Friday, 16 August 1562 at Merchant Taylors' School; the visitation does not mention Spenser by name, but it occurred while he was enrolled at Merchant Taylors' School and included examiners who were later connected with Spenser's life or his verse.[29] The examination was conducted by a distinguished group of churchmen and scholars: David Whitehead; John Calfhill, Canon of Christ Church; Thomas Watts, Archdeacon of Middlesex; and, particularly important, Archbishop Edmund Grindal, later portrayed sympathetically as Algrind in Spenser's *Shepheardes Calender*. The participation of Thomas Watts is also significant because, after his death, his widow Grace married Spenser's 'Roffy', i.e., John Young, former Master of Pembroke, Bishop of Rochester, and an important employer of Spenser.

These men evaluated the ushers whom Mulcaster had selected and then examined the boys in their respective forms. They reported to the master and wardens of the school that Richard Mulcaster, the schoolmaster, was 'worthy of great commendation' and that 'some of the boys had made a proficiency equal to the attainments of the scholars of any school in the realm'. The examiners were critical of the 'Cumbrian accents' of the masters and students and attributed this problem to the masters who were 'Northern men borne'. Richard Mulcaster, the headmaster, was born in Carlisle within eight miles of the Scottish border; he is likely to have had many acquaintances from the north and to have selected them as assistants in spite of their accents.[30] Further, Spenser's exposure to northern forms during his early schooling may have intrigued him and awakened an interest in dialect forms that later expressed itself in the linguistic exuberance of the *Shepheardes Calender*.

On 13 November 1564, Grindal again visited the school accompanied by Alexander Nowell, Dean of St Paul's, brother of the Robert Nowell who gave scholarship money to Spenser. Grindal and Nowell were accompanied by John Mullins, Archdeacon of London; Miles Coverdale, formerly Bishop of Exeter but now rector of St Magnus's by London Bridge; Whitehead; Calfhill; and other learned men.[31] They were joined by the entire court of the Merchant Taylors Company. A boy named King delivered an oration, and other unnamed scholars delivered copies of verse epistles. It is possible, in fact extremely likely, that Spenser, who was selected to act as the principal representative from Merchant Taylors' School at Robert Nowell's funeral, distinguished himself during one of these examinations when the school was visited by Alexander Nowell.

Although Grosart accurately identified references to Spenser in the 'Nowell Account Book', he sometimes misinterpreted their contexts. He, for example, was unaware of the conventions of Elizabethan and Jacobean funeral processions and so did not recognize the signal honour that Spenser had received when he was selected to represent Merchant Taylors' School at Robert Nowell's funeral. Grosart even comments that '[i]t has an odd look to find, as here and elsewhere, the foremost men in the State and Church allowing their "servantes" to receive gifts of "coattes" and the like' (33).³² Elizabethan conventions required that Robert Nowell should pay for the apparel worn by those who walked in his funeral procession. The very next bequest, after the one Grosart objects to, is for 'blacke coattes geuen to gentellmen srvantes & ptly to the poore in numbr 64' (32). Bequests of gowns to scholars and coats to servants were a traditional part of the ritual. Funds were also set aside for choir members and for those preparing the funeral dinner.

One particular entry in the 'Nowell Account Book' listed later during Spenser's collegiate years is of particular importance because Grosart thought that it might be in the hand of Alexander Nowell. I was able to confirm Grosart's suspicions by comparing this entry with Nowell's handwriting in A.6.49 (62), a theological commonplace book at Chetham's Library.³³ This entry regarding Spenser is indeed in Alexander Nowell's hand and thus makes it virtually certain that Edmund Spenser was personally known to Alexander Nowell.

In the 1560s Spenser's contemporaries had no way of knowing that he would later write the *Faerie Queene* (1590, 1596). Consequently, the entries in the 'Nowell Account Book' are important because they demonstrate that early in his career Spenser was regarded as a particularly promising academic talent among the most talented of his generation of students. In an important entry relating to Nowell's funeral we are told that certain scholars from Merchant Taylors' School, Westminster, St Anthony's, St Saviour's, and St Paul's were selected to represent their respective schools. That Spenser was selected to walk first among the representatives of his school was an impressive academic achievement.³⁴

In the entry dated 28 April 1569, on folio 50, Spenser is singled out by name to receive a scholarship along with students from Westminster and Eton whose names are unknown and left blank. Spenser received 10s. The next heading grants lesser stipends of 'vjs' to six scholars who are unnamed. The general heading for all of these bequests reads '[g]even to poor Schollers of Dyvers gramare Scholles.' The entries appear as follows:

i4 April   To mr Jervis, chaplin to my L. of canturbury to the vse of a poor schollore as apperethe by his accquitance. . . . . .x^s

28 April   To Edmond Spensore scholler of the m'chante tayler scholl^r at his gowinge to Penbrocke hall in chambridge. . . . . . .x^s

Geven to sex poor schollers of the m'chante tayler schole wch hade gownes. . . . . .vj^s.³⁵

(fol. 50, Grosart, 160-1)

This entry shows that Spenser already had sufficient reputation with the London clergy to be designated by name; in other cases, where that kind of name recognition did not exist, a general or anonymous bequest was made to someone, such as Mr Jervis, chaplain to the Archbishop of Canterbury, who was in a position to identify gifted students.

Grosart's interpretation of the 'Nowell Account Book' has promoted the view that scholarships were awarded specifically to the poor and needy. The Nowell scholarships are described as bequests to 'poor' boys, but the names of the recipients, in fact, demonstrate that scholarships were awarded on the basis of merit. If need was considered, it figured in only after the criterion of merit was met. Recognizing that 'poor' was a formulaic phrase, in 1947 Douglas Hamer argued against Grosart's insistence on Spenser's poverty concluding that 'the gift of a gown and a shilling to him while at school was certainly not because of either scholastic or real poverty'.[36]

To Hamer's argument, I will add conclusive evidence that academic promise was the principal consideration in awarding scholarships. In these accounts, poverty is a very elastic term. When John Fletcher, future playwright and younger son of Dr Richard Fletcher, matriculated at Merchant Taylors' School, he was given a partial tuition scholarship. Fletcher, whose prominent father later became Bishop of London, could have qualified for a scholarship only if such grants were awarded on merit. We should understand that Spenser received scholarships because a circle of London schoolmasters and clergymen, who represented a powerful social network, regarded him as worthy.

The first of the Spenser entries in the manuscript is introduced with a marginal note stating, 'Gownes geuen to carteyn poor scholler[s] of the scholls about London in numbr xxxjth':

Edmund Spenser
Richard Bitese
George hunte
Thomas Curley
henry Ive
Gregorie Donnhill schollers of the
    M'chante Taylers schole xij yardes di.
    at vj^s the yarde.

[Total cloth used] xij yardes & a di.
[Total expenditure for scholars from Merchant Taylors' School] iiij^{li}xv^s
(fol. 25, Grosart, 28–9)

As noted above, references to a 'poor scholler' should be interpreted within the context of the record in which it appears. Gregory Donnhill (or Downhall), who was referenced in the above record, was named a Watts scholar at Pembroke College in 1572 and later became a Master in Chancery.

This list of bequests to poor students continues and includes six representatives from Westminster School, two of whom, John Beaumont and Richard Hakluyt, became authors. They are described as 'poor' scholars, but their later achievements indicate their academic distinction. Beaumont matriculated from Westminster to Trinity College, Cambridge, where he was elected a Fellow. After earning three degrees beyond the B.A. (M.A. 1576; B.D. 1583; D.D. 1592), he served as the rector of Hadleigh, Suffolk. Hakluyt, the younger cousin of a bencher at the Middle Temple who had the same name, was a friend of the poet Sir Edward Dyer, the diplomat Daniel Rogers, and the astrologer John Dee. He came from a family with property in Hereford.[37] Hakluyt's own father was a London merchant and sufficiently affluent to be able to afford excellent educations for his four sons. They each went to Westminster School and then on to Cambridge or Oxford. Even though his background was comfortable, Hakluyt received financial support as a Queen's scholar at Westminster and was then elected to a fellowship at Christ Church.[38] Nevertheless, Hakluyt, like Spenser, is described as a 'poor scholler' in the 'Nowell Account Book'.

The statutes of the Merchant Taylors' School themselves illustrate the ambiguity of the term 'poor scholler': article four specifies that 'one hundreth schollers ... being poore men's sonnes and coming thether to be taught (yf such be meete & apte to learne,) without any thing to be paid by the parents of the said one hundreth poore children for their instruction & learnyng'. Article five, however, uses precisely the same designation of 'poore men's children' for those, like John Fletcher, asked to pay half of the costs of instruction.[39] Among the students paying half tuition were people who came from demonstrably affluent families. Edwin Sandys and George Cranmer received half-tuition scholarships. Edwin Sandys was admitted to Merchant Taylors' School on 23 March 1571 when his father was Bishop of London. Poor does not mean poor when an Elizabethan bishop's son is given a scholarship! George Cranmer, nephew of the martyred archbishop, entered Merchant Taylors' School at about the same time and received a scholarship. From these examples, it is clear that merit was the principal consideration in awarding scholarships; need, if it counted, was at best a secondary criterion.

The wording of the entries often suggests how to interpret them. In one entry, the name of the recipient is deliberately left blank, suggesting that grants were made to unknown individuals to be awarded on the basis of a schoolmaster's recommendation:

> To one [blank] Bacheler of arte before m^r mulcaster whoe was some tyme his scholmaister, gyven more the xixth of Maye A° 1575. . . . . .xx^s
> (Grosart, 188)

This entry illustrates the credibility that Mulcaster had with the executors of the Nowell estate. He is assumed to be able to identify students worthy of scholarship support; thus, his recommendation alone could have ensured Spenser's academic future. Another member of the Nowell circle, Dr John Young, Master of Pembroke College during Spenser's tenure, was like Mulcaster singled out to deliver grants and stipends to worthy recipients:

> Itm sent vnto one Sr Doue, of Pembrocke hall in cambridge the ixth of november 1575: by thandes of mr Doctor yonge. . . . . .x^s.
> (Grosart, 188)

The reference here to 'Sir' is a courtesy title given to those who had obtained the Bachelor of Arts degree. 'Sr Doue' is likely to have been Thomas Dove, who was described as a poor student at Merchant Taylors' School before going on to Pembroke College. He matriculated as a Watts scholar and was later appointed Bishop of Peterborough in 1601.

Public exhibitions or recitations also seem to have served as 'auditions' for scholarship support. When Sir William Pickering endowed scholarships with his estate, an additional sum was set aside by the executors of the Nowell estate to sponsor an exhibition or examination to determine those who would be selected as recipients of the Pickering scholarships:

> Item sent ∧ the vijth of november Anno 1575: by mr Still to the vse of Sr willm Pickringe Knighte his scholers for theyr exhibition due at. . . . . .vij^{li}.x^s (Grosart, 188)

The Mr Still identified here illustrates the far-reaching importance of the kinds of academic networks forged in grammar schools. John Still was the son of William Still, Esq., a merchant tailor who owned property and so could style himself esquire. Still matriculated as a pensioner of Christ College where he was elected a Fellow in 1562. He was acquainted with the Nowell family and with John Young, Master of Pembroke. At Pembroke, he interceded for Gabriel Harvey when he had trouble getting his M.A. degree approved. Still, a friend of Humphrey Tyndall, also served as the chaplain of the Earl of Leicester; it was Tyndall who performed the ceremony for Leicester's secret marriage to Lettice Knollys, widow of the Earl of Essex. Still received numerous preferments and was later appointed Bishop of Bath and Wells in 1592. He is also well known in literary history as the author of *Gammer Gurton's Needle*, one of the earliest English comedies. From the perspective of Spenser's biography, however, it is important to note that Spenser's excellent performance as a grammar-school student could have forged the connections that later resulted in his association with Leicester House.

Nowell was not the only benefactor of scholars at London schools. Scholarship support was available to students at Merchant Taylors' School from a number of recorded sources. In 1564, only three years after its founding, the company agreed to keep a scholar at Oxford or Cambridge at the expense of £5. The scholar was to be designated as the Merchant Taylors' Scholar, but the beneficiary had to be a student of divinity.[40] In 1567 Sir Thomas White created St John's College, Oxford, and endowed fifty scholarships: two were to be chosen from Coventry, two from Bristol, two from Reading, one from Tunbridge; the remaining forty-three were to be chosen from Merchant Taylors' School with the provision that six of these were reserved for kindred of the founder. White's portrait was hanging in the school library during Spenser's residence, and it is possible that he benefited from White's bequest. Unfortunately, we have no records regarding how White's bequest was used until 1572, three years after Spenser had matriculated at Pembroke College, Cambridge, in 1569.[41]

Archdeacon Watts, who along with Grindal, Nowell, and others had participated in many of the early visitations, endowed Greek scholarships at Pembroke College, Spenser's alma mater, with a preference to be given to students educated in London. In 1571 Lancelot Andrewes and Thomas Dove were Watts scholars. Spenser was probably not a Watts scholar; these scholarships were established after he had already matriculated at Pembroke, but he is likely to have profited from a similar endowment. We have ample evidence that a circle of well-to-do men, including Nowell, White, Watts, Pickering, and others, were interested in supporting the education of gifted students and that Spenser, like Lancelot Andrewes, was one of their protégés.

That merit motivated these bequests is substantiated by the later achievements of the various recipients. The distinguished contemporaries of Spenser's who received funds from the Nowell estate included Lancelot Andrewes, Richard Hooker, Richard Hakluyt, William Whitaker, Giles Fletcher, and three previously unmentioned recipients who later became bishops: Henry Parry, Myles Smith, and John Wolton. Of these men, Lancelot Andrewes affords the best comparison with Spenser. Andrewes attended Merchant Taylors' School and then matriculated at Pembroke College. Andrewes was a year younger than Spenser; he was born in London in 1555, the eldest child of Thomas and Joan Andrewes. His father was a London merchant and a seafaring man who is variously described as a 'member of the commercial or middle class' and as a 'rich London merchant'.[42] According to John Buckeridge, who preached Andrewes's funeral sermon, his parents left him a 'sufficient patrimony and inheritance which descended to his heir at Rawreth in Essex'.[43] Andrewes's parents had the vision and means to arrange for his education. At eight, he was sent to Coopers' Free School at Radcliffe; two years later he went to Merchant Taylors' School where Edmund Spenser was already in residence. Incidentally, the financial status of Andrewes's parents was not sufficient to deter his being called poor in the 'Nowell Account Book':

> Too one Lancelet Androwes poor scholler of Penbroke hall the xxviij of martch Ao 1573 at the sute of Mr Lewes my Lorde of Lacester gent. . . . . .x^s. (Grosart, 184)

When Spenser left Merchant Taylors' School, he was on a similar academic trajectory to Lancelot Andrewes. Spenser's poverty, like his kinship with the wealthy Spencers of Althorp, has been overstated while his academic prowess has been underestimated.

Intellectual promise

Spenser's early life records have never been fully contextualized. The argument that Spenser was admitted to Merchant Taylors' School because of his father's association with a guild misrepresents the very liberal traditions of that school in the sixteenth century and obscures the fact that Spenser was a truly exceptional student. In the sixteenth century, Merchant Taylors' School was not a trade school for the 'middling sort', but a preparatory school for Cambridge and Oxford. The sixteenth-century graduates of Merchant Taylors' School were expected to compete with those of Eton and Westminster. The statutes of Merchant Taylors' School in no way suggest that this school preferentially admitted children whose fathers were merchant tailors. In fact, the statutes of the Merchant Taylors' School are so liberal that they do not even impose geographical constraints.[44] They specify that foreign applicants will receive the same consideration as domestic applicants. Statute 25 specifically states that 'children of all nations & countryes indifferently' are to be admitted on the condition that they can 'read perfectly & write competently'.[45] Those admitted were to know the catechism in English or Latin and be 'apt & meete to learne' (20).

The admission records of Merchant Taylors' School are incomplete, particularly for the early years, and Spenser's name does not appear in these records.It is unlikely that, as Grosart assumed, Spenser received preferential admission. Of the students admitted in the first four years to Merchant Taylors' School, only twenty per cent are identified as sons of merchant tailors.[46] In his edition of Richard Mulcaster's *Positions*, William Barker independently and using different criteria examined the records and concluded that over fifty-five per cent are identified as sons of tradesmen, gentlemen, or esquires; for over thirty per cent no social status or trade is listed.[47]

Spenser's education at Merchant Taylors' School was equivalent, if not superior, to what he would have experienced at Westminster or Eton. Hebrew was included in his programme of study, and, significantly, seven of the translators of the 1611 King James's version of the Bible studied under Mulcaster, including Lancelot Andrewes, Thomas Dove, Ralph Huchenson, John Peryn, Ralph Ravens, John Spencer, and Giles Thompson. Ben Jonson's much quoted dismissal of Shakespeare's grammar-school education, that he had 'little Latin' and 'less Greek', has to be put in perspective. Jonson received his grammar-school education from William Camden, and Jonson himself became a formidable classical scholar who was awarded honorary M.A. degrees by both Oxford and Cambridge. Shakespeare's 'little Latin and less Greek' may not have impressed Jonson, but it would be a mistake to assume that Spenser, Shakespeare, and certainly Jonson were not extremely well served by their grammar-school educations.

Notes

1 *Shorter Poems*, ed. McCabe, *Shepheardes Calender*, p. 24.
2 For Drayton's background, see my *Michael Drayton Revisited* (Boston: G.K. Hall, 1990), 3–7.
3 Andrew Hadfield, 'Edmund Spenser (1552?–1599)', *ODNB* (2008); Ruth Mohl, 'Edmund Spenser', *Spenser Encyclopedia*, 668–71; Willy Maley, 'Spenser's Life',

in *The Oxford Handbook of Edmund Spenser*, ed. Richard A. McCabe (Oxford: Oxford University Press, 2010), 13–29.
4 For further discussion, see my 'Revising Edmund Spenser's Birth Date to 1554', *Notes and Queries*, New Series, 56, No. 4 (2009), 523–8.
5 W.L. Renwick, ed., Edmund Spenser, *Daphnaida and Other Poems* (Cambridge: Cambridge University Press, 1929), 201.
6 Mohl, 'Edmund Spenser', 668.
7 Damian Riehl Leader, *A History of the University of Cambridge* (Cambridge: Cambridge Unversity Press, 1988), I: 36. See, also, M.B. Hackett, *The Original Statutes of Cambridge University: The Text and Its History* (Cambridge: Cambridge University Press, 1970), 167, and J.A. Weisheipl, 'The Structure of the Arts Faculty in the Medieval University', *British Journal of Educational Studies*, 19 (1971), 266.
8 Judson, *Life*, 8.
9 See A.Kent Hieatt, *Short Time's Endless Monument* (New York: Columbia University Press, 1960), and Carol V. Kaske, 'Spenser's *Amoretti* and *Epithalamion* of 1595: Structure Genre and Numerology', *English Literary Renaissance*, 8 (1978), 271–95.
10 Although the *Amoretti* and *Epithalamion* were not actually published until 1595, these poems left Spenser's hands by September 1594. William Ponsonby, Spenser's publisher, addressed his 'Epistle Dedicatory' to 'Sir Robart Needham, Knight', saying that the poems crossed the 'Seas in your happy campanye (though to your selfe vnknowne)' (*Shorter Works*, ed. McCabe, p. 386). Needham was knighted on 1 September 1594 by Lord Deputy Russell prior to his departure for England on 25 September 1594. The potential political significance of the *Amoretti* is discussed by Catherine Bates, *The Rhetoric of Courtship in Elizabethan Language and Literature* (Cambridge: Cambridge University Press, 1992), 138–51.
11 Hadfield accepts Grosart's assertion that Spenser's father was a merchant tailor, disputes his claim that Spenser's family originated in Lancashire, and emphasizes Spenser's connections with Northamptonshire, the residence of the Spencers of Althorp and of Elizabeth Boyle, his second wife (*Life*, 19–21).
12 Grosart, *Life*.
13 Please note the publication date of 1945. Judson, a North American, wrote his biography during the Second World War and did not consult archival sources; he worked from notes transcribed earlier by Ray Heffner, another Indiana University professor, who had passed away.
14 Judson (8) cites Knowles, *HMC*, 407, rather than Grosart, and does not mention the fact that Knowles later retracted this identification.
15 The Spencers remain well known today because of their descendant, the late Lady Diana Spencer ('Princess Di'). For a family history, see Mary E. Finch, *The Wealth of Five Northamptonshire Families, 1540–1640*, Northamptonshire Record Society 19 (Oxford: Charles Batey at the University Press, 1956), esp. 38. Sir John Spencer spent more than £6,000 on the marriages of his six daughters.
16 *Calendar of State Papers, Domestic, 1619–23*, 254.
17 Sir John Harington, *A New Discourse of a Stale Subject, Called the Metamorphosis of Ajax*, ed. Elizabeth Story Donno (London: Routledge & Kegan Paul, 1962), 228–9. On Harington's authorship of the 'Apologie', see pp. 13–14.
18 For details on the possibility that Spenser grew up in East Smithfield near the Tower, see British library, MS Add. 23089, D.1. MS collections by Mr George Vertue Engraver, fos 115–34, and an evaluation by Grosart, *Life*, 4–6.

19 Critics commenting on Spenser's life in relation to his work have followed articles in reference works such as the ODNB, *Oxford Dictionary of National Biography* (2004), *Spenser Encyclopedia* (1990), and *Spenser Handbook* (2010), all of which privilege Grosart's identification of Spenser as the son of John Spenser, journeyman tailor. Judson's genteel Spenser is subordinated to this middle-class Spenser.
20 Harvey, *Foure Letters*. Harvey spells Spenser with a 'c' on E4v, K1r, K2r.
21 Knowles, *HMC*, prints his retraction in a 'Supplementary Note' added on p. 613. In contrast to Judson, Grosart prints Knowles's retraction in his life of Spenser (*Life*, xxxiv).
22 Mark Eccles, 'Elizabethan Edmund Spensers', *Modern Language Quarterly*, 5 (1944), 413–27.
23 The 'Nowell Account Book' is described as the Towneley Hall manuscript because it passed to Townley, Nowell's half-brother. My examination may be the first since Grosart had it in his possession.
24 Colonel Towneley's manuscripts were located at Towneley Hall, Burnley, and were described by R.B. Knowles in *HMC*, xvi–xvii, 406–16.
25 The manuscript was printed by Charles E. Simms, Manchester, in 1877. Grosart, who probably had the Towneley manuscript in his possession from 1874 to 1877, says that he has given the manuscript, '*literatim et punctatim*' and adds that the 'student may rely on the fidelity of the text to the original' (x), but does not supply a physical description.
26 Some of the leaves are cropped, measuring 287 by 185 mm, but a typical leaf measures 290 by 202 mm. The cover measures 304c by 207 mm. The nineteenth-century brown cloth binding was by Thomas Carter, Bookbinder, Manchester. The title, Nowell MSS, appears in gold letters on the spine.
27 *Townley Hall MSS*, ed. Grosart. Grosart sometimes but not always records the page and folio numbers of the manuscript at the top of each page of his edition; his own pagination appears at the bottom of the page. Grosart's page numbers (bottom of the page) will be cited parenthetically in my text. For any entry concerning Spenser, I supply my own transcription, the actual foliation of the manuscript, and cite Grosart's page number parenthetically. Unfortunately, I had no printed edition of Grosart's edition when I made these transcriptions; I was unable to compare the manuscript with Grosart's edition.
28 Knowles, *HMC*, 411. Knowles's foliation differs from Grosart's and from the present state of Chetham's Library MS A.6.50.
29 Rev. H.B. Wilson, *History of Merchant-Taylors' School*, 2 vols (London: Marchant and Galabin, 1814), I: 23–5. Hereafter, Wilson, *Merchant Taylors' School*.
30 To support his argument that Spenser's family derived from the Hurstwood Spensers, he usefully identifies northern dialect words in his works. Grosart, *Life*, 408–21.
31 Wilson, *Merchant Taylors' School*, I: 25–8.
32 *Towneley Hall MSS*, ed. Grosart, 33; see 17, n. 2. For Alexander Nowell's own bequest of coats to clerics and servants for his funeral procession, see Ralph Churton, *The Life of Alexander Nowell, Dean of St. Paul's* (Oxford: Oxford University Press, 1809), 433–4.
33 Manchester, Chetham's Library, A.6.49 is a theological commonplace book consisting of 42 folios with a watermark of a hand with a star at the end of the fingers. Nowell's hand is distinguished by a tail on the y and a horned g.

34 See Douglas Hamer, 'Edmund Spenser's Gown and Shilling', *Review of English Studies*, 23 (1947), 218–25: Hamer's reference to seniority may be misleading: 'As his name appears first in the list from that school he was probably the senior boy of the contingent, perhaps, indeed, the senior boy of the school'. The point is that Spenser was academically outstanding, not that he was older.
35 Grosart reports that this entry is on p. 87 and that it is fol. 71; it is paginated as 71, but currently appears on fol. 50; it is printed and discussed in Grosart, *Life*, 160.
36 Compare Hamer, 'Spenser's Gown and Shilling', with Grosart, *Life*, 13.
37 E.G.R. Taylor, *Late Tudor and Early Stuart Geography, 1583–1650* (London: Methuen & Co. Ltd, 1934), 4.
38 George Bruner Parks, *Richard Hakluyt and the English Voyages*, ed. James A. Williamson, American Geographical Society Serial Publication No. 10 (Lancaster, PA: Lancaster Press, 1928), 57–65.
39 Wilson, *Merchant Taylors' School*, I: 12–13.
40 Wilson, *Merchant Taylors' School*, I: 30–1.
41 Frederick M. Fry, Master of the Company for 1895–6, *A Historical Catalogue of the Pictures, Herse-Cloths & Tapestry at Merchant Taylors' Hall* (London: Chapman and Hall, Ltd, 1907), 93–6.
42 Paul A. Welsby, *Lancelot Andrewes, The Preacher, 1555–1626* (London: SPCK, 1958), 8–9; see also Nicholas Lossky, *Lancelot Andrewes, The Preacher (1555–1626)*, trans. Andrew Louth (Oxford: Clarendon Press, 1991), 8.
43 John Buckeridge, 'Sermon Preached at the Funeral of ... Lancelot late Lord Bishop of Winchester ... On Saturday being the XI. Of November, A.D. MDCXXVI', included in the 1629 edition of *XCVI Sermons*, ed. Archbishop Laud and John Buckeridge (London: George Miller for Richard Badger, 1629). RB 43440. The Huntington Library, San Marino, CA.
44 The statutes of Merchant Taylors' School were taken almost verbatim from those drawn up by John Colet for St Paul's. Cited from William Barker, ed., Richard Mulcaster, *Positions Concerning the Training Up of Children* (Toronto: University of Toronto Press, 1994), lxxiv.
45 Wilson, *Merchant Taylors' School*, 16.
46 *A Register of the Scholars Admitted into Merchant Taylors' School, from A.D. 1562 to 1874*, ed. Rev. Charles J. Robinson, 2 vols (London: Lewes Farncombe & Co., 1882), I: 2–10.
47 For an analysis based on figures from *Merchant Taylors' School Register 1561–1934*, ed. E.P. Hart, 2 vols (London: Merchant Taylors' Company, 1936), and compared by Natalie Johnson with the company records, see William Barker, ed., Richard Mulcaster, *Positions*, lxvi, lxxv. My statistics are based on Robinson's edition of the admission records, and I attempt to distinguish the sons of merchant tailors from those belonging to other guilds involved in the cloth trade. The number of students in the school was not to exceed 250 scholars, but, since the records are incomplete, we do not know how many students attended the school (Wilson, *Merchant Taylors' School*, 565).

2

Spenser's education and Merchant Taylors' School

The Elizabethans valued education.[1] There were four times as many grammar schools per capita in Spenser's as in Dickens's London. There is virtually no reliable evidence enabling us to draw statistical conclusions about mass literacy in the English Renaissance. We do know that Edmund Spenser, William Shakespeare, Ben Jonson – and those fortunate enough to receive a grammar-school education – were very well educated. Shakespeare attended a grammar school in Stratford where students were literate in English when they entered, and at school they learned Latin and were introduced to Greek. Spenser attended Merchant Taylors' School in London where Hebrew was also part of the curriculum.[2] A number of graduates of this distinguished grammar school contributed to the celebrated King James's translation of the Bible. Students were trained to write and speak Latin, and they read Greek and Roman history in texts written in those languages.

The printed word fascinated early modern society in part because of the phenomenal impact of the printing press; books previously produced laboriously in scriptoria and monasteries could be mass-produced for the first time. Religion offered incentives for literacy. In the aftermath to the translation of the Bible into English, the Protestant clergy supported literacy. Reading the scripture could not ensure salvation, but literacy might make the godly less susceptible to error. Knowledge of the Bible was a blessing to the ungodly as well as the godly. A thief or murderer could plead 'benefit of clergy' and have his sentence commuted. Benefit of clergy contributed substantively to Jacobean literary achievement. Early in his career, two days after the opening of his *Every Man in His Humour*,

Ben Jonson killed Gabriel Spencer. The actor Spencer was a member of the Lord Admiral's Men, the company of Philip Henslowe. Henslowe, whose *Diary* is the source of much that we know of Renaissance drama, reported news of the duel to Edward Alleyn, his son-in-law. He describes Jonson not as a playwright but as a bricklayer, an uncelebrated occupation even among the trades: 'I have lost one of my company, which hurteth me greatly – that is, Gabriel, for he is slain in Hogsden Fields by the hands of Benjamin Jonson, bricklayer'.[3] Jonson was convicted and left prison a branded felon, but, because he could read Latin, escaped the gallows.

To the Elizabethans, in spite of their largely egalitarian approach to educating those who lacked money and titles, birth and background remained immensely important markers of gentility. Like many of those who were not well-born, Edmund Spenser was attracted to and repelled by the mystique of gentle blood. Ben Jonson made it clear to posterity that he was a clergyman's son even if his stepfather was a bricklayer. Michael Drayton presented himself as the protégé of Sir Henry Goodere of Polesworth even though he was a servant in the household of Sir Henry's younger brother.[4] Though we do not have evidence that Spenser was born into the gentry, like all university graduates he became a gentleman when he received his degree. Even after receiving the degree and becoming a gentleman, he, however, continued to be self-deprecating. In addition to using 'Clout' as his surname for his artistic persona in the *Shepheardes Calender* and the *Faerie Queene*, he signs himself 'Immerito' in the *Shepheardes Calender*, another epithet emphasizing his unworthiness. Edmund Spenser was successful, even brilliant, as a student, and so his insecurity must have developed from self-consciousness about his lineage. Class mattered immensely to the Elizabethans and especially to men like Spenser, who were 'new' men. William Shakespeare, also a 'new' man, purchased a coat of arms for his father once he was in a position to do so. Gabriel Harvey, a fellow student of Spenser's at Pembroke College, Cambridge, matriculated as a gentleman pensioner, making him at least upper middle class by our standards. Harvey's wealthy father, however, was a rope-maker, branding him, like Spenser and Shakespeare, as a new man.

Wealth and power were not enough to make an Elizabethan a great man. A title and estate had to have been in the family for generations for such assets to confer unqualified distinction. The seventeenth Earl of Oxford, whose character troubled many, was still the seventeenth earl and so a suitable match for the upwardly mobile Cecils.[5] When the powerful and affluent William Cecil, Lord Burghley, was slandered in tracts accusing him of being an upstart and of amassing a fortune at the expense of the realm, he was as injured by the insinuation that he was a 'new' man as he was by the charge that he had misappropriated funds. Likewise, Sir Philip Sidney, when he set out to write a defence of his uncle, Robert Dudley, Earl of Leicester, was as concerned about defending any slight to his uncle's, and his own, lineage as he was in proving Leicester innocent of charges that he had murdered his first wife and poisoned the husband of his second wife.[6] Noble birth carried with it privileged treatment. A man who matriculated as a gentleman pensioner dined at the fellows' table. Members of the aristocracy (unlike commoners whom we have seen earlier) came to Oxford and Cambridge at ten or eleven years old – accompanied by their tutors and retainers. It was unnecessary for them to earn a B.A; they proceeded immediately to the M.A.

Although we lack the documentary evidence to draw any reliable conclusions about Spenser's parentage and social status, we know from his work that lineage and rank were matters of concern to him, as indeed they were to his contemporaries. In his poetry Spenser repeatedly comments upon the relative importance of nature and nurture, birth and education. In *Teares of the Muses* (1591), he censures 'mightie Peeres' (80), who pride themselves on rank:

> But they doo onely striue themselues to raise
> Through pompous pride, and foolish vanitie;
> In th'eyes of people they put all their praise,
> And onely boast of Armes and Aunscestrie:
> But vertuous deeds, which did those Armes first giue
> To their Grandsyres, they care not to atchiue.
>
> (Clio, 91–6)[7]

His scepticism about the virtue conferred by noble ancestry is rarely expressed this directly. In the *Faerie Queene* (1596) gentle manners seem a natural accompaniment to gentle blood. The 'salvage man' who lives 'mongst saluage beasts, both rudely borne and bred' treats Serena generously, but later this generosity seems as if it may have proceeded from his own 'gentle blood' (VI.v.2, 5).[8]

Using an analogy frequently made in Italian courtesy books, Spenser cites the concept of the thoroughbred horse as an illustration of the importance of natural instinct:

> For seldome seene, a trotting Stalion get
> An ambling Colt, that is his proper owne:
> So seldome seene, that one in basenesse set
> Doth noble courage shew with curteous manners met.
>
> (*Faerie Queene*, VI.iii.1, 6–9)

By inference, the nature conferred by heredity may be more important than the nurture supplied by upbringing or education. The kindness of the Hermit who ministers to Serena and Timias in Book VI of the *Faerie Queene* is also explained by his breeding and blood lines:

> For well it seem'd, that whilome he had beene
> Some goodly person, and of gentle race.
> (*Faerie Queene*, VI.v.36, 6–7)

Nevertheless, the author of the *Faerie Queene* is fully conscious of the ironic potential of his narrator's comment that 'courtesy' is 'rightly named of court'. Meliboe, Calidore's peasant host in Book VI, is specifically and emphatically depicted as a model of good manners.

Italian courtesy books preach that ancestry is an asset to the courtier, but it is unlikely that anyone seriously subscribed to the view that all noblemen were virtuous and civil. Stephano Guazzo's *La Civile Conversation*, translated by George Pettie (1581) and Bartholomew Young (1586), makes this point:

> And truely I knowe many men of meane calling, who in Gentlemanlike and courteous conditions, in good bringing up, and all their talke and behaviour excell many Gentlemen. And contrariwise, I am sure you know many Gentlemen more uncivill then the Clownes themselves. (175)[9]

Comments such as these, and of course Chaucer's verdict that 'gentle is as gentle does', were certainly available to Spenser, but his works, like those of Shakespeare, seem to have been influenced by the conventions of medieval romance. In romances, it is common for heroines or heroes of gentle birth to be born or bred in wild or rural conditions but later revealed as aristocrats; Perdita in Shakespeare's *Winter's Tale* is a case in point. Spenser, too, depicts foundlings bred in wilderness or country settings whose gentility is revealed by later events.[10] The use of these conventional romance motifs does not signify that either Spenser or Shakespeare subscribed to the aristocratic bias that blood will tell, but we need to be aware that their culture was at home with these ideas.

Spenser, we may be sure, remained convinced that education was the foundation of civil society. Of the *Faerie Queene* he says: 'The generall end ... of all the booke is to fashion a gentleman or noble person in vertuous and gentle discipline' (p. 714). Spenser is convinced that his reader will welcome this 'fashioning' in virtue and and 'gentle discipline', and this conviction was shared by his contemporaries. A grammar-school education may later have become a nod at literacy and a guarantee only that an individual had a smattering of information. An Elizabethan grammar-school education ensured that a young man was well grounded in the classics, and this excellent formal education was intended to serve as a springboard to a student's own reading and possibly writing.

Elizabethan schoolmasters, all of whom had received the traditional Christian humanist education in the Bible and the classics, endorsed their own educational background; they advocated educating the lower classes and, some, like Richard Mulcaster, Spenser's very liberal schoolmaster, supported teaching women as well as men. In his *Utopia* (1516), Thomas More, noteworthy for having educated his daughters, envisions an educated society in which all classes study literature. Under Henry VIII, there was concern about extending literacy to the lower classes. In the Act of 1543 for the Advancement of True Religion, the government held that 'no women nor artificers, prentices, journeymen, serving men of the degrees of yeomen or under, husbandmen, nor labourers' were to be permitted to read the Bible in English.[11] Apparently, women and workers were regarded as too volatile to be allowed access to the stimulation of the scriptures. The Elizabethan educational establishment was less suspicious of the lower classes; the power structure supported education more strongly than it had in the 1540s.

Spenser was fortunate to have been born during Elizabeth's reign (1558–1603). Less than a decade after Elizabeth's death and the accession of the Stuart king, Sir Francis Bacon was to counsel James I against increasing educational opportunities. By 1611 Bacon subscribed to the opinion that there were too many grammar schools and that an excessive number could be dangerous: 'Many persons will be bred unfit for other vocations, and unprofitable for that in which they are brought up, which fills the realm full of indigent, idle and wanton people which are but *materia rerum novarum*'.[12] In the decades after the English Civil War, most people were even less progressive about educating the poor. They feared that to overproduce intellectuals by educating the humbly born beyond their station in life would breed social unrest. Lawrence Stone concludes that, in quantitative terms, it was not until the First World War that English higher education was as egalitarian as it was in the 1630s and that it was not until after the Second World War that modern society was as committed as they had been in the sixteenth and early seventeenth century to educating the lower classes.[13] Elizabeth was educated in the classics and spoke several modern languages. King James's remark that 'one tongue is enough for a woman' suggests that his own views of female learning were less enlightened than those of sixteenth-century fathers and schoolmasters.

Spenser received his early education under the guidance of Richard Mulcaster and other teachers at Merchant Taylors' School, but he was also supported by the clergymen who visited and examined students at London grammar schools. These teachers and clergymen supplied an educational network for promising students. In *The Description of England*, Chapter 3 'Of Universities' (1577), William Harrison states that in addition to the universities, 'there are a great number of grammar schools throughout the realm, and those very liberally endowed for the better relief of poor scholars, so that there are not many corporate towns now under the Queen's dominion, that have not one grammar school at the least, with a sufficient living for a master and usher appointed to the same'.[14] Earlier in the same chapter, Harrison is less optimistic about the number of university fellowships likely to trickle down to the lower classes: 'it is in my time a hard matter for a poor man's child to come by a fellowship (though he be never so good a scholar, and worthy of that room)' (71). Although in 1577 Harrison is sceptical about how fairly educational opportunities are in practice distributed, neither he nor his contemporaries questions the principle that the poor should be educated. A century later in 1678, Christopher Wase is forced to acknowledge that there is widespread opposition to educating the lower classes. He concedes that 'there is an opinion commonly receiv'd that the Scholars of England are overproportion'd to the preferments for letter'd Persons':

> Hereupon the Constitution of Free-Schools cometh to be question'd, as diverting those, whom Nature or Fortune had determin'd to the Plough, the Oar, or other Handicrafts, from their proper design, to the study of the Liberal Arts ... multiplying ... Foundations is ... represented as dangerous to the Government.[15]

The quality and quantity of educational opportunities available to the lower classes, and perhaps to women as well, decreased as the seventeenth century came to an end.

Our picture of how well educated the average man or woman was in the sixteenth century remains uncertain, but we are remarkably well informed about what was the theory and very likely the practice when Spenser went to Merchant Taylors' School or Shakespeare entered his Stratford grammar school. Educational manuals indicate that there was considerable agreement on curriculum and methodology. Children first attended a petty school where they learned reading, writing, and counting;

girls might be taught needlework instead of writing and arithmetic. The boy was to begin by learning his *ABC*, probably from a hornbook, and then, in 'good reformation style', he was introduced to the *Catechism*, *Psalter*, and *Primer*. The petty school was frequently under the jurisdiction of the church, but that mattered little in terms of curriculum: the drive toward religious uniformity deeply influenced early education. Nine years before Spenser was born, in 1545 King Henry's authorized *Primer* was published in English to supply 'one vniforme maner or course of praiying throughout all our dominions'.[16] A translation was made available for those who knew Latin. All agreed that the *ABC* and *Catechism* should be the first texts and that religious uniformity was essential; there was less consensus about which religious doctrines and practices should be uniformly accepted. As T.W. Baldwin concludes about the curriculum of the petty school: 'The emphasis here is on Reformation, not on Renaissance' (32).

Alexander Nowell, the same clergyman who examined Spenser at Merchant Taylors' School and whose brother was Spenser's early benefactor, was the author of the basic *Catechism*, which existed in three Latin versions of increasing difficulty. Nowell's *Catechism* was approved by the bishops in 1562, but not published until eight years later. Between 1570 and 1647 Nowell's *Catechism* went through forty-four editions in Latin, English, and Greek.

Nowell's *Catechism* had a major impact on the way texts were interpreted because it emphasized a typological approach to reading. The master asked a question to which the student supplied a memorized answer. In addition to inculcating specific and uniform doctrines, such as justification by faith, the catechism guided the student to pay attention to correspondences between the Old and New Testaments. In Romans 5:14, 'type' is used in a strict theological sense when Paul calls Adam the *typos* of Christ, literally 'the figure of him that was to come'. A type in the Old Testament foreshadows its antitype in the New. If, for example, the master asks why the Decalogue refers to the Christians of the New Testament as well as the Israelites of the Old Testament, then the student is supposed to reply that the pharaoh of Egypt is a type of the devil and that Moses' delivery of the Israelites from bondage in Egypt is a type of Christ's delivery of the faithful Christian from the bondage of sin.

This system of reading influenced Spenser as it was later to influence John Milton, George Herbert, and other seventeenth-century writers. Spenser and his readers were conditioned to expect a multiplicity of levels of meanings. In the first book of the *Faerie Queene* Redcrosse Knight, as an individual, is the Protestant Everyman, but he also represents the collective people of England. Historically, he is St George, England's patron saint, and he is a pilgrim who hopes to achieve the virtue of holiness; his adventures illustrate the path to holiness for the reader, and these typological layers invite Spenser's reader, too, to become a pilgrim. The overarching quest for Redcrosse, as an individual, is to behold a vision of the New Jerusalem. The knight of holiness, however, is also engaged in a holy quest involving the lady Una, who represents the one true faith. To liberate Una's parents, who are a king and queen as well as Adam and Eve, Redcrosse must slay the Dragon who holds them prisoner. When Spenser describes the battle between Redcrosse Knight and the dragon, we are invited to see this combat as a re-enactment of victories of good over evil. The dragon represents sin, the Spanish Armada, the beast of the Apocalypse; when Redcrosse defeats the dragon, he is in effect restoring Eden. Redcrosse is then deemed worthy of union with Una. Studying the early modern catechism helped to establish typology as a system for reading the Bible, but, as had been true of the medieval allegorical tradition, its approach to making cross-references and to reading symbolically also influenced the reading and writing of secular texts.

The uniformity prized in religious instruction in the petty school extended into the grammar-school curriculum. In addition to authorizing a prayer book, Henry VIII decreed that William Lyly's *Grammar* was to be the standard introduction to Latin. We prize the term 'innovative' and laud innovation, but that was not the case in Spenser's culture. English Renaissance educators distrusted innovation and used the term 'new-fangled' to deride change. Lyly's *Grammar* remained the standard grammar-school text throughout the sixteenth and seventeenth centuries.[17] After concentrating on Lyly's *Grammar* in the lower grammar school (approximately the first three years), the study of rhetoric began in the fourth form. Students composed elegant letters in Latin and began Greek. The dramatist Terence was particularly important as a text. Charles Hoole says that students must make him 'wholly their own':

> *Terence*, of all the School-Authors that we read, doth deservedly challenge the first place, not only because *Tully* [Cicero] himself hath seemed to derive his eloquence from him ... The matter of it is full of morality, and the several Actors therein, most lively seem to personate the behaviour and properties ... of people, even in this age of ours. (137–8)[18]

In *Staple of News*, Jonson satirizes schoolmasters for not spending enough time on the catechism and for letting the children speak plays and act fables, but Terence is exempted from this censure: 'We send them to learn their grammar and their Terence, and they learn their play-books' (I intermean 3 after Act III.iv).

The lower forms of the grammar school concentrated on grammar while the upper emphasized rhetoric.[19] Throughout all of the forms most of the ushers and school masters would have used the 'double translation' method advocated by Roger Ascham in *The Schoolmaster* (1570). Students were given verses from a text, such as Ovid's *Metamorphoses*, and asked to parse them grammatically, identify tropes and figures, produce Latin synonyms. The student would then turn the passage into English prose and translate it back into Latin, taking care to place each word grammatically and rhetorically; finally, the passage was turned into English verse. In some schools, grammatical translations were used. Students were asked to translate words and phrases into normal English word order before they returned the passage to Latin.

From this intensive syntactical work with Latin, students learned a case-structure grammar in which endings made clear syntactic positions in the sentence. Early exposure to Latin and so to a case-structure grammar encouraged students to experiment with variations on the subject-verb word order characteristic of an English sentence. The subject-verb order of 'the knight slays the dragon' could be transformed in a case grammar to 'the dragon the knight slays' or 'the knight the dragon slays'. The double translation method ensured that students would engage in close reading and that even those without a natural sensitivity to language would learn to pay close attention to specific word choice.

The fifth form introduced the comparative grammar of Latin and Greek and focused on oratory, especially Demosthenes, Isocrates, and the all-important Cicero. Poetry was not neglected: students read Vergil's *Eclogues* and *Georgics* with their schoolmasters. Hoole memorably comments that, after students had memorized sections of the *Eclogues* and worked with their schoolmaster on the *Georgics*, they might be left to read the *Aeneid* by themselves (180). In the fifth form students also prepared a commonplace book, a kind of mini-Bartlett's *Quotations*, in which witty or apt phrases were arranged under headings such as friendship, liberty, law. These sayings and stylistic set pieces could later be used in compositions and speeches. Hoole concludes his section on 'The Masters Method' in A *New Discovery of the Old Art of Teaching Schoole* by announcing that he has described what is 'commonly *practised*' in England and foreign countries and that the curriculum and pedagogy are '*proportioned to the ordinary capacities of children* under fifteen years of age'

(204–5). Following this grammar-school education, a student of fifteen, if he had the means, or the kind of network that we can document as existing for Edmund Spenser, would enter a university.

Richard Mulcaster, Spenser's schoolmaster

Richard Mulcaster, Spenser's schoolmaster at Merchants' Taylor School, probably influenced Spenser's decision to become an English rather than a Latin poet. The great Italian Renaissance poet Petrarch is remembered for his vernacular sonnets to 'Laura'; his serious work, his unfinished epic *Africa* on Scipio Africanus, was composed in Latin. It is important to note that, for many of the well-educated, Latin was a spoken language in the Renaissance. Montaigne, for example, was not allowed to speak vernacular French until he was six; his family, servants, and tutors spoke only Latin to him. Neo-Latin literature is formidable.[20] Thomas More wrote his *Utopia* in Latin. Gabriel Harvey, Spenser's schoolmate at Cambridge, may have begun a Latin epic and did publish Latin tracts and verse. Thomas Campion wrote verses in both Latin and English. Sir Francis Bacon began publishing his terse and epigrammatic vernacular *Essays* in 1597, but his more ambitious works, *Novum organum* (1620), a systematic treatise on methodology, and *De augmentis scientarum*, on the advancement of learning, are more complete in Latin. William Camden wrote his history of Elizabeth's reign *Annales Rerum Gestarum Angliae et Hiberniae Regnate Elizabetha* in Latin and left it to others to supply translations. Spenser's success at Merchant Taylors' School indicates that he knew Latin well, and so would have had the choice of writing either in the vernacular or in Latin. It was Spenser's contact with Mulcaster that may have tipped the scale towards English.

In manuals for training children in reading and writing, Richard Mulcaster wholeheartedly celebrated the English language:

> I take this present period of our English tung to be the verie height thereof, bycause I find it so excellentlie well fined, both for the bodie of the tung itself, and for the customarie writing therof, as either foren workmanship can giue it glosse, or as homewrought handling can giue it grace.

Mulcaster recognized that language changes over time and that a new age will introduce new vocabulary and syntactic conventions:

> When the age of our peple, which now vse the tung so well, is dead and departed there will another succede, and with the peple the tung will alter and change. Which change in the full haruest thereof maie proue

comparable to this, but sure for this which we now vse, it semeth euen now to be at the best for substance, and the brauest for circumstance, and whatsoeuer shall becom of the English state, the English tung canot proue fairer, then it is at this daie.[21]

Mulcaster can envision a future in which the English state may decline but insists that 'the English tung canot proue fairer, then it is at this daie'. No student studying under Mulcaster would be likely to miss this message. Judging from the number of major literary figures produced in his age, there was substance to Mulcaster's claim that the English tongue would never 'proue fairer' than in the age of Sidney, Spenser, Shakespeare, Jonson, Donne, and Milton.

In addition to being a passionate advocate for the English language, Richard Mulcaster supported education for the children of tradesmen and merchants. He himself seems to have derived from a prominent landowning family and was educated at Eton as a King's Scholar. He matriculated at King's College, Cambridge, and graduated with a B.A. from Peterhouse. He then matriculated in 1556 at Christ Church, Oxford, where he completed his M.A. He had relocated to London by 1559. In 1561, when Merchant Taylors' School opened, he became the first headmaster, a position that he held for twenty-five years. During his tenure as headmaster, Mulcaster published his two books, *Positions Concerning the Training Up of Children* (1581) and the *The First Part of the Elementary, which entreateth Chiefly of the Right Writing of our English Tongue Positions* (1581). *Positions* was entered in the Stationers' Register on 6 March 1581 to Thomas Chard with an interesting provision suggesting that Mulcaster or his views on education were regarded as controversial: 'That yf this booke conteine any thinge preiudiciall or hurtfull to the booke of maister Askham that was printed by master Daie / Called *the Scolemayster* That then theis Lycence shalbe voyd'.[22] Ascham, author of *The Scholemaster, Or plaine and perfite way of teachyng children ... the Latin tong* (1570), had been the pupil of the notable humanist Sir John Cheke and the tutor of Queen Elizabeth, and he focused more on educating the privileged than the more egalitarian Mulcaster.

Spenser exhibits little interest in the drama in his work, but his schooling was not responsible for this omission.[23] In *The First Part of the Elementary, Which Entreateth Chiefly of the Right Writing of our English Tongue Positions* (1582), Mulcaster explains what skills are to be taught and includes drawing, singing, and acting along with reading and writing. This training in drama influenced the development of two notable authors. Both Thomas Kyd, author of *The Spanish Tragedy*, an important Senecan drama, and Thomas Lodge, the physician and poet whose *Rosalynde* influenced Shakespeare's *As You Like It*, were educated at Merchant Taylors' School.[24]

In addition to including the fine arts in the curriculum, Mulcaster seems to have encouraged active participation in civic entertainment by precept and example. He was invited by a London committee consisting of Richard Hilles, M.P. and a merchant tailor; Lionel Duckett, a mercer; Francis Robinson, a grocer; and Richard Grafton, a printer and chronicler to write a principal pageant for the Queen's entrance into London on the day prior to her coronation.[25] Over the years Mulcaster appears to have continued to contribute to the Lord Mayors' Pageants and to various court entertainments.[26] In July 1575 we find him participating in the festivities at Kenilworth organized by George Gascoigne and described by both Gascoigne and Robert Laneham, the Clerk and Keeper of the Council Chamber Door.[27] Those who contributed to the entertainment included Gascoigne, Laneham, Mulcaster, George Ferrers, poet and M.P., and William Hunnis, master of the children of the Chapel Royal.[28] Mulcaster wrote a Latin poem on a tablet explaining the identity and significance of the gifts which the Queen received. The Queen passed over a bridge about twenty feet wide with pillars on each side. On the first pair were birds from Sylvanus, on the second bowls of fruit from Pomona, on the third wheat and grain from Ceres, on the fourth grapes and vines from Bacchus, on the fifth grass and fresh fish from Neptune, on the sixth arms on a ragged staff as gifts from Mars, and on the seventh musical instruments as gifts from Apollo. Since it was dark, a finely dressed poet, possibly Mulcaster, read the verses from a scroll in his hand. Gascoigne said farewell to the Queen under the figure of Sylvanus, a name used by Mulcaster for one of his sons and later also used by Spenser for his elder son.

We know that Mulcaster included music in the curriculum of Merchant Taylors' School. Sir James Whitelock, later Justice of the Common Pleas and the King's Bench, describes the school as 'famous' and recounts the kinds of activities in which he participated as a schoolboy.

> I was brought up at school under mr. Mulcaster, in the famous school of the Marchantaylors in London, whear I continued untill I was well instructed in the Hebrew, Greek, and Latin tongs. His care was also to encreas my skill in musique, in whiche I was brought up by dayly exercise in it, as in singing and playing upon instruments, and yeerly he presented sum playes to the court, in whiche his scholers wear only actors, and I

on[e] among them, and by that meanes taughte them good behaviour and audacitye.[29]

Between 1572 and 1583 we have records of eight performances at court by the boys at Merchant Taylors' School under the direction of Mulcaster.[30]

Although we cannot be sure where or when Spenser was first exposed to Italian authors, it is likely that Mulcaster was responsible for awakening his interest in Tasso and Ariosto before he went to the university. Mulcaster was himself interested in Ariosto. He adapted an episode from Ariosto's *Orlando Furioso*, 'A historie of Ariodante and Geneuora', for performance at Richmond in 1583. This performance took place after Spenser had graduated, but it testifies to Mulcaster's enthusiasm for Italian authors. This, too, distinguishes him from Roger Ascham. In his *Schoolmaster*, Ascham inveighs mightily against the 'Englishman Italianated' but also deplores the publication of Italian books:

> These be the enchantments of Circes, brought out of Italy, to mar men's manners in England: much by example of ill life but more by precepts of fond books, of late translated out of Italian into English, sold in every shop in London; commended by honest titles the sooner to corrupt honest manners; dedicated overboldly to virtuous and honorable personages, the easilier to beguile simple and innocent wits. It is a pity that those which have authority and charge to allow and disallow books to be printed be no more circumspect herein than they are. Ten sermons at Paul's Cross do not so much good for moving men to true doctrine as one of those books do harm with inticing men to ill living.[31]

Ariosto was available in an English translation by Peter Beverley as early as 1566, but Mulcaster, unlike many of the more staunchly anti-Catholic schoolmasters, may have introduced Spenser and other students to Ariosto and other Italian authors before they were available in English.

Mulcaster appears to have had difficulty living within his means; he is reported to have been unscrupulous in trying to reduce his debts.[32] These character flaws did not keep him from being loved by his students. He earned the lifelong respect of Lancelot Andrewes, Spenser's classmate at Pembroke, whose fondness for his schoolmaster was remembered in the sermon delivered by John Buckeridge at Andrewes's funeral:

> Master Mulcaster, whom he ever reverently respected during his life, in all companies, and placed him ever at the upper end of his table; and after his death (having but few other in his House) [caused his picture] to be set over his Study door.

Andrewes also assisted his schoolmaster financially and helped to educate Mulcaster's son:

> 'And not onely shewed he this outward thankfulness to him, but supplyed his wants many time also, privately, ... bequeathed a Legacy to his son – having bestowed a scholarship in Pembroke'.[33]

We do not have anecdotes of this kind concerning Spenser and Mulcaster, but Mulcaster's views of language are likely to have had a significant impact on Spenser's own experimentation with language.[34] Indeed, Mulcaster's discussion of orthography in the *Elementarie* might prove a fruitful context for analysing Spenser's linguistic experimentation in the *Shepheardes Calender* and his archaism in the *Faerie Queene*.[35]

Mulcaster, too, was acquainted with the Dutch and French immigrant communities in London, and it is likely that his connections with Emanuel van Meteren and others led Spenser to become involved in the production of an early emblem book. *A Theatre for Worldlings* (1569) was entered in the Stationers' Register on 22 July 1569.[36] The English version was entitled *A Theatre for Worldlings wherein be represented as wel the miseries & calamities that follow the voluptuous Worldlings, As also the great joyes and pleasures which the faithfull do enioy*; it was printed in 1569 by Henry Bynneman, who was later to print the early works of Gabriel Harvey. This version translates the Dutch and French versions printed a year earlier in London in 1568. It can only be conjectured how much or how little Spenser participated in this project, but the later publication history is quite suggestive. Jan van der Noot, who describes himself as the 'devisor' rather than the author, prepared the original Dutch text. It was published in London with a dedication dated 18 September 1568 and addressed to Roger Martin, Lord Mayor of London, who had befriended Dutch refugees, such as van der Noot. In the same year as this Dutch edition, John Day printed a French edition in London with a dedication to Elizabeth signed 28 October 1568.

The texts consisted of seven translations from Petrarch by Clement Marot, eleven from *Songe* in *Antiquitez del Rome* by Du Bellay, and four apocalyptic poems by van der Noot. The poems are followed by a long prose commentary headed 'A briefe declaration of the Authour upon his visions ... Translated out of the French into Englishe by Theodore Roest.'[37] Etchings, possibly by the Flemish artist Lucas de Heere of Ghent, were used to illustrate the Dutch and English editions, but a set of woodcuts imitating the etchings was used for the English edition and for a later German edition. For the French version John Day prints the original

French poems; in the Dutch version they are translated into Dutch. The English translations may have been based on the French, although commentators have suggested influences from Dutch and from the Italian originals.

Van der Noot planned three groups: Petrarch's poems in French guise represent the rejection of earthly love and worldliness; the selections from Du Bellay contain a vision of self-destructiveness; and the apocalyptic poems show the punishment of those who persecute their brethren in Christ. In his commentary, van der Noot offers specific interpretations of the images, suggesting that Laura is represented by the ship and the laurel tree; the singing birds signify her fair speech, and lightning and the storm her death. Van der Noot's sonnets combine the traditional themes of Antichrist with the promise of redemption. The beast of Revelations and the woman on the beast are juxtaposed with the word of God and the New Jerusalem.

These English translations from Italian and French poems were first printed with Spenser's works by Henry John Todd in 1806; Todd identified the poems with the 'Dreames', one of several purportedly lost works. The principal reason for attributing them to Spenser, however, is that William Ponsonby, the publisher of the *Faerie Queene*, collects them and publishes them with Spenser's *Complaints* (1591). This led W.L. Renwick and other editors of Spenser to agonize that Spenser might have plagiarized or passed someone else's work off as his own. Renwick, concerned with what he feared might be fraud on Spenser's part, was able to reassure himself that there were hints of genius in the translations, making Spenser's authorship assured.

> If Spenser was not the author of the *Theatre* translations, he committed a monstrous theft in the *Complaints*, and – what is more important to us who know more about his art than his morals – performed an unprecedented kind of work. We may continue to accept these translations as the first offspring of Spenser's Muse.[38]

Other critics have not been as impressed by these poems as Renwick, and some have been rejected on the grounds that Spenser was too fine a poet to have written them.[39] In the preface to the *Complaints*, which first attributed the translations to Spenser, the printer William Ponsonby states that he assembled this volume in Spenser's absence.[40] Ponsonby may have acquired manuscripts of van der Noot's 'Sonets' and 'Epigrams' and printed them as 'The Visions of Du Bellay' and 'The Visions of Petrarch formerly translated' and then included them in the *Complaints*

(1591).⁴¹ No definitive case has yet been made for or against Spenser's authorship of each and every one of the translations from *A Theatre for Wordlings*. Nevertheless, 'The Visions of Du Bellay' and 'The Visions of Petrarch' were printed with his work while he was alive, and it is likely that he translated other poems from *A Threatre for Worldlings* when he was a schoolboy. We know that he was thoroughly familiar with the works of Petrarch, Marot, and Du Bellay.⁴² Spenser's stature as a poet is not dependent on the attribution to him of *A Theatre for Worldlings*, but these poems, at the very least, offer insight into his early intellectual milieu. Spenser's interest in this kind of poetry supports the likelihood that he seriously considered taking holy orders.

Notes

1. See my earlier 'Literacy and Education', in *A Companion to English Renaissance Literature and Culture*, ed. Michael Hattaway (Oxford: Blackwell Publishers, 2000), 95–105.
2. In the 1572 visitation, Dean Nowell of St Paul's examined them in Horace, Archdeacon Watts continued with Homer, and the Bishop of Winchester took them through the Hebrew psalms. See Richard L. DeMolen, *Richard Mulcaster and Educational Reform in the Renaissance* (Nieukoop: De Graaf Publishers, 1991), 17.
3. Henslowe's *Diary*, cited in Ben Jonson, *Works*, ed. C.H. Herford and Percy Simpson (Oxford: Clarendon Press, 1925), I: 18.
4. For a biographical overview of Drayton, see my *Michael Drayton Revisited* (Boston: G.K. Hall, 1990), 1–23, esp. 5–7.
5. The seventeenth Earl was considered a better match than Philip Sidney, the son of a knight. For a documentary biography of Oxford, see Allen H. Nelson, *Monstrous Adversary: The Life of Edward de Vere, 17th Earl of Oxford* (Liverpool: Liverpool University Press, 2003), esp. 68–79.
6. *Leicester's Commonwealth: The Copy of a Letter Written by a Master of Art of Cambridge (1584) and Related Documents*, ed. D.C. Peck (Athens: Ohio University Press, 1985). Sidney's *Defence of Leicester* is printed with this edition, e.g.,'Now to the Dudleys such is his bounty that when he hath poured all his flood of scolding eloquence, he saith they are no gentlemen, affirming that John Duke of Northumberland was not born so' (256).
7. *Shorter Poems*, ed. McCabe, 193–4.
8. Spenser, *Faerie Queene*, 632.
9. Stephano Guazzo, *The Civile Conversation*, trans. George Pettie and ed. Charles Whibley. 2 vols. The Tudor Translations (New York: AMS Press, 1967), 175.
10. According to William Oram, the comments on Calepine's bear-baby (*FQ*, VI.iv.) might be tongue-in-cheek, taking as they do the extreme view that you can form a baby by his education.

11 34 and 35 Henry VIII.c.1. Cited in David Cressy, *Literacy and the Social Order: Reading and Writing in Tudor and Stuart England* (Cambridge: Cambridge University Press, 1980), 44.
12 *The Letters and Life of Francis Bacon*, ed. J. Spedding, 14 vols (London, 1868), 4: 252-3.
13 Lawrence Stone, 'The Educational Revolution in England, 1560-1640', *Past and Present*, 28 (1964), 41-80, esp. 69 on lack of progress.
14 *The Description of England* by William Harrison, ed. Georges Edelen, Folger Shakespeare Library (Ithaca: Cornell University Press, 1968), 76. This text was first published in 1577 as part of Holinshed's *Chronicles*, now available as a free e-book from www.gutenberg.org.
15 Christopher Wase, *Considerations Concerning Free Schools as Settled in England* (London: Mr Simon Millers, 1678), 1. RB 349367, The Huntington Library, San Marino, CA.
16 T.W. Baldwin, *William Shakespeare's Petty School* (Urbana: Univesity of Illinois Press, 1943), 44.
17 After the Restoration, in the House of Lords (Convocations of Canterbury in 1664 and 1675), attempts were made to end the privileged status of Lyly's *Grammar*, but to no avail.
18 John Hoole (1610-67), *A New Discovery of the Old Art of Teaching Schoole*, "The Master's Method'. Available online from the Hathi Trust Digital Library, based on 1913 rpt (Liverpool: Liverpool University Press).
19 Peter Mack, *Elizabethan Rhetoric: Theory and Practice* (Cambridge: Cambridge University Press, 2002).
20 For numerous translations of neo-Latin literature by Dana Sutton and others, see the philological museum at www.philological.bham.ac.uk.
21 Mulcaster's *Elementarie*, ed. E.T. Campagnac (Oxford: Clarendon Press, 1925), N2r (179).
22 *A Transcript of the Registers of the Company of Stationers of London*, ed. Edward Arber (1875; rpt Gloucester, MA: Peter Smith, 1967), 2.
23 In *Familiar Letters*, there is an allusion to Spenser's 'nine Englishe Commoedies', and a 'Latine *Stemmata Dudleiana*', but, if these works ever existed, they have not survived.
24 On including playacting in the curriculum, see Foster Watson, *The English Grammar Schools to 1660: Their Curriculum and Practice* (1908; rpt New York: Augustus M. Kelley, 1970), 318-24. For an account of the Chapel Royal, see Mrs C.C. Stopes, *William Hunnis and the Revels of the Chapel Royal* (Louvain and London: A. Uystpruyst and David Nutt, 1910), 226-33. Plays were also presented at court by the children of the Chapel, St Paul's, and Westminster where Ben Jonson studied under William Camden.
25 DeMolen, *Mulcaster*, 133. The resulting pageants were printed as *The Quenes Maiesties Passage through the Citie of London To Westminster the Day before her Coronacion* (London: Richard Tottel, 1559). Reprinted by John Nichols, *The Progresses and Public Processions of Queen Elizabeth*, 2 vols (London, 1788-1805, 1823; New York: Burt Franklin, 1966), I: 38-60. Reprinted by Arthur F. Kinney, ed., *Elizabethan Backgrounds* (Hamden, CT: Archon Books, 1975), 7-59.
26 DeMolen, *Mulcaster*, 139-44.

27 Both were printed in Nichols, *The Progresses and Public Processions of Queen Elizabeth*; see also C.T. Prouty, *George Gascoigne: Elizabethan Courtier, Soldier, and Poet* (New York: Columbia University Press, 1942), 86–9.
28 For a study of William Hunnis, see Stopes, *William Hunnis and the Revels*, 234–44.
29 *Liber Famelicus of Sir James Whitelocke*, ed. John Bruce, Camden Society, No. 70 (Westminster: J.B. Nichols and Sons, 1858), 12.
30 *Documents Relating to the Office of the Revels in the Time of Queen Elizabeth*, ed. Albert Feuillerat (rpt Louvain: A. Uystpruyst, 1963), 174, 350. The boys also performed for the general public. On 16 March 1573/4 the company decreed that 'playes and such lyke exercises ... exposed to be seane for money' could not be presented in the common hall to any 'lewed persone [who] thinketh himself (for his penny) worthy of the cheif and most comodious place'.
31 Ascham, *Schoolmaster* (1570), ed. Lawrence V. Ryan. (Ithaca: Published for the Folger Shakespeare Library by Cornell University Press, 1967), 67.
32 Barker (Mulcaster, *Positions*), lxxii, cites his possible robbery of Dr Caius, as does De Molen, *Mulcaster*, 25.
33 John Buckeridge, 'Sermon Preached at the Funeral of ... Lancelot Late Lord Bishop of Winchester', 6 November 1626, in *XCVI Sermons* (London: Richard Badger, 1634), 15.
34 For Mulcaster as a linguistic theorist, see Maria O'Neill, 'Forgotten Figure on the Bridge: Richard Mulcaster', *Sederi*, VII (1996), 93–7.
35 It should be possible to produce a regularized or modernized text for Spenser's works using the orthography of the letters he wrote for Lord Grey and Mulcaster's *Elementarie*.
36 William Barker states that there are no records documenting the acquaintanceship of van Meteren and Mulcaster before the 1570s. See Barker (Mulcaster, *Positions*), lxvii, lxxvi.
37 On the translator, see Leonard Forster, 'The Translator of the "Theatre for Worldlings"', *English Studies*, 48 (1967), 27–34; for arguments on authorship, see W.J.B. Pienaar, 'Edmund Spenser and Jonker Jan van der Noot', *English Studies*, 8 (1926), 33–44 and 67–76.
38 W.L. Renwick, ed. *Complaints* (London: Scholartis Press, 1928), 260.
39 For an argument that Spenser translated eleven sonnets from Du Bellay, but did not translate the 'sonets from the Apocalypse', see Alfred W. Satterwaite, *Spenser, Ronsard, and Du Bellay: A Renaissance Comparison* (Princeton: Princeton University Press, 1960), appendix 1: 255–63.
40 On this preface, see my 'Who Fashioned Edmund Spenser?: The Textual History of *Complaints*', *Studies in Philology*, 88 (1991): 153–68.
41 Gabriel Harvey is likely to have had copies of early works by Spenser and was in London at this time. According to Thomas Nashe, he was employed sporadically as a proofreader by the printer and publisher John Wolfe.
42 On French influences, see Anne Lake Prescott, *French Poets and the English Renaissance: Studies in Fame and Transformation* (New Haven: Yale University Press, 1978); for Italian, see William J. Kennedy, *Authorizing Petrarch* (Ithaca: Cornell University Press, 1994), 195–280; for Dutch, see Jan van Dorsten, *The Radical Arts: First Decade of an Elizabethan Renaissance* (Leiden: Sir Thomas Browne Institute, 1970).

3

Pembroke College (1569–74)

To understand the atmosphere of Spenser's undergraduate residence at Cambridge we need to recognize that universities were far from being ivory towers. During the English Reformation, battles over ritual and church government played themselves out at Cambridge as fiercely as, or more fiercely than, they did in society at large. After the accession of Elizabeth, universities served as havens to the liberal intellectuals returning from the Continent, but at the same time figured as bastions of the established church. The stakes were very high: it was the universities that would educate the clergymen who would shape the future of Protestantism. The returning Marian exiles were suspicious of ecclesiastical hierarchy and objected to vestments and ceremonies; they believed that scripture should determine church government. The more radical, associated with what was later called the Puritan party, disapproved of what they viewed as the government's conciliatory attitude towards the Roman rituals in the Elizabethan church and the Queen's policy of toleration. The liberties and franchises of the universities, confirmed in the Elizabethan charter of April 1561, were repeatedly questioned and threatened by ecclesiastical commissions.

Pembroke and the Reformation

Pembroke, the Cambridge college at which Spenser matriculated, was central to Reformation history. Of the men with close ties to Pembroke who played major roles in contemporary church politics, the most prominent was Edmund Grindal (1519?–1583; appointed Archbishop of

Canterbury 1575 and served until 1583). He appears in Spenser's early literary work *Shepheardes Calender* (1579) under the anagram Algrind and as representative of the view that the clergy should be held to a higher standard of conduct and '[m]ought not live ylike, as men of the laye' (*Maye*, 75–6). Grindal, himself a Master of Pembroke, was the protégé of Nicholas Ridley, a former Master of Pembroke and an important Protestant martyr catalogued by John Foxe. In 1547, Ridley became first Bishop of Rochester and then in 1550 Bishop of London. During the Marian persecutions, on 16 October 1555, Ridley refused to recant his Protestant faith and was burned at the stake along with Hugh Latimer.[1] John Rogers, John Bradford, and Edmund Grindal were Fellows of Pembroke while Ridley was Master. Rogers was burned at Smithfield, where Spenser reportedly grew up; both he and Bradford left accounts of their martyrdom. Grindal, who escaped to the Continent, became a symbol of Protestant heroism and a revered senior statesman of Pembroke College.

Grindal seems to have controlled senior appointments at Pembroke before, during, and after Spenser's residence. Prior to his falling out with the Queen in 1577, from 1562 to 1577 his favour guaranteed advancement at Pembroke and probably in the church as well. After resigning as Master of Pembroke in 1562, he was succeeded by one of his chaplains, Matthew Hutton, Lady Margaret Professor of Divinity at Trinity. When Hutton was appointed Dean of York in 1567 (subsequently Bishop of Durham in 1589 and Archbishop of York in 1596), he too resigned. Grindal then recommended John Whitgift, another of his chaplains, as the next Master of Pembroke. Whitgift, a Fellow of Peterhouse, was Master from April to July 1567, but then became Master of Trinity, an office which he held until he, too, became a bishop.

John Young: Spenser's patron

After Whitgift left Pembroke for Trinity, Grindal proposed John Young as Master of Pembroke, a position in which Young was to serve for eleven years, from 1567 to 1578, until he was created Bishop of Rochester. It is this John Young, a protégé of Grindal's, and an heir to the Pembroke tradition extending from Ridley to Grindal, who became Spenser's most important early patron. In the *September* eclogue of Spenser's *Shepheardes Calender*, Young, Bishop of Rochester, figures as Roffy or Roffyn (derived from the Latin *Roffensis* for Rochester) and is approvingly characterized as 'meeke, wise, and merciable, / And with his word his worke is conuenable' (174–5).

In 1567, two years before Spenser matriculated at Pembroke, Young became Master of Pembroke but continued to reside in London and to serve as Rector of St Magnus the Martyr, London Bridge, and as a prebendary of both St Paul's and Southwell Minster in Nottinghamshire. In 1572 he was also a Canon of Westminster. In 1569, the year that Spenser matriculated, John Young, already Master of Pembroke for two years, became Vice-Chancellor of the university. Though William Cecil, Lord Burghley, was officially the Chancellor, the Vice-Chancellor was the principal administrator. During Young's tenure as Vice-Chancellor, a dispute arose because Thomas Aldrich failed to proceed to Bachelor of Divinity within three years after he became Master of Corpus Christi. Aldrich was summoned to Lambeth by Archbishop Mathew Parker to account for his failure to abide by statutes. Vice-Chancellor John Young ordered Aldrich to ignore the summons.

Burghley was called in to adjudicate, but his position seems to be unknown. A hearing was held with Young and other university officials, and the actions of Vice-Chancellor Young were vindicated. In the meantime, Archbishop Parker disclaimed any desire to abridge the privileges of the universities. Once Vice-Chancellor Young and the heads of colleges had won their point, they notified Burghley that, in their judgement, Aldrich should not remain in his position. They stipulated that they were reluctant to render a final decision until they had received the direction of Archbishop Parker. The dispute was thus resolved with graciousness on all sides, but Young had maintained the principle that the university had the privilege and responsibility for disciplining its own. Young's victory may have earned him respect within the academic community, but his independence is unlikely to have enhanced his stature in the circles of power.[2] Even when self-interest might have dictated caution, Young, like Grindal, was not a compromiser, and so he opposed Archbishop Matthew Parker on an issue involving the franchise of the university.

Sizar at Pembroke

Spenser matriculated as a sizar, indicating that he worked for his room and board and for his tuition. The term 'sizar' is thought to have derived from 'assize' and to refer to the 'sizes' or 'sizings' that were the ordinary portions of food and drink allotted as part of the fixed fee or pension. One of a sizar's duties was to serve the 'sizes' to the 'pensioners' who paid for their room and board – much the same as would happen with modern-day 'board jobs'. Most students entered as pensioners. Gabriel Harvey, for example, was admitted as a gentleman pensioner at Easter 1566. An Edward Spencer, the fifth son of Sir John Spencer of Althorp, was admitted as a gentleman pensioner at Caius College on 15 November 1575. This Edward Spencer was the brother of the sisters who were to act as patrons to Spenser in the 1590s, and care should be taken to distinguish his publications from those of Edmund.

We know that Spenser was at least fourteen years old when he matriculated, or he would have been entered as *'impubes'*, younger than fourteen. Those who were admitted as fellow commoners paid double fees; for this they were allowed to sit at the high table along with the fellows and to graduate in three years. Edward de Vere, Earl of Oxford, for example, matriculated at Queen's College as a fellow commoner when he was only eight years old; his youthful admission was not so much a sign of intellectual precocity as it was a marker of rank and financial resources. De Vere subsequently seems to have been educated in the household of Sir Thomas Smith, later Elizabeth's Secretary of State, and a patron of Gabriel Harvey.

In addition to the support Spenser received as a sizar at Cambridge, he also continued to receive bequests from the estate of Robert Nowell. On 7 November 1570, Spenser and Richard Langherne, the son of a clergyman, are mentioned as follows:

> To Richard Langher and Edmond Spenser / towe poore scholars of Pembrock haule vj^s a peace in the whole xij^s. by the handes of Mr Thomas Newce felow of the same house. (fol. 75; *Townley Hall MSS*, ed. Grosart, 172)

Richard Langherne (Langher) was the son of Richard Langherne, vicar of Edmonton, who died in 1570.[3] The following spring Spenser again received a grant from the 'Nowell Account Book' in an entry dated 24 April 1571:

> To Edmonde Spensere the xxiiijth of aprill A^o i57i. . . . .
> ij^{s}vj^d. (fol. 72; *Townley Hall MSS*, ed. Grosart, 164)

The continuation of these bequests to Spenser demonstrates that his benefactors were pleased by his academic progress.

The Pembroke College account books, along with records of continuing bequests in the 'Nowell Account Book', are the principal extant documents relating specifically to Spenser for the years 1569–74. In supplement to these records of scholarships that Spenser received from the Nowell estate, we have entries in the Pembroke College account books that shed light on Spenser's academic standing while at Cambridge. These records have survived, and they were printed, but not very clearly, in Grosart's biography.[4] In addition, Grosart ignored the context in which the references appeared and interpreted the entries themselves too literally. The term *aegrotat* (lit. he is sick) was used to describe a student who had been ill but was still allowed to receive a degree. Grosart interprets these entries as evidence of Spenser's ill-health: 'I fear that he was valetudinarian' (*Life*, 36–7). Percy Long thought that the entries were proof of academic graft and evidence of partiality towards graduates from Merchant Taylors' School.[5] However, in the account books of Pembroke College, *aegrotat* was interpreted broadly and used as a filler. For example, John Young, Master of Pembroke, when he was Vice-Chancellor, was out of commons for twenty-two weeks in 1568. He was granted an allowance for the entire year in lieu of commons; this allowance is described as *praefecto aegrotanti*. From this example and from other entries in the records, Aubrey Attwater, historian of Pembroke, concluded that *aegrotat* was a catch-all term used when a student or fellow was away from the university, or ill, and so did not participate in meals or commons.[6]

To this I want to add my independent assessment of the records. There is evidence that *aegrotat* also functioned in the account books as a convenient way of listing sums paid out of discretionary funds, particularly as scholarships or grants to meritorious students. Five names appear very frequently in connection with *aegrotats*: Edmund Spenser, Richard Langherne, Lancelot Andrewes, Thomas Dove, and Gregory Downhall. Each of these scholars had attended Merchant Taylors' School; each was a beneficiary of bequests from the will of Robert Nowell. In addition, Andrewes, Downhall, and Dove were awarded Watts scholarships. Thomas Watts, Archdeacon of Middlesex, was one of Grindal's chaplains, and he founded seven Greek scholarships at Pembroke with elaborate requirements that the scholars be examined in Greek, Hebrew, and Latin. The scholars had to be able to compose Latin and Greek epigrams on scriptural topics for presentation on Sundays and at festivals.

In the Pembroke account books, grants described as *aegrotats* are related to the Watts scholarships and other occasional awards for scholarship or presentations. Both Langherne and Spenser matriculated prior to the establishment of the Watts scholarships, but it is reasonable to assume that since both matriculated as sizars and both received *aegrotat* funds, they benefited from a similar endowment. Watts specified a preference for residents of London, and so it is not evidence of graft that many students from Merchant Taylors' School benefited from his bequest.

The relevant lists appear in the manuscript account book of Pembroke College where the allowance for *aegrotat* is approximately 10d per week. Entries relating to Spenser appear on folios 55, 58, and 66 with payments for eleven and a half weeks in 1570, seven weeks in 1571, and six weeks for 1573.[7] A number of entries appear as 'Dom. Langhorne & Spenser'; Spenser is thus linked with Richard Langherne. These entries and the fact that they both entered as sizars may indicate that they shared chambers.

It seems to have been customary to supply an *aegrotat* allowance to all of the scholars and many of the Fellows during Lent, and these allowances for Lent explain two, but not all, of the grants to Spenser.[8] The other grants can be accounted for if we assume that the term *aegrotat* was also used to record grants out of discretionary funds deriving from bequests or gifts to the College. This seems likely because we find references to Spenser, Langherne, Dove, Andrewes, and Downhall (Downell, Downall) at times other than Lent. Among this high-achieving group receiving *aegrotat* funds, both Dove and Andrewes went on to become bishops recognized for their learning. Richard Langherne was awarded a Fellowship as soon as he received the B.A. in 1572; he received the M.A. in 1575. Another frequent recipient of *aegrotat* allowances, Gregory Downhall, seems not to have received the B.A. Like John Donne, who later took the same post, Downhall became a secretary to Sir Thomas Egerton, Lord Keeper. He went on to become a Master in Chancery and benefactor to the Pembroke College Library.

Far from suggesting that Spenser was sickly (Grosart) or the beneficiary of Elizabethan graft (Long), the Pembroke account books, like the 'Nowell Account Book', show that Spenser was regarded as an exceptionally talented performer among an already outstanding group of students. Spenser's B.A. was awarded in 1573; he ranked eleventh in the Ordo Senioritatis, and third from Pembroke College.[9]

Cartwright, Whitgift, and university governance

Spenser and his classmates may not have become actively involved in the Vestment or the Admonition controversies, but the theological debates and accompanying political struggles affected their lives as undergraduates, and, in the case of Gabriel Harvey may even have had a lasting impact on his career. While Spenser was at Pembroke the uneasiness between conservative supporters of the established church and Protestant liberals, sometimes labelled Puritans, erupted into a public confrontation between the liberal Thomas Cartwright and the conservative John Whitgift.

It is even possible that Cartwright's story had a bearing on Spenser's decision not to pursue an academic career. Prior to Spenser's matriculation at Pembroke, Cartwright, to escape the religious contention at Cambridge which he himself had done something to provoke, retired in 1565 to Ireland. Adam Loftus, a Cambridge man and former Fellow of Trinity College, had been appointed Archbishop of Armagh in Ireland at a relatively youthful age. Following the appointment, Cartwright accompanied Loftus to Ireland as his chaplain. In March 1567, when Loftus was translated to the see of Dublin, he took advantage of that occasion to urge that his chaplain Cartwright be appointed his successor in the see of Armagh. In a letter written 5 December 1567, Loftus declares that Cartwright had 'used hym self so godlly, during his abode with me in Ireland, bothe in lyfe and doctryne, that his absence from hence is no small greef and sorowe to all the godly and faythfull heare'.[10]

Cartwright, a Fellow of Trinity College, was accorded the distinction of being elected Lady Margaret Professor of Divinity in 1569, the year that Spenser matriculated at Pembroke. Cartwright's enemy, John Whitgift, now Master of Trinity, was a protégé of the influential Andrew Perne, who was notorious for his willingness to accommodate to whatever happened to be the national religion. In 1556 Perne preached the sermon when the bodies of Bucer and Fagius were disinterred and burnt for heresy; in 1560 when these proceedings were reversed under Elizabeth, he preached a second sermon – this time rehabilitating them. Campus wags advertised that, if a coat had been turned, it had been 'perned'. In the Martin Marprelate tracts he was later labelled 'old Andrew Turncoat'. Even so, Perne was a force to be reckoned with at Cambridge; he was five times Vice-Chancellor of the university.

Initially, Whitgift may have feared that Cartwright, who was generally conceded to be a better orator than Whitgift, was so popular that he might become a serious candidate for Vice-Chancellor of the University and then stage a Puritan takeover. Whitgift prized quiet, and he was more concerned with order and uniformity than theology. In contrast, Cartwright welcomed the intellectual ferment of a continuing reformation along the liberal lines later advocated in Milton's *Areopagitica*. Cartwright particularly challenged the establishment because he was dealing with the highly explosive issue of church government, rather than less volatile matters, such as wearing the appropriate clerical attire or kneeling at communion. His concern with licensing for pluralities and non-residence had financial implications for the economic status of the clergy, but even this was a less volatile issue than church governance.[11] Cartwright claimed that he was the true conservative and that he was conserving the democratic organization of the early church. He lectured in favour of holding presbyterian elections to select bishops and so antagonized even those who sympathized with other tenets of Puritanism. On 11 June 1570, William Chadderton wrote to Burghley charging that Cartwright intended to overthrow all ecclesiastical and civil governance, and even Edmund Grindal complained that Cartwright's unsound doctrines proceeded from a head 'stuffed full of singularities'.[12]

Cambridge authorities appealed to Burghley, honorary Chancellor of Cambridge, but Burghley with characteristic shrewdness refused to intervene. He opposed persecution on practical grounds because it made martyrs and then heroes of the opposition. Even so, rather than ignoring Cartwright, university authorities led by Whitgift decided to refuse Cartwright his degree as Doctor of Divinity. Once this became generally known, Cartwright's supporters organized to confront the administration. In the Congregation of 29 June 1570, they vetoed the name of every candidate proposed for membership in the *caput*, the governing body of the university, who did not favour Cartwright.

Spenser was in his second year at the university when this familiar academic drama played itself out. Dissension over religion and politics erupted into a power struggle over university governance.[13] The University was technically governed by six men, the Vice-Chancellor and the *caput senatus*. At the beginning of Elizabeth's reign the relatively liberal statutes of Edward's reign were reinstituted.[14] The *caput*, elected at each congregation, consisted of five members: three doctors from the traditional faculties of law, physic, and divinity and two representatives selected on the basis of seniority rather than specialization: 'a non-regent', who represented masters of arts with at least five years' standing or doctors with two years' standing, and a 'regent', who was a master of arts with less than five years' standing. These designations are counterintuitive because the non-regents are senior to the regents; the regents, even though they had held the M.A. for less than five years, were very influential because they were responsible for teaching. Proctors were elected from non-regents, and scrutators were elected from regents.

In 1570, Whitgift began a battle to establish new statutes that not only departed from the Edwardian model but were even more conservative than those that had prevailed during the reign of Catholic Mary. Whitgift wanted to vest governance entirely in the hands of the Vice-Chancellor and the Masters of colleges by limiting the right to nominate candidates for Vice-Chancellor to the heads of colleges. The procedures for electing the caput were to be similarly restrictive. The Vice-Chancellor would draw up a list of five names: a Doctor of Divinity, a graduate in law and another in medicine, a non-regent, and a regent. Each of the two proctors made out a similar list. The Masters of colleges, doctors, and scrutators selected five of the fifteen nominees to serve on the caput for the entire following year. Since the heads of colleges, quite naturally, would endorse the nominees of the Vice-Chancellor, whom they had themselves elected, their control over the university was assured. Significantly, the Vice-Chancellor was to have veto power over every grace offered to the senate and thus could block the award of any degree. A clause was also included giving the master of each house a veto to all internal elections, even though this provision violated the statutes of many of the colleges. Statute 45 aimed at Cartwright, of course, legislated against criticism of the established religion.

Not surprisingly, the new statutes received royal approval. Opposition to the new statutes was coloured by attitudes towards the perceived disenfranchisement of teaching fellows, i.e., the junior faculty.[15] Most of the regents and non-regents, who had all received the M.A., acted as tutors; they assisted their undergraduate pupils in finding lodging and even sometimes lived with them. In December 1570, after Whitgift was elected Vice-Chancellor, he immediately created a crisis concerning religious toleration and faculty governance. With the support of the Masters of colleges and under the authority of new statutes, he deprived Cartwright of his Lady Margaret lectureship. This spectacular event radicalized students and junior faculty.

Whitgift, who wanted to eradicate Puritanism from Cambridge, appears to have thought he could accomplish this by getting rid of Cartwright. By September, he had managed to deprive Cartwright of his Fellowship. He used as grounds Cartwright's failure to observe the college statute, requiring that, within seven years of receiving the M.A., a Fellow should take clerical orders. A similar statute was later used to force Gabriel Harvey out of his fellowship at Pembroke. Whitgift's actions against Cartwright were viewed not only as a crackdown on reformist Protestantism but also as a declaration of war on faculty and student governance. Many who were not Puritan sympathizers opposed the new statutes. Lancelot Brown, a Pembroke fellow and an opposition leader, circulated a protest document. By 6 May 1572, the opposition had collected 134 names. Among those signing were a number of unlikely names, including

Humphrey Tyndall, Lawrence Chadderton, and, most ironically, Richard Bancroft, who later joined Whitgift's crusade against Puritanism and succeeded him as Archbishop of Canterbury.[16]

Gabriel Harvey and the Pembroke Fellows

The battle over the new statutes supplies the context for a confrontation between the resident Fellows and John Young, Master of Pembroke College. The issue at stake became who, the Master or the Fellows, was to have the final authority in granting degrees. Young clearly had the final authority under the new statutes, but the Pembroke Fellows used their resentment of Gabriel Harvey, whose demeanour had antagonized them, to challenge Young. Harvey, unlike Spenser, came from a wealthy family; before becoming a Fellow at Pembroke, he had matriculated as a pensioner at King's College. His father, whom Thomas Nashe was later to describe as a rope-maker, was engaged in trade, and so Harvey, whatever his financial resources, was regarded as socially inferior by the more genteel of his fellows. His advertisement of his connections to patrons, such as Sir Thomas Smith, who was prominent in the government, may also have antagonized the Pembroke Fellows. After receiving his B.A. from King's College, he was granted the fellowship at Pembroke in 1570; he credited Sir Thomas Smith, a neighbour, perhaps even a kinsman, with assistance in gaining this appointment.[17]

In the marginalia to his Livy that can be dated in 1570 or early 1571 Harvey reports witnessing a fascinating debate on Elizabethan military strategy deriving from Livy's 'Marcellus' and 'Fabius Maximus'. Representing 'Fabius Maximus', Sir Thomas Smith, Secretary of State, and Walter Haddon, a distinguished Latinist and civil lawyer, won the contest in which Sir Humphrey Gilbert, recently knighted for service in Ireland, and Thomas Smith the younger, represented 'Marcellus'. Keenly sensitive to issues of class, Harvey describes the audience as 'myself, John Wood, and several others of gentle birth'.[18] Only a person insecure of his own social status would be likely to add the phrase 'others of gentle birth' to a marginal comment. Later in his Livy, Harvey describes another occasion upon which he read Livy, this time with the younger Thomas Smith. This reading occurred early in 1571, just prior to Smith's being sent to Ireland as a royal deputy in the Ardes, where his family had colonial interests.[19] In Foure Letters (1592), Harvey later corroborates the patronage that he received from the Smiths and also alludes to the benevolence of the Earl of Oxford, reporting that Oxford bestowed golden coins on him at Cambridge (17) 'at the affectionate commendation of my Cosen, M. Thomas Smith, the sonne of Sir Thomas, shortly after Colonel of the Ards in Ireland'.[20] As this passage indicates, Harvey likes to point out the importance of his connections, but his success in attracting the attention of learned men, who also occupied centre stage in Elizabethan politics, may not have endeared him to his peers. Harvey is likely to have publicly touted his triumphs as well as recording them in the margins of his books.

In 1573, Harvey had technically fulfilled the three years' residence requirement for the Master of Arts, and his degree was thus to be awarded. The Pembroke Fellows, however, refused to pass Harvey's supplication for the degree. Resentment of Harvey may not have been the only motivating factor. The Fellows may also have been eager to challenge the master's sole authority to authorize degrees under the new statutes. Spenser was in his fourth year when this confrontation occurred, and he would have known all of the players in this drama.

Even though he denied being a Puritan, Harvey was widely regarded as a Puritan sympathizer because of his enthusiasm for intellectual innovation. In 1549, the Cambridge statutes had required lecturers on rhetoric to cover Cicero, Hermogenes, and Quintilian. Harvey's interest in the modern views of Peter Ramus may have been enough to make him appear radical. Sir Roger Ascham, Elizabeth's tutor, explains the connection that Harvey's contemporaries made between intellectual innovation and political dissidence. In the *Scholemaster* (1570), Ascham chides Ramus and Talaeus for their criticism of Aristotle and Cicero. He implies that those attracted to these innovators are likely to be subversive in religion and politics:

> For he, that can neither like *Aristotle* in Logicke and Philoosphie, nor *Tullie* in *Rhetor*icke and Eloquence, will from these steppes likelie enough presume by, like pride, to mount hier, to the misliking of greater matters: that is either in Religion, to have a dissentious head, or in the common wealth, to have a factious hart.[21]

Harvey's Cambridge contemporaries, like Ascham, may have associated innovation in rhetoric with 'faction' in religion and politics, and these prejudices may explain why the combination of Harvey's intellectual liberalism and his social class may have made his peers suspicious of his politics.

Nearly everything that we know about these events is presented from Harvey's point of view. We have eight letters written by Harvey dating from 21 March to 1 November 1573 preserved in a collection of manuscripts, now known as Harvey's *Letter-Book*.[22] Letters 1, 4, 5, 6, and 8 are addressed to Dr John Young; letters 2 and 3 are to Humphrey Tyndall, Fellow of Pembroke; Letter 7 is to Harvey's father. We know that Harvey composed these letters; they are copied into Sloane 93 in a very fair version of his hand, but we cannot be certain if these are copies, or merely drafts, of letters that Harvey later sent.

The story of Harvey's conflicts with his Cambridge colleagues is important to Spenser's biography because it makes us aware of Harvey as a figure in his own right and introduces us to his somewhat quirky personality. Convinced of his own intellectual superiority, Harvey was treated as a social inferior by many at the university. In the correspondence preserved in his private *Letter-Book*, he reveals character traits that are more publicly displayed in *Familiar Letters* and more than twenty years later during his pamphlet warfare with Thomas Nashe. A more nuanced approach to the differences, as well as the similarities, between Spenser and Harvey's personalities, is needed, and this early conflict with authority is suggestive. Harvey wanted to play a figure on the world stage; his published, and even unpublished, writing focuses on advancing his career. Even in the presumably private marginalia of his personal library, Harvey created personae who represented various aspects of his personality, and he used these fictional avatars to imagine and work out strategies for self-promotion, e.g., 'Axiophilus', a writer and critic of poetry; 'Chrysotechnus', a philosopher; and even 'Anonymus'.[23]

> No marvell, thowgh Axiophilus be so slowe in publishing his exercises, that is so hastie in dispatching them: being one that rigorously censures himself; unpartially examines other; & deemes nothing honorable, or commendable in a poet, that is not divine, or illuminate, singular, or rare; excellent, or sum way notable.[24]

At the conclusion of the volume he wistfully imagines 'sum heroical thing in the clowdes ... Axiophilus ... will remember to leave sum memorials behinde him: & to make use of so manie rhapsodies, cantos, hymnes, odes, epigrams, sonets, & discourses, as at idle howers, or at flowing fitts he hath compiled'.[25] Harvey, apparently, thought of himself as quick to 'dispatch' but slow to 'publish' and dreamed that he would indeed 'leave sum memorials behinde him'.

The sizar Spenser experienced economic pressures that Harvey would not have encountered, but the social pressures that they faced were similar. Though Spenser lacked Harvey's economic assets, he shared with him the stigma of being a new man, but they handled social pressure differently. Judging from his later ironic presentations of himself as Immerito and Colin Clout, Spenser disarmed criticism by accepting and even dramatizing his own unworthiness. Harvey defied those of his peers who scorned him, and, as a result, was regarded as arrogant and self-important long before Thomas Nashe took up his pen.

As Harvey relates the story of the events at Pembroke, he was the innocent victim of the other Pembroke Fellows who arbitrarily decided to block the award of his Master of Arts degree. Even from Harvey's account, it is clear that he had gone out of his way to identify himself with avant-garde ideas and so managed to give credence to the charge that he sympathized with Puritan positions. On 21 March 1573, Harvey wrote to John Young, Master of Pembroke, to protest against the blocking of his M.A.: 'this is mi year to commens master of art: and you know how ordinari a thing it is, that everi on at his time should inioie his degree, unles there be sum wunderful great let to the contrari' (2). Harvey identifies Thomas Neville, Thomas Nuce, Richard Osburn (Osborne), the tutor, and Sir Lawhorne (Langherne) as the principal opponents to his receiving the degree. The ringleader Thomas Neville had received a fellowship from Pembroke in 1570, the same year that Harvey received his, but he had been awarded the M.A. a year earlier in 1572. Neville, a descendant of the poet Barnabe Googe, was from a well-to-do and staunchly Church of England family. His brother Alexander Neville served as a secretary to Archbishop Parker. Far from opposing the new statutes, Neville aligned himself with Whitgift, whose protégé he was to become. He later succeeded Whitgift as Master of Trinity College (1593–1615) and was an executor of Whitgift's estate. Harvey's opponents were not philistines, but intellectuals who shared the literary interests of Spenser and Harvey. Thomas's brother Alexander Neville (1544–1614) and Thomas Nuce were both early translators of Seneca.

Harvey himself says nothing about the social class of his adversaries and downplays the influence of religion and politics on their actions. To Young he reports that Neville has lodged four charges against him:

> He laid against me mi commun behaviur, that I was not familiar like a fellow, and that I did disdain everi mans cumpani … The secund point that he stud uppon was, that I culd hardly find in mi hart to commend of ani man; and that I have misliked those which bi commun consent and agrement of al have bene veri wel thout of for there lerning … I hapned to kast out thus mutch, that althouh thei were both veri il, yit of the two it were better for a man to be thout arrogant then foolish. [According

to Harvey, Neville repeated the remark out of context in a large company as evidence that Harvey preferred arrogance before folly.] ... M. Nevils third reason was, that I made but smal and liht account of mi felloushop. That he gatherid uppon certain talk that a litle before fil out betwixt him and me at the table. The talk was this: he said he wuld not for a hundrith pounds but have bene fellou of the hous: and I said merrely, that a hundrith pound was a great deal of moni in a schollars purs ... I said also, that I made as great account of the bennefit as ethir he or ani man els did, or coold. Marri so, that I wuld have bene loth to have bouht it so dear as he spake of. (4–8)

According to Harvey, Neville's fourth and principal academic objection to him was that he was 'a great and continual patron of paradoxis and a main defender of straung opinions, and that communly against Aristotle too' (10).

To refute the charge that he is anti-Aristotelian, Harvey cites Melanchthon, Ramus, Valerius, and Foxius as the sources for his paradoxes, but unconsciously reveals his disdain for old-fashioned approaches to rhetoric and logic:

> Sutch matters have bene thurrouly canvissid long ago: and everi on that can do ani thing is able to write hole volumes of them, and make glorius shows with them. I cannot tel, but me thinks it were more fruteful for us and commodius for our auditors to handle sum sad and witti controversi. But I never found ani fault with them for duelling in there own stale quaestions. (11)

Harvey's interest in Ramus seems to have been regarded with suspicion:

> But thai f[e]are that this singulariti in philosophi is like to grow to a shrode matter, if I onc convert mi studdi to diuiniti. Belike thai are aferd les I shuld proove sum noble heretick like Arrius and Pelagius: and so disturb and disquiet the Church as I now do the Chappel. (11)

It is clear even from his own report that Harvey had already caused 'disquiet' in the 'Chappel' and had identified himself as unorthodox. Rightly or wrongly, he was viewed as having Puritan leanings. Thomas Nuce, the senior Fellow and Young's deputy, talked with him about his philosophical questions and told him that he 'seemid to be givin over mutch to nu opinions' (16).

Richard Langherne, a fourth-year student but one who was immediately elected to a fellowship, is mentioned in Harvey's *Letter-Book*, but Spenser is not (2, 26, 28, 33, 35, 36). Even so, we can be sure that Spenser knew that Harvey was under attack. Harvey vividly described the libels that were circulated about him throughout Cambridge:

> And now tales run up and down the town that Sr Harvi of Pembrook Hale hath dun thus and thus, abusid thes men, and thes men, behavid himself after this manner and this manner ... and thai that knew me too (unles it be sum of mi nearist acquaintanc) mai now begin to dout of me. (17)

Harvey concluded his letter on 21 March 1573 with apologies to Young for the trouble that he was causing him.

In April, Harvey, having retreated to his family home at Saffron Walden, wrote and asked Humphrey Tyndall, a senior Fellow at Pembroke, to ride to London and discuss the matter with John Young. Either Tyndall returned with letters from Young or Young had already dispatched letters to his deputy Thomas Nuce and the other Fellows. On 4 April Nuce brought up Harvey's grace in chapel but indicated to the assembly that while previously 'he had bene sumwhat ernest to further [Harvey], he wuld now be veri indifferent only' (25). Humphrey Tyndall discussed the matter privately with Nuce who, according to Harvey, was offended by Young's tone: 'M. Nuce ... seemid to take it in marvelus great duggin that your wurship had written so sharply and bitterly unto him, as he thouht, saiing he wuld not have written so to ani servant' (28). Again, we have evidence that tensions regarding social class underpinned these quarrels. Harvey, although his principal goal was to vindicate himself, could not resist showing off. Lancelot Brown, a senior fellow studying medicine and a recent opponent of the new statutes, supposedly added to the charges against Harvey that he had 'dispraisid al men saving physicians' and had 'greatly commendid thos whitch men call praecisions and puritanes' (29).

Accusations that a man was a Puritan could be used to brand him as intolerant of authority. William Camden, unsympathetically but suggestively, summarizes the politics of Puritan intellectuals: 'Incredible it is how much the followers of this sect increased everywhere through a certain obstinate wilfulness in them, indiscretion of the bishops, and secret favour of certain noblemen who gaped after the wealth of the Church, which sect began presently to be known by the odious name of Puritans'.[26] Harvey preens himself on exposing the fallacy in the charge that he is a Puritan:

> And as for puritanes I wuld fain know what those same puritanes ar and what quallities thai have, that I have so hihly and usually commendid. Let M. Phisician name the persons and then shew that I have praisid

them, in that respect thai ar puritanes or that ever I have maintainid ani
od point of puritanism, or praecisionism mi self, and I shal be contentid
to be bard of mi mastership and iointid of my fellowship too. (30)

Satisfied that he has exposed Brown's vacuity, Harvey then accuses Nuce
of betraying Young's confidence by charging that Nuce has shown Young's
letters to Neville and Osburn and that they have read them aloud at the
Bear's Inn to undergraduates:

A pretti matter that your wurships letters shuld be blasid thus abroad in
the town as thai ar: and whatsoever you have writ and dun in the matter,
as wel and better known, not to on fellow of ye Queenes Collidg, but to
a great cumpani of iunior regents of everi collidg then to sum senior
fellows of our own collidg. (32–3)

After a month of correspondence and postings back and forth between
Cambridge and London, Young decided to take matters into his own
hands.

John Young arrived in Cambridge on Thursday, 14 May 1573. On the
following Monday, Young arranged for Harvey to be nominated in the
Congregation. Even this action by Young generated opposition. At the
next Congregation, John Gawber of Pembroke unsuccessfully tried to
block the award of Harvey's degree, but Harvey was admitted Master of
Arts by the Congregation. Harvey wrote to his father that Young had
told Gawber to leave the College and that Tyndall had put him out of
Commons. Harvey gleefully boasts about having caused the downfall
of Gawber:

[He] lingerith about ye Colledg like a masterles howne, bycause he wuld
not seem to be thrust out: but in deed lookith like a dog that had lost his
taile, or, to make ye [the] best of it, like an unbidden geste that knowes
not where to sitt him downe. (42)

Young's actions could be interpreted as opposition to a group of conservative Church of England Fellows, but he may have acted as he did because
he decided that their actions were unjust. Harvey's right to the M.A. was
publicly vindicated when he was given first place in the Ordo Senioritatis,
a position usually assigned on the basis of accomplishment or noble
birth.[27]

Young also arranged for Harvey to be elected Greek lecturer and to
begin his duties on 10 October 1573. Harvey thanked him and considered
himself bound to him for the appointment 'by caus it was frely offrid of
yow, not ambitiusly souht of me' (45). His enemies seem to have continued

to conspire against him. On 1 November he wrote in detail to Young about their actions. He first informed Young that Gawber, whom Young had expelled, was back in Commons. Then, he explained that Nuce had organized a new election for the Greek lecturer and had assured the Fellows that Young was willing for a new election to take place if 'a met [meet, i.e. appropriate] man were chosen to it' (46). After Harvey began his lecture, he was confronted by Brown, who told the scholars that he was only 'Sir Harvi'. Undergraduates were addressed by their last names prefaced by 'Sir', and so Brown was challenging the validity of Harvey's having the M.A. degree and the right to lecture. Brown told the scholars that Harvey could not read because 'he bi his Proctoral autoriti had suspendid me before, and I as yit had not bene absolvid' (47):

> in the hearing of al the schollars, in despite calid me Sir Harvi, and to mend the matter said flatly, that I shuld wel understand inded that I was but batcheler of art, and that he wuld stand in it, I was no more, and that he wuld pronouns me so openly in the schools. (47–8)

Harvey reports that he remained calm, but asked Brown to dismiss the undergraduate scholars to avoid gossip (48).

Harvey was told by others that Brown had insulted him by calling him 'boy' (48), the epithet so profoundly offensive to Shakespeare's Coriolanus. Harvey warns Young that Nuce and Osburn are plotting to reverse Young's decisions, but urges Young to do what he thinks best for the 'behoof of the collidg'. He plaintively adds that he desired the lectureship because of the stipend (54) but adds that he would try to foster learning even if there were no stipend at all (54). Apparently, Young again intervened in support of Harvey because he continued his readings in Greek and then became University Praelector of Rhetoric on 23 April 1574. The granting of Harvey's M.A. degree remained an issue at Cambridge, and, significantly, his degree in civil law was later awarded by Oxford, though he prepared for the degree at Cambridge.

Spenser's far less flamboyant academic career offers a contrast to Harvey's battles with his peers. Spenser quietly received the B.A. in 1573, the same year that Harvey melodramatically completed his master's degree. After receiving the bachelor's degree, Spenser spent the next academic year, 1573–74, at Cambridge working on his master's degree. The plague picked up force and ravaged Cambridge in the summer of 1574. In the Pembroke College account books, Spenser's name, like that of numerous others, appears in a list of those out of commons during the last six weeks of the academic year 1573–74. The accounts state that allowances for maintenance were given to seven Fellows and eight boys for the plague. This is the last reference to Spenser in the Pembroke College records. When plague caused the university to adjourn in the autumn of 1574, Spenser appears to have left Cambridge. No references of any kind to Spenser appear in the account books after the summer adjournment in 1574.

Spenser's academic achievement suggests that, if he had wished, he could have remained at Cambridge in 1574 or returned on a fellowship after receiving the M.A. in 1576. His record compares favourably with those of his contemporaries who became university dons. When Spenser's B.A. was awarded in 1573, four of his Pembroke classmates were elected as Fellows, and, of these, three had ranked below him in the graduation list. It is possible that, after witnessing the Whitgift and Cartwright controversy and the academic power struggle over Harvey's degree, he was disenchanted with the university. It is also conceivable that the celibacy requirements of an academic life discouraged him, and, of course, it may have been that a university career was not attractive to a poet who wanted to write about chivalric encounters.

Spenser and celibacy

Spenser's interest in women – he was married first to Machabyas Chylde and then to Elizabeth Boyle – may also have influenced his decisions not to pursue a career at the university. The narrator of the *Faerie Queene* seems to suggest that the author is physically attracted to women:

> The loue of women not to entertaine;
> A lesson too too hard for liuing clay.
>
> (III.iv.26)[28]

Universities did not encourage men who were serious about their academic careers to 'entertain' the 'loue of women'. The celibacy of Fellows at Oxford and Cambridge was conventional in all colleges until the latter half of the nineteenth century. Like many clergymen who wished to progress in the church hierarchy, scholars were supposed to be single in order to devote themselves to their studies. This convention was so pervasive that there were no statutes forbidding marriage in the charters of colleges that were founded before the Reformation.

Since Protestantism, in contrast to Roman Catholicism, favoured the idea of a married clergy, colleges founded after the Reformation faced a dilemma. In 1585 the strict Protestant Sir Walter Mildmay, one of the dedicatees of Harvey's *Smithus*, set out to frame the statutes for Emmanuel College. Like a staunch Protestant, Mildmay disparaged celibacy and praised marriage: 'Although we willingly concede to marriage that honour which is accorded to it by the Holy Spirit in Holy Writ, and reject the opinion of those who have held that matrimony ought to be forbidden to a certain order of men'.[29] Mildmay then, inconsistently but very explicitly, prohibits any member of Emmanuel from marrying:

> yet there are many and grave causes why we should suffer no one of those who shall be numbered among the members of our College to be married. We therefore desire and decree that if anyone hereafter who has a wife shall be elected in the College aforesaid, his election shall be held void, as of one unable to have any rights in the College aforesaid; and if he shall take a wife after his election, he shall forever lose all rights he may have obtained by such election. (89)

Technically, the Master of a College was allowed to marry. The Queen, however, opposed the marriage of senior fellows and masters. In a royal decree of 9 August 1561, she observed that cathedral churches and colleges were founded to house societies of 'learned Men professing Study and Prayer for the Edification of the Church of God, & so consequently to serve the Commonwealth'.[30] She had learned that 'Prebendaries, Students, and Members' as well as 'cheif Governors' kept wives, children, and nurses. So, she had decided to command that no one who was either the head or a member of a college or cathedral church might house a wife and family within its precincts or even have a woman dwelling there. Anyone violating this order would by her express order 'forfeit all ecclesiasticall Promotions in any Cathedrall or Collegiate Church or College within this realm'. In practice, however, Brett Usher has documented that marriage did not necessarily disqualify a man from becoming a bishop.[31]

Spenser's M.A. was not awarded until 1576, but it is likely, as noted above, that he left the university prior to that date. Aubrey Attwater, the archivist and historian of Pembroke College, concluded that, though three years of residence were technically required for the M.A. degree, in practice students had begun to leave after one year.[32] At Oxford by 1600 the granting of dispensations for non-residence was so common that it represented normal procedure. By 1608 the custom of leaving after one year had become academic policy at Cambridge. The Vice-Chancellor and Masters of colleges interpreted the Elizabethan statutes as excusing candidates from all residence requirements and attendance at lectures and exercises. Their rationale was that 'a man once grounded so far in learning as to deserve a Bachelor in Arts is sufficiently furnished to proceed in study by himself'.[33] Candidates, however, had to supply testimonials from three clergymen regarding their moral character. Spenser's grace was passed on 26 June 1576; he ranked sixty-seventh in a class of seventy – probably in part because of his non-residence.[34] By the time that the university reopened in the autumn of 1574, Spenser had already moved to London where it is likely that he was employed in the household of John Young, Master of Pembroke.

Notes

1 Reported in *Foxe's Book of Martyrs*, ed. G.A. Williamson (Boston and Toronto: Little, Brown and Company, 1965), 311.
2 Mark H. Curtis, *Oxford and Cambridge in Transition, 1558–1642* (Oxford: Clarendon Press, 1959), 180–1.
3 Cambridge University manuscripts associated with Langherne (Langhorne) seemed to offer no information on Spenser, but Edmonton archives might prove more useful.
4 Grosart, *Life*, 36–7.
5 Percy W. Long, 'Spenser and the Bishop of Rochester', *Publications of the Modern Language Association*, 31 (1916) 713–35.
6 Aubrey Attwater, *A Short History of Pembroke College* (1936; rpt Cambridge University Press, 1973), 44, 48–9.
7 'Account Books', Pembroke College Archives. I am indebted to Miss Jane S. Ringrose, Pembroke College Archivist, for allowing me to examine the accounts in order to interpret and contextualize the records.
8 Attwater, *History of Pembroke College*, 48.
9 *Grace Book Delta Containing the Records of the University of Cambridge for the Years 1542–1589*, ed. John Venn (Cambridge: Cambridge University Press, 1910), 274.
10 Evelyn Philip Shirley, ed., *Original Letters and Papers in Illustration of the History of the Church in Ireland* (London: Francis and John Rivington, 1851), 321–3. Cited also in the *ODNB* article on Adam Loftus, Archbishop of Dublin.
11 Powel Mills Dawley, *John Whitgift and the English Reformation* (New York: Charles Scribner's Sons, 1954), 82–3. V.J.K. Brook, *Whitgift and the English Church* (London: The English Universities Press Ltd, 1957), 27.
12 For Chadderton's letter to Burghley on 11 June 1570, see PRO, SP 12 71/11, and, for Grindal, see PRO, SP 12 71/23.
13 The relevant documents have been reprinted in *Cambridge University Transactions during the Puritan Controversies*, ed. James Heywood and Thomas Wright (London: Henry G. Bohn, 1854), I: 9, 19–20, 26–8.
14 *Collection of Statutes for the University and the Colleges of Cambridge*, ed. James Heywood (London: William Clowes & Sons, 1840), 31–7.
15 The youth of the regents probably influenced some supporters of the 1570 statutes. In a list of 132 regents dating from 1572, the ages ranged from twenty-one to

twenty-eight; only twelve were older than twenty-five (British Library, Lansdowne MS 15l, No. 60, cited in *Grace Book Delta*, ed. Venn, viii).
16 *Cambridge University Transactions*, I: 60-2.
17 Harvey, *Letter-Book*, 162.
18 Lisa Jardine and Anthony Grafton, '"Studied for Action"': How Gabriel Harvey Read His Livy', *Past & Present*, 129 (1990), 30-78, esp. 40.
19 Jardine and Grafton, 'Studied for Action', 41.
20 Harvey, *Foure Letters*, C4r.
21 Roger Ascham, *The Schoolmaster* (1570; rpt Edward Arber, 1870), 93.
22 Harvey, *Letter-Book*, vii.
23 Stern, *Harvey*, 126-7. Cited from Stern's transcription of Harvey's copy of Chaucer ed. Thomas Speght (1598), fols 421v.
24 Harvey's marginalia in James VI, *The essayes of a prentise in the divine art of poesie* (Edinburgh: T. Vautrollier, 1585). Harvey wrote original poems signed 'Axiophilus'. See Stern, *Harvey*, 126, n. 145.
25 Stern, *Harvey*, 128.
26 Cited in William Haller, *The Elect Nation: The Meaning and Relevance of Foxe's Book of Martyrs* (New York: Harper & Row, 1963), 231.
27 *Grace Book Delta*, ed. Venn, viii-x. Venn comments that 'some notion of merit, in the sense of intellectual superiority, must have been recognized all along; at least so far as the men toward the top of the list are concerned' (ix).
28 *Faerie Queene*, III.iv.26.
29 *The Statutes of Sir Walter Mildmay, Kt Chancellor of the Exchequer and one of Her Majesty's Privy Councillors; authorized by him for the government of Emmanuel College founded by him*, ed. and trans. Frank Stubbings (Cambridge: Cambridge University Press, 1983), 89.
30 London, Inner Temple, Petyt MS 47, fol. 373. See also British Library, Lansdowne MS 487/7. In *Marriage and the English Reformation* (Cambridge, MA: Blackwell, 1994), 46-66, esp. 49-50, Eric Josef Carlson argues that Elizabeth was motivated by considerations of decorum rather than opposition to clerical marriage. See also Carlson, 'Clerical Marriage and the English Reformation', *Journal of British Studies*, 31 (1992), 1-31. For the view that Elizabeth was motivated by an aversion to marriage, see Nancy Basler Bjorklund, '"A Godly Wyfe is a Helper": Matthew Parker and the Defence of Clerical Marriage', *Sixteenth Century Journal*, 34 (2003), 347-65, esp. 358.
31 Brett Usher, 'Queen Elizabeth and Mrs Bishop', in *The Myth of Elizabeth*, ed. Susan Doran and Thomas S. Freeman (New York: Palgrave Macmillan, 2003), 200-20.
32 Attwater, *History of Pembroke College*, 49.
33 Cited in Curtis, *Oxford and Cambridge in Transition, 1558-1642*, 97.
34 *Grace Book Delta*, ed. Venn, 290.

4

'Southerne shepheardes boye' (1574–79)

We have virtually no documentary evidence regarding Spenser's whereabouts from summer 1574, when he is last mentioned in the Pembroke College Account Books, until 1578. In 1578, we can document by two independent sources that he was employed by John Young, Master of Pembroke and then Bishop of Rochester. It seems likely that Spenser was employed in London from 1574 to 1578 by John Young, Master of Pembroke. This continuity of appointment seems more probable than that, after a four-year interval, Young would summon Spenser back to his side after being appointed Bishop of Rochester in 1578.

When Young was Master of Pembroke (1567–78), he did not relocate to Cambridge. Presumably, Young, who grew up in London, maintained London lodgings and a staff to handle his ecclesiastical livings in London and Westminster.[1] For over fifteen years, Young held a prebend in London under another of Spenser's early patrons, Alexander Nowell, Dean of St Paul's; he did not resign it until a year after he became a bishop.[2] Young was also installed as prebendary of Westminster on 26 April 1571, a position he retained until his death in 1605, six years after Spenser died. On 31 January 1578, Young was nominated to the bishopric of Rochester; he was elected on 18 February, confirmed 15 March, consecrated the next day, but not installed until 1 April.

The supposition that Spenser went to work for Young in London after leaving Pembroke College also seems plausible because Spenser's relationship to Young was very close; his allusions in the *Shepheardes Calender* (1579) suggest that Young figured as more than an employer to Spenser:

Aprill: '*Colin* thou kenst, the Southerne shepheardes boye' (21)

September: 'Colin clout I wene be his selfe boye' (176)[3]

It is difficult to imagine epithets that would suggest more commonality of purpose. The relationship underlying such warmly descriptive phrases as 'Southerne shepheardes boye' and 'his selfe boye', merits further research on Young and his papers.[4] For the present, we should assume that Spenser was Young's protégé and put our emphasis upon this bond of affection rather than on his precise position or duties in Young's household.

To fill in the blanks between 1574 and 1578, early biographers followed Grosart in portraying Spenser as visiting relatives located in the north[5] (the Lancashire Spensers, who were supposedly related to the poet because they spelled Spencer with an 's' rather than a 'c'). It is during Spenser's conjectured visit to these northern relatives that he is supposed to have met and fallen in love with Rosalind, Colin Clout's Petrarchan mistress.[6] Grosart thinks that Spenser spent three or four years visiting this extended family in 'north-east Lancashire'.[7] In addition to being unsubstantiated by any documentary evidence, this northern sojourn is unlikely for the very practical reason that the twenty-year old Spenser, who had entered Cambridge as a sizar, would have needed gainful employment in 1574.

Of the documents putting Spenser in Young's employment, the more important is a rental receipt which is in Spenser's hand and dated 24 November 1578.

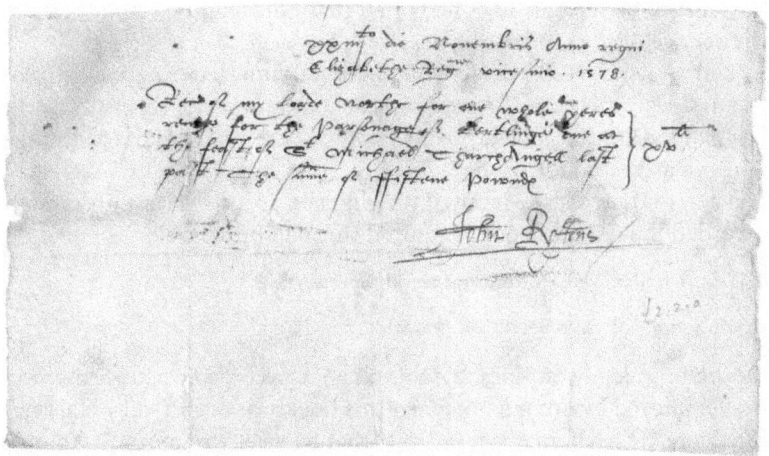

Receipt for Quit Rent. Kirtling, Cambridgeshire. 24 November 1578. North Family. Estate Papers. Reproduced courtesy of Special Collections, Kenneth Spencer Research Library, University of Kansas Libraries. MS 240A: 1024.

24th day of November in the twentieth year of the reign of Queen Elizabeth 1578.

Received of my Lorde North for one whole yeares rente for the parsonage of Kertlinge and at the feast of St. Michael the archangel last past the summe of fifteen pownds.

John Roffens[8]

While this document in Spenser's hand does not identify Spenser as Young's secretary, it does show that by November 1578 Spenser had been in Young's employment long enough to be entrusted with handling a financial transaction involving a prominent nobleman. The date of this receipt thus argues in favour of the continuity and longevity of Spenser's employment by Young.

The only documentary evidence we have specifically identifying Spenser as Young's secretary derives from an inscription which Gabriel Harvey, not Spenser, wrote in one of Harvey's books. At Christmas 1578, Spenser gave Harvey a copy of Jerome Turler's *The Traveiler ... devided into two Bookes. The first conteyning a notable discourse of the maner and order of travelling oversea, or into straunge and forein Countreys. The second comprehending an excellent description of the most delicious Realme of Naples in Italy* (London: William How for Abraham Veale, 1575). As Chapter 5 will indicate, an Italian travel book was an appropriate gift for Harvey because in 1578 he hoped that he would be sent to Italy in the service of the Queen or Leicester.

Harvey acknowledged Spenser's gift by carefully lettering a note inside the first leaf of Jerome Turler's *Traveiler*, and this note seems to be the basis for the identification of Spenser as Young's secretary. Harvey identifies Spenser as the donor of the book, describes him as Young's secretary, and lists the date that he received the gift from Spenser (Harvey habitually recorded the dates of books acquired through purchase or as gifts):

Gabrielis Harveij. ex dono Edmundi Spenserii,

Episcopi Roffensis Secretarii. 1578.[9]

Judson mistakenly assumes that this note was recorded when Spenser was first employed by Young, not when this book was acquired by Harvey.[10] This note, by itself, may not indicate that Spenser was officially Young's secretary. Harvey, who later was to describe himself as having written more in one year than any man in England, was prone to exaggerating in matters related to status and achievement; on the other hand, Harvey had no reason to exaggerate Spenser's importance in Young's household.

Considering Spenser's employment from Young's perspective, it seems clear that his motivation for employing Spenser must have been that he, like the churchmen who administered the funds in the 'Nowell Account Book', expected Spenser to take holy orders.[11] Rochester was a relatively modest diocese, and so we would expect Young, who could ill afford a large staff, to have employed a chaplain rather than a secretary. A chaplain would have taken holy orders and so could have more fully assisted him with clerical responsibilities.[12] There is no record, however, that Spenser took holy orders.[13]

Part of the explanation of why Spenser may have baulked at taking holy orders may lie with his preference for marriage over celibacy, but the ecclesiastical eclogues of the *Shepheardes Calender* also show that Spenser became disenchanted with the Church of England. In an article on Spenser as priest, Jeffrey Knapp comments, 'Aside from the "meek, wise, and merciable" Roffy, Spenser offers no clearly positive model of a living cleric in the entire *Calender*'; he succinctly concludes that Spenser 'loathed the clergy'.[14] Even if we give full credence to Harvey's note and suppose he officially served as the secretary for an Elizabethan bishop, he did not occupy this position for very long – probably less than a year.[15] He may then have been affiliated with the Sidneys and possibly Leicester, who was widely acknowledged to be a patron of Puritans. Without any equivocation, we can then document Spenser's association with a militant Puritan sympathizer, Arthur Lord Grey of Wilton.[16] The pendulum seems to have swung too far to the right and there may be too much insistence on Spenser's conformity.[17]

We need to consider the agency of John Young, who, even if he agreed with Spenser's politics, would not, and probably could not, have supported him once the poet began to write anything for public consumption that could even vaguely be interpreted as an attack on the episcopacy. As it is, John Young did not prosper as a bishop. He followed the very same career path as that laid out by Ridley and Grindal; he served first as Master of Pembroke (1567–78) and then in 1578 became Bishop of Rochester, the bishopric that they had held before him. In contrast to his mentors, Young did not move from Rochester to a more lucrative bishopric, such as London or Winchester. He served at Rochester for twenty-seven years. To cite the *ODNB* article by Brett Usher on John Young, of the twenty-two bishops of Rochester between 1472 and 1629, he was one of the four who were not translated to a wealthier see.[18] Of course, there were many reasons why Young may not have prospered, including his marriage to Grace Watts, but his sponsorship of Spenser may have been one. After Spenser left Young's service, his residual loyalty to the man John Young (he was the self-styled 'Southerne shepheardes boye') may have caused him to avoid publicly proclaiming himself as opposed to the established church.

It is conceivable that Spenser's studied anonymity in presenting the *Shepheardes Calender* as a 'child whose parent is vnkent' was a strategy on his part intended to spare Young the embarrassment of having a protégé publish satire on the church. (There is no ambiguity about Spenser's authorship of the *Faerie Queene*.) It is also possible that Spenser resisted identification as Catholic, Protestant, or Puritan and preferred to adopt what he pleased from each of these religious traditions. In keeping with concealing his authorship of the *Shepheardes Calender*, Spenser, as we shall see below, uses a dialogical structure in the ecclesiastical eclogues to counter and resist attempts to categorize him as either a conservative in the Church of England tradition or a liberal veering in the direction of Puritanism. Critics as varied as Jerome Dees, Harold L. Weatherby, Darryl J. Gless, Linda Gregerson, Richard Mallette, and Carol Kaske have reached some consensus that Spenser's theology was eclectic.[19]

Whitgift, Perne, Spenser, and the Elizabethan settlement

While living in London, Spenser experienced at first hand what has been called the Elizabethan settlement, but Spenser experienced more than the disparity between ideals and practice which many encounter when they enter practically into a profession. As a young man considering a clerical career, he observed the consummation of the political event that had most troubled the statesman Sir Thomas More – the union of church and state.[20] At Cambridge, as an undergraduate, he had witnessed the revision of the university statutes and the success of Whitgift and Perne in silencing Cartwright's independent voice. After leaving Cambridge, he watched the established church develop into a political institution increasingly dominated by the state and dedicated to suppressing dissent. Spenser's decision to accompany Lord Grey to Ireland should be informed by a full understanding of the politics of this religious context.

After Matthew Parker's death in 1575, he was succeeded by Edmund Grindal, who was named Archbishop of Canterbury and confirmed on 15 February 1576. Spenser is likely to have been personally acquainted with Grindal, not only because he was a legend at Pembroke College but also because Grindal had served on examination boards for Merchant Taylors' School while Bishop of London. Spenser may also have encountered him while he was employed by Grindal's former chaplain and protégé, John Young. In less than a year after Grindal was created archbishop, he lost the favour of the Queen. On 20 December 1576, Grindal wrote to Elizabeth defending 'prophesyings', clerical meetings in which the scripture was debated, and reminding her that she was 'a mortal creature' and that although she was a 'mighty prince, yet ... He that dwelleth in heaven is mightier'.[21] Annoyed by his presumption, Elizabeth maintained her conviction that 'prophesyings' might lead to insurrection and directed the bishops to suppress them. Attempts to broker a compromise by limiting attendance at the 'prophesyings' to licensed clergy were unsuccessful. In June 1577 she suspended Grindal for non-compliance; he was sequestered for six years, from 1577 until shortly before his death in 1583.

Standing in the wings was John Whitgift, a very familiar figure to a Cambridge graduate such as Spenser. Also, from the moment of Grindal's sequestration, it was John Aylmer, Bishop of London, who took over most of his responsibilities. Whitgift, who valued church hierarchy and endorsed uniformity, was increasingly viewed as the likely successor to Grindal. He held that there should be no distinction between the church of Christ and the Christian commonwealth. The Queen, as supreme governor, should 'govern the church in ecclesiastical affairs as she doth the commonwealth in civil' (*Defense of the Aunswere to the Admonition Against the Replie of T.C.*, II: 264 (1574)). Whitgift was on a different side from Spenser in Cambridge and in London. In Cambridge, Whitgift promoted the career of Thomas Neville, who led the battle to deprive Harvey of his M.A. We do not know if Gabriel Harvey held Whitgift responsible for Neville's vendetta against him, but there is ample evidence that Harvey loathed Andrew Perne and thought that he had blocked his advancement at Cambridge.

Whitgift had entered Pembroke College in 1550 when Ridley was Master and had earned his B.A. He was twenty-three and a Fellow at Peterhouse, the oldest of the Cambridge colleges, when Andrew Perne became the new Master at thirty-six. In 1567 Whitgift left Peterhouse for a brief stint as Master of Pembroke before moving on to the better endowed Trinity, where he remained as Master until he was appointed Bishop of Worcester in 1577. While serving as Bishop of Worcester, Whitgift also served under Sir Henry Sidney as vice-president of the

Council of the Marches of Wales, and, predictably, opposed Sidney by taking a harder line against Catholics. Whitgift's willingness, however, to defer to and promote the Queen's authority made it increasingly likely that he would be appointed Archbishop of Canterbury in succession to Edmund Grindal.

After becoming Archbishop of Canterbury, Whitgift became the Queen's clerical favourite and was the very first Elizabethan clergyman to sit on the Privy Council, taking his seat on 2 February 1585/6. Leicester, a sponsor of Puritan clerics, was not a fan of Whitgift's, and gossip had it that Whitgift succeeded in obtaining a seat on the Privy Council only because Leicester was away in the Netherlands. Throughout his career Whitgift remained close to his mentor Perne, who spent the last three years of his life living in his protégé's establishments. The Marprelate tracts use this longstanding relationship to attack Dr Perne and Archbishop Whitgift as homosexual lovers: 'Doctor Perne, thou knowest, was thy joy, and thou his darling'.[22]

Shepheardes Calender

From a political perspective, the *Shepheardes Calender* was not the kind of safe production that would inspire confidence in a patron – at least in any courtier, churchman, or civil servant who wished to stand well in 1579 with the controlling political Burghley–Sussex faction or the church hierarchy headed by Whitgiftt. The harping on 'secrets' in the Gloss to the *Shepheardes Calender* would have been likely to discourage patronage from any patron who valued discretion in his clients. At the same time, nothing could be more likely to stimulate salacious interest in a readership excited about hearing the latest gossip than the harping on 'secrets' and the suggestion that the text contained allusions to prominent figures in the church or government. Unfortunately, we do not have easy access to Elizabethan gossip. To address this problem, it is necessary to pay attention to how names were pronounced as well as spelled. Also, we should consider any and all evidence of how the *Shepheardes Calender* was read and interpreted including texts, such as the Marprelate tracts, which were printed almost a decade later. In fact, it says much about the topicality of the *Shepheardes Calender* that the names of characters in it are used a decade later in these anti-prelatical tracts.

From a biographical perspective, two aspects of the *Shepheardes Calender* are especially useful: first, Spenser's intentionally dialogic structure, in which the author resists being fitted neatly into a religious group, and, second, the handling and function of topical allusions. That is not because the eclogues are primarily concerned with Spenser's religious position or intended as gossip; far from it, the *Shepheardes Calender* invites highly sophisticated literary analysis.[23]

Maye

In the Argument for *Maye*, E.K. states that the two shepherds, Piers and Palinode, represent two 'formes of pastoures or Ministers or the protestant and the Catholique' (72). Scholars have rightly insisted that *Maye*, a dialogic masterpiece, is more complex than E.K.'s 'Argvment' suggests. The name Palinode means 'retraction' or 'recantation', and the name alone may explain why the Marprelate pamphleteers borrowed it to satirize Andrew Perne, who was notorious for having recanted his Edwardian Protestantism under Mary Tudor and then recanting his Catholicism under Elizabeth Tudor.[24] It is soon clear that, in *Maye*, Palinode will represent the Catholic and Piers the Protestant 'formes of pastoures', but Spenser's presentation is hardly simple.

Spenser's Palinode waxes sentimental about the advent of spring and savours the rituals of the season, 'the mery moneth of May, / When loue lads masken in fresh aray' (1–2). In diction and rhythms that recall the Prologue to Chaucer's *Canterbury Tales*, Palinode describes the piping and dancing and the procession to the 'greene Wood' (27):

> For thilke same season, when all is ycladd
> With pleasaunce: the grownd with grasse, the Wods
> With greene leaues, the bushes with bloosming Buds.
> Yougthes folke now flocken in euery where,
> To gather may buskets and smelling brere.
>
> (6–10)

Piers scolds Palinode, who sounds like Spenser's mentor Chaucer, for relishing the season and reminds him that they are 'men of elder witt' (18). Palinode responds that since 'God his good does them send', shepherds should 'reapen the fruite thereof, that is pleasure' (64–5).

The Protestant Piers is harshly ascetic and even seems to oppose marriage for clerics, but not on theological grounds. Traditionally, Roman Catholic clergy are celibate while Protestants endorse marriage, even allowing the clergy to marry. The Protestant Piers, who is less charitable than the tradition represented by Langland's *Piers Plowman*, reproves Palinode as a 'worldes childe' (73).[25] Since the Argument tells us that Piers and Palinode represent two kinds of pastors, Protestant and Catholic, we would expect Piers to celebrate wedded love, but Spenser quite resoundingly turns the tables on our expectations. Piers the Protestant even quotes Archbishop Grindal as seeming to advocate a celibate clergy (74–6). Critics have sometimes interpreted this to mean that Spenser wants to impose Roman Catholic requirements of celibacy on priests ordained in the Church of England. We know that Spenser was not attracted to celibacy, but it is also possible that Piers the fiercely celibate Protestant may not necessarily be the spokesman for Spenser's views, particularly because Palinode so blatantly echoes Chaucer.

Piers, as we would expect, counters Palinode's *carpe diem*, but he has quite a bit more to say about parents and offspring. He condemns soundly the idea of inherited wealth for the children of priests as 'heaping vp waues of welth and woe, / The floddes whereof shall them ouerflowe' (93–4). There is little doubt that this passage is a hit at John Aylmer, Bishop of London, who had ten children and employed a household of sixty; Aylmer was frequently accused of despoiling church lands by cutting down timber and of using his clerical positions to make his children rich. Spenser's Piers rails against 'welth', because it may lead to 'leudnes and lust' (87) but goes further and opposes a married clergy on the grounds that domestic responsibilities will impede religious vocation.

> They must prouide for meanes of maintenaunce,
> And to continue their wont countenaunce.
> But shepheard must walke another way,
> Sike worldly souenance he must foresay.
>
> (79–82)

Piers favours clerical celibacy because, faced with the practical responsibilities of feeding their offspring, married clergymen may divert their energy away from their flocks. A similar complaint is offered by Diggon Davie in *September*: 'All for they casten too much of worlds care, / To deck her Dame, and enrich her heyre' (114–15). On quite secular grounds, the shepherd-priest 'must walke another way' and 'worldly souenance' forswear.

The asceticism of Spenser's Piers is less attractive than that of his fourteenth-century namesake. He offers an appalling warning of what will be the consequences if priests marry and become parents. Piers tells us that it will be like the folly of an ape who is so enamoured of her offspring that she hugs it to death:

> Sike mens follie I cannot compare
> Better, then to the Apes folish care,
> That is so enamoured of her young one,
> (And yet God wote, such cause hath she none)
> That with her hard hold, and straight embracing,
> She stoppeth the breath of her youngling.
>
> (95–100)

Piers summons up the disquieting image of a foolish female ape 'so enamoured of her young one' that she embraces it to death. This insistence that maternal love is like the folly of an ape who smothers her 'youngling' will alienate some readers and leave many uneasy. Having offered this cruel image of parental love and infanticide, he moralizes blandly: 'So often times, when as good is meant, / Euil ensueth of wrong entent' (101–2). Piers's ironic detachment is chilling.

After giving us this disturbing lesson in celibacy, Piers retells the history of the early church when *'Pan* himselfe' was the 'shepheard's inheritaunce' (111). Piers describes a past golden age that 'may againe retorne' (103) in which 'shepheards had none inheritaunce, / Ne of land, nor fee' (105–6). These shepherds, who own no private property, are carefree because 'nought hauing, nought feared they to forgoe' (110), but their very security leads to their undoing. After 'tract of time, and long prosperitie' (117), the shepherds became discontent with 'loyal obeysaunce' (120).

In *Maye* Spenser imaginatively coalesces the end of the Golden Age with the conclusion of this pastoral idyll, and he portrays them both as ending in 1579 when Elizabeth is considering a French match:

> Some gan to gape for greedie gouernaunce,
> And match them selfe with mighty potentates,
> Louers of Lordship and troublers of states.
>
> (121–3)

The principal references here may be political. In the phrase 'gan to gape for greedie gouernaunce' followed by 'match … with mighty potentates', Spenser may be alluding to John Stubbs's *Gaping Gulf* (1579), a denunciation of Elizabeth's projected French match with the Duke of Anjou, published in the same year as the *Shepheardes Calender*. We should note in passing that the Puritan printer John Singleton printed the *Shepheardes Calender* shortly after he printed Stubbs's tract.

Just in case, we might have missed the phrase 'Louers of Lordship' (123), E.K. chimes in to reassure us that Spenser is not attacking the bishops:

> Peters counterfet keyes, open a wide gate to al wickednesse and insolent gouernment. Nought here spoken, as of purpose, to deny fatherly rule and godly gouernaunce (as some malitiously of late haue done to the great vnreste and hinderaunce of the Churche) but to display the pride and disorder of such, as in stead of feeding their sheepe, indeed feede of theyr sheepe. (p. 84)

By reassuring the reader that Spenser values 'the fatherly rule and godly gouernance' of the bishops, E.K., in effect, insinuates the possibility that the author of the *Shepheardes Calender* may be as anti-prelatical as the text itself has suggested.

From any conceivable topical perspective, the reader cannot satisfactorily place Spenser's religious allegiance. Some aspects of Piers's arguments align with the liberal Protestant position, but can we safely assume that Piers is Spenser's spokesman? Or, does Spenser think that Palinode has a point when he exclaims that Piers 'raylest on right withouten reason' (147)? *Maye* is an exemplary example of Spenser's dialogic technique. Palinode may be high Anglican, or even Roman Catholic, but his message is more attractive than that of the ascetic Piers. Piers registers as the more Puritanical of the two speakers, but he seems to favour the Catholic doctrine of clerical celibacy. It is no wonder that scholars have cited the *Maye* eclogue as evidence of Spenser's Catholicism, his Church of England orthodoxy, and his Puritanism! And, any contemporary would have recognized the censure of Bishop John Aylmer's excesses in the passages deploring marriage on secular grounds.

March

To examine the problematical relationship between topical allusions, audiences, and meaning, we can turn to one of the recreative eclogues, *March*. According to the Argvment of *March*, Thomalin and Willye, two shepherd boys, 'make purpose of loue and other plesaunce, which to springtime is most agreeable' (p. 52). Willye calls attention to the signs of spring:

> *Flora* now calleth forth eche flower,
> And bids make ready *Maias* bowre,
> That newe is vpryst from bedde.
> Tho shall we sporten in delight,
> And learne with Lettice to wexe light.
>
> (16–20)

Lettice may be an allusion to Lettice Knollys, married to Leicester and formerly the wife of William Devereux, the first Earl of Essex. The potential topicality of this allusion, as argued originally by Charles E. Mounts (1952) and more recently by Richard E. Lynn (2011), seems clear, particularly because 'Lettice' (20) is glossed by E.K. as 'the name of some country lasse' (57).[26] The word 'country' also had connotations of promiscuity in the sixteenth century. This topical allusion is titillating enough to figure as gossip, but not so pointed as to register as slander. The potential topicality is persuasive in part because E.K. unnecessarily calls attention to Lettice as waxing 'light' with the coming of spring by glossing 'Lettice' (20) as a 'country lasse' (p. 57). If we consider the politics, then Sidney is likely to have been disappointed by Leicester's marriage to Lettice Devereux, widow of the Earl of Essex, a marriage that jeopardized his position as Leicester's heir. Both he and Spenser were well aware that Leicester's marriage had undermined the position of the liberal Protestant party of which Leicester was the titular head, but this topical information seems too much ballast for the reference to 'Lettice'.

In the conclusion to *March*, there may be another overtly political allusion in Thomalin's emblem: '*Of Hony and of Gaule in loue there is store:/The Honye is much, but the Gaule is more*' (122–3, 56). In this emblem, Spenser departs from Italian and uses English to underscore the message. As Richard McCabe has noted, 'Gaule' is substituted for gall to create a pun that may be a topical allusion to Elizabeth's unpopular French suitor (p. 527). From an interpretative perspective, neither of these topical allusions is central to the meaning of *March*.[27] These allusions are likely to have piqued the interest of contemporary readers, but they do little other than add a topical edge to the *March* eclogue, an edge that becomes sharper in the ecclesiastical eclogues.

Julye

Turning to the *Julye* eclogue, scholars have noted that Spenser transparently reverses the name of Grindal as Algrind, but some have been reluctant to accept that Morell is John Aylmer, Bishop of London – perhaps because even an ambiguous attack by Spenser on an important clergyman was very daring. In this regard, it is important to note that Aylmer's name was pronounced 'Elmer'. John Strype, that formidable church historian of bishops, thought that he might be a descendant of Aylmer's and so does his best to sanitize Aylmer, including honouring his preference for Aylmer over Elmer. In his *ODNB* article, the historian Brett Usher notes that prior to ordination he emphasized his putative Anglo-Saxon origins by signing himself 'Ælmer'; otherwise his name is usually found in contemporary sources as 'Elmer'.[28] Usher also describes Spenser as characterizing Morrell as a goatherd, not a true pastor, and satirizing him for his ambition, signified by his emblem, *In summo foelicitas*.

Aylmer was widely criticized for his sale of timber on Church lands to amass a fortune for his eight sons and two daughters. He was later a favourite target in the *Marprelate tracts*, where he is attacked for his harsh treatment of both Puritans and Papists. He was characterized as 'Dumb John' for his infrequent preaching and 'Mar-elm' for his misappropriation of timber on church lands. The epithet Mar-elm also glances back at Spenser because Morrill was pronounced as Mer/el (Elmer transposed). Early in his career, he got into a dispute with Thomas Cooper, Bishop of Lincoln and then Winchester (Thom +Lin or Thomalin), who was celebrated for his patience and humility. He came from a very poor background, beginning as a menial servant at Magdalen College, but becoming a bishop. He took over the task of modernizing Thomas Elyot's dictionary, but his wife, Amy, threw early drafts into the fire; Cooper patiently redid his work. Amy later committed adultery with at least two men in Oxford, but, in spite of the circulation of ribald verses, Cooper refused to divorce her. Sir John Harington said that his 'lyfe in Oxford was saint-lyke; for if it be saintlike to live unreproachable, to bear a cross patientlie, to forgive injuries freely this man's example is sampleless in this age' (Harington, *Nugae Antiquae*, 2.88–9).[29] The contemporary reputations of Aylmer and Cooper are the context for *Julye*.

Morrell has a debate over pride and humility with Thomalin, and the Argument tells us that this eclogue commends good shepherds and censures 'proude and ambitious Pastours. Such as Morrell is here imagined to bee' (p. 95). The qualifer 'here imagined to bee' probably enables Spenser to sidestep any danger of libelling. Thomalin says that he has been 'taught by *Algrins* ill, / to loue the lowe degree' (219–20) because Algrind now 'lyes in lingring payne' (228). This event is based on the classical legend that Aeschylus, the father of Greek tragedy, was killed when an eagle, mistaking his bald head for a rock, dropped a tortoise on him. In Spenser's version, the Eagle, significantly, is female, and so must be identified as Elizabeth. The symbolism of substituting a shellfish for the tortoise has not been solved. Most editors have followed Ben Jonson in glossing the shellfish as the Puritan party, but the connection between the Puritans and Grindal's 'lingring payne' (228) seems tenuous.

Percy Long points out that the Bishops of Rochester used the scallop shell as an emblem and implies that Young was implicated in Grindal's fall, but we would need more information for this to be persuasive.[30] Among the conclusions we can safely draw, it seems that Morrell is typical of the bishops who not only sat with the lords in the House of Lords but regarded themselves as great lords. Spenser seems to prefer Thomalin who says that '*Algrins* ill' has made him prefer the anonymity of 'lowe degree' (220). In *Julye*, as in *Februarie*, Spenser seems sceptical about an ambition that leads to worldly prominence.

If there are unanswered questions in *Julye*, *September* seems even more resistant to topical explanation.[31] In the dialogue between Diggon Davie (Diggon is Welsh dialect for Diccon or Richard) and Hobbinol, there may be allusions to contemporary churchmen, but, if so, the significance of the topical references is not immediately clear.[32] According to the Argvment, Diggon Davie, 'in hope of more gayne, droue his sheepe into a farre countrye' (Argvment, p. 116). He relates to Hobbinol the 'abuses' and 'loose liuing of Popish prelates'. Diggon then concludes with the tale of 'Roffy', John Young, Bishop of Rochester, who apprehends a wolf disguised as a sheep.

Roffy has the assistance of his dog Lowder, but the 'Wolfish sheepe' waits until Lowder is far away and then catches his prey. The wolf also counterfeits Roffy's voice and attempts to trap Lowder. Roffy, however, penetrates the disguise of the wolfish sheep and 'let[s] out the sheepes bloud at his throte' (207). Spenser's recent editors gloss the account of Roffy's discovery and slaughter of a disguised wolf as an unidentified response to the Jesuit Mission.[33]

Spenser may have invented this fictional episode to emphasize the loyalty of Bishop Young to the Elizabethan settlement, but he may also be using it to mock readers looking for topical allusions. E.K.'s Gloss pointedly insists on the story's topicality: 'This tale of Roffy seemeth to coloure some particular Action of his. But what, I certeinlye know not' (p. 127). Spenser may be treating literally a shepherd's strategies for guarding his flock. A dog, realistically named Lowder, is very improbably imitated by a wolf who has disguised himself as a sheep. And, even though E.K. insists on the reality behind the image, no such reality may exist. It may have amused Spenser to set his readers in chase of Lowder.

Even though the topicality of allusions may explain why the *Shepheardes Calender* went through more editions than the *Faerie Queene*, this topicality is far from transparent to modern readers. Much of the scholarship on the ecclesiastical eclogues has concerned Spenser's orthodoxy or lack thereof. It might be more useful to know why he borrows the legend of an eagle's dropping a tortoise on Aeschylus's head, but changes the story so that the eagle drops a shellfish rather than a tortoise. In *Maye* Piers seems to oppose a married clergy but does so on secular rather than theological grounds. Although scholarship has emphasized Spenser's theology, the ecclesiastical eclogues investigate social ills and allude to church politics, not theological disputes. It is possible that Spenser decided not to take holy orders because both camps – the Puritans and the Church of England – devoted too much energy to theological disputation.

Notes

1. Aubrey Attwater, *A Short History of Pembroke* College (1936: rpt Cambridge: Cambridge University Press, 1973), 48–9. See, also, Percy W. Long, 'Spenser and the Bishop of Rochester', *Publications of the Modern Language Association*, 31 (1916), 718.
2. Alexander C. Judson, *A Biographical Sketch of John Young, Bishop of Rochester, with Emphasis on His Relations with Edmund Spenser* (Bloomington: Indiana University Studies, 1934), 8. Emphasizing the theology of Young, Grindal, and Spenser, this study is based only on printed sources.
3. , *Shorter Poems*, ed. McCabe, 193–4.
4. Further research in Young's papers and those of his correspondents is likely to uncover more documents. The rental receipt in Spenser's hand was discovered among the North Family Estate Papers now at the Kenneth Spencer Research Library, at the University of Kansas.
5. Hadfield, *Life*, and I agree on finding Spenser's supposed trip to the north to visit relatives improbable (83). Labelling the period from 1574 to 1579 Spenser's 'Lost Years', Hadfield has suggested a number of possible employers, 83–118.
6. Spenser's residence in London from 1574 to 1578 would have given him an occasion to meet and woo Machabyas Chylde. On the marriage, see Hadfield, *Life*, 140–7. See also my 'Spenser's Romances: From "Lying Shepherd's Tongues" to Wedded Love', *Sidney Journal*, 26, No. 2 (2008), 101–10.
7. Grosart, *Life*, 3–61. Recent accounts have favoured filling in these 'lost' years with service in Ireland or France, but we have no evidence connecting any of these Mr Spencers with Edmund Spenser.
8. MS 240A: 1024. Receipt for Quit Rent. Kirtling, Cambridgeshire. 24 November 1587. North Family Estate Papers.. My thanks also to Richard Hardin, who assisted me in obtaining a photostat to verify the handwriting.
9. Now in the Rosenbach Library, Philadelphia, PA. This annotation is reprinted along with a catalogue of Harvey's library, in Stern, *Harvey*, 237. At the bottom of the final page of this book, Harvey wrote 'Legi pridie Cal. Decembrus. 1578. Gabriel Harvey'.
10. Judson, *Life*, states: 'The first preferment in the south of which we have any real knowledge occurred in 1578, when Spenser became secretary to Bishop Young, whose official residence was at Bromley, Kent, ten miles from London' (47). See, also, Hadfield, *Life*, 110: 'He [Spenser] probably moved to north Kent to work for

John Young at some point in 1578, perhaps joining his new employer when he was consecrated as bishop of Rochester on 16 March 1578. Spenser remained in the bishop's service until the middle of the following year when the correspondence with Harvey indicates that he had entered – or returned to – the service of Leicester' (110).

11 For the view that Harvey's note and the text of *Familiar Letters* show that Spenser aspired to find a position as a secretary, see, for example, Hadfield, *Life*, 147: 'It is quite likely that Spenser planned to pursue a career as a secretary, and he may have acted in this capacity for Leicester in 1579, a possibility made more likely if we assume that he had already worked for Leicester carrying letters earlier in the 1570s (after the publication of the *Calender* it is unlikely that such a relationship could continue)'.

12 For background on duties, see *Chaplains in Early Modern England: Patronage, Literature and Religion*, ed. Hugh Adlington, Tom Lockwood, and Gillian Wright (Manchester: Manchester University Press, 2013).

13 Percy Long suggests that Young may have violated church protocol by asking Spenser to perform duties reserved for those who had been ordained, for example chaplains, 730–5.

14 Jeffrey Knapp, 'Spenser the Priest', *Representations*, 81 (2003), 61–78.

15 Spenser's religious allegiance has been inferred from Harvey's note describing him as Young's secretary. For example, see John King, 'Reformation', *Spenser Encyclopedia*, 594: 'Spenser's service in 1578 as secretary to Young renders improbable contentions that the work endorses anti-prelatical attitudes'.

16 On Leicester's patronage of Puritans, see Eleanor Rosenberg, *Leicester Patron of Letters* (New York: Columbia University Press, 1955), 184–229, 340–1. Grey gave a living to the cleric Thomas Sparke who, along with Walter Travers, defended the Puritan cause against Whitgift in the Conference of 1584.

17 Much of this disagreement seems to be over terminology. For the view that Spenser shared the aims of Puritan divines, see Anthea Hume, *Edmund Spenser: Protestant Poet* (Cambridge: Cambridge University Press, 1984), 59–71. David Norbrook, *Poetry and Politics in the English Renaissance* (London: Routledge and Kegan Paul, 1984), 36, describes Spenser as a 'moderate Puritan'. In an article entitled 'Was Spenser a Puritan?', *Spenser Studies*, 6 (1986), 1–31, John King objects to Norbrook's and Hume's characterization of Spenser as a Puritan. In *Spenser's Poetry and the Reformation Tradition* (Princeton: Princeton University Press, 1990), 9, King describes Spenser as a 'progressive Protestant' in contrast to Norbrook's 'moderate Puritan'.

18 Brett Ussher, 'John Young', *ODNB* (2008).

19 On Spenser's theology, see Jerome Dees, 'Homiletics', *Spenser Encyclopedia*, 376–7; Harold L. Weatherby, *Mirrors of Celestial Grace: Patristic Theology in Spenser's Allegory* (Toronto: University of Toronto Press, 1994); Daryl J. Gless, *Interpretation and Theology in Spenser* (Cambridge: Cambridge University Press, 1994); Linda Gregerson, *The Reformation of the Subject: Spenser, Milton and the English Protestant Epic* (Cambridge: Cambridge University Press, 1995); Richard Mallette, *Spenser and the Discourses of Reformation England* (Lincoln: Nebraska University Press, 1997); Carol V. Kaske, *Spenser and Biblical Poetics* (Ithaca, NY: Cornell University Press, 1999).

20 More's son-in-law, William Roper, reports that More stated to Cromwell that he should advise Henry what he ought to do, but never tell him what he was able to do. 'For if the lion knew his own strength, hard were it for any man to rule him.' *The Life of Sir Thomas More* in *Two Early Tudor Lives*, ed. Richard S. Sylvester and Davis P. Harding (New Haven: Yale University Press, 1962), 228.
21 *Remains of Archbishop Grindal* (Cambridge: Cambridge Univesity Press, 1843). Letter 99: 'To the Queen Concerning Suppressing the Prophecies ...', Lansdowne MS 23, No. 12. Documents relating to the Archbishop's Sequestration, p. 389.
22 *The Marprelate Tracts: A Modernized and Annotated Edition*, ed. Joseph L. Black. Cambridge: Cambridge University Press, 2008), xxviii; 239, n. 84; 226-7, n. 144.
23 For exemplary studies of Spenser's complicated interplay with sources and analogues, see Judith Anderson, *Reading the Allegorical Intertext: Chaucer, Spenser, Shakespeare, Milton* (New York: Fordham University Press, 2008), and John Watkins, *The Specter of Dido: Spenser and the Virgilian Epic* (New Haven: Yale University Press, 1995). In the *Shepheardes Calender*, we find gamesmanship involving classical and continental pastorals, resounding statements about writing poetry, appreciations of nature, and much else – probably even interpretations yet to be formulated.
24 *The Marprelate Tracts*, ed. Black, 217, n. 53. Discussed in Patrick Collinson, 'Andrew Perne and His Times', in *Andrew Perne: Quatercentenary Studies* (Cambridge: Printed for Cambridge Bibliographical Society by Cambridge University Press, 1991), 1-34 (34). For further discussion of the use Puritan pamphleteers made of the *Shepheardes Calender*, see James Jackson Higginson, *Spenser's Shepherd's Calender in Relation to Contemporary Affairs* (New York: Columbia University Press, 1912), 181-4.
25 The reference is uncertain, but the figure of Piers may allude to John Piers, Bishop of Salisbury (1523-94), a clergyman celebrated for his virtue and character. Politically, Bishop Piers was also associated with the militant policies of Leicester and Walsingham and shared their desire to aid the Protestant Low Countries in their revolt against the Catholic Spanish. Strype, *Whitgift*, I: 437; and III: 165, cited in Paul E. McLane, *Spenser's Shepheardes Calender: A Study in Elizabethan Allegory* (Notre Dame: Notre Dame University Press, 1961), 185.
26 Richard E. Lynn, 'Ewe/Who?: Recreating Spenser's March Eclogue', *Spenser Studies*, 26 (2011), 153-78. Charles E. Mounts, 'Spenser and the Countess of Leicester', in *That Soueraine Light: Essays in Honor of Edmund Spenser, 1552-1952*, ed. William Mueller and Don Cameron Allen (Baltimore: Johns Hopkins University Press, 1952), 111-22.
27 For the view that this allusion annoyed Leicester, who retaliated, see Hadfield, *Life*, 128-30, 235.
28 On the satire against Aylmer, see Hadfield, *Life*, 138-39, who thinks Young may be implicated in the satire on Aylmer (Morell). See, also, p. 471, n. 126, on contemporaries referring to Aylmer as Elmore.
29 Cited from Brett Usher, 'John Aylmer', *ODNB* (2008).
30 Long, 'Spenser and the Bishop of Rochester', 733-5.
31 See Scott Lucas, 'Diggon Davie and Davy Dicar: Edmund Spenser, Thomas Churchyard, and the Poetics of Public Protest', *Spenser Studies*, 16 (2002), 151-65.
32 Davies, along with Thomas Cooper, Bishop of Lincoln, signed a letter in support of Grindal at the time of his fall. For a cogent summary see McCabe, *Shorter*

Poems, 553. For background, see Viola Hulbert, 'Diggon Davie', *Journal of English and Germanic Philology*, 42 (1942), 349–67, and McLane, *Spenser's Shepheardes Calender:A Study in Elizabethan Allegory*, 216–34.
33 For the suggestion that Spenser may disagree with Young's tactics, see Hadfield, *Life*, 115–18.

5

Gabriel Harvey and Immerito (1569–78)

In Gabriel Harvey's *Gratulationes Valdinenses* (1578), a work that could be described as his *Shepheardes Calender*, he reveals his approach to securing patronage. This text, written without a collaborator and published prior to *Familiar Letters*, enables us to understand how Harvey was viewed by his contemporaries.[1] The task of distinguishing Spenser from Harvey is far from simple because much that we know about the early Spenser is filtered through Harvey's texts, and these texts are not readily accessible. There is still no complete edition of Harvey's works. There have been a few facsimile reprints of his contributions to the pamphlet war with Thomas Nashe, but there is no complete edition of his substantial body of Latin and English writing. Grosart prints only selected excerpts of his Latin works in his poorly annotated three-volume edition.[2] We have a new translation of Harvey's *Gratulationes Valdinenses*, but few of his other texts have been satisfactorily edited.[3]

To compound these problems, Harvey's original texts have survived in very few copies, and not even facsimile reprints are available in most libraries. Even with the advent of Early English Books On-Line (EEBO) the original texts pose difficulties because Harvey published in black letter and his texts require annotation.[4] With the exception of *Familiar Letters*, Harvey's works have been inaccessible to most scholars.[5] And even *Familiar Letters*, a very significant text, is available only in poorly annotated and textually unsatisfactory editions.[6] The inaccessibility of texts may explain in part why there has been little effort to distinguish Spenser's voice from that of Harvey.

The story of Harvey and his relationship to Spenser and to the publication of Spenser's early works is involuted and convoluted. It cannot be told coherently unless it is arranged chronologically, and, even then, it remains confusing. Harvey tells one version of his relationships with Andrew Perne and Sir Thomas Smith in 1577, another in 1580, and yet another when these events are revisited more than a decade later during the Harvey–Nashe pamphlet warfare of the 1590s. For this reason, no text of Harvey's can be safely commented upon without knowledge of his complete output. On his side, Thomas Nashe conflates *Three Letters* (hereafter *Familiar Letters*) with Harvey's subsequent publication, *Foure Letters*, but this conflation should not lead us to underestimate Nashe's knowledge of Harvey's works. Nashe had done considerable homework, reading closely the *Shepheardes Calender* and studying *Familiar Letters*. He was also familiar with Harvey's independent publications, particularly *Gratulationes Valdinenses* (1578). Nashe, in addition, had the advantage of being a party to contemporary gossip and hearsay.

To make sense of these flashbacks and reinterpretations, I have constructed a chronologically organized narrative of key events in the lives of Harvey and Spenser prior to 1580. Harvey, though less important for our purposes, dominates this narrative because he left so much autobiographical data. He revealed himself in his *Letter-Book* and in the marginal notations inscribed in the extant books of his large library. In contrast to this wealth of information about Harvey and his ambitions, our knowledge of Spenser is limited. The partisan Thomas Nashe, though unsympathetic to Harvey, deeply admired Spenser, and so his comments may assist us in reconstructing contemporary assessments of Harvey's relationship to Spenser.

Harvey matriculated at Cambridge as a pensioner, just after he had turned fifteen on 28 June 1566; he matriculated three years prior to Spenser. As is the case with Spenser, his birth date has been queried. In her 1979 study of Harvey and his marginalia, Virginia Stern, apparently influenced by Harold Wilson, and others, says that Harvey was born in July 1550, but in her 1990 biography of Harvey written for the *Spenser Encyclopedia* (1990) she gives his birth date as 1552.[7] In a letter preserved in his *Letter-Book* written in 26 April 1573 Harvey says: 'And if Mai proove no better with me then March and April have dun, I must needs sai, and mai sai it truly, it wilbe the worst spring, yea the wurst and rouhist winter for me that hapnid this xxii. Years'.[8] This letter, written in 1573, suggests that Harvey, in fact, was born in 1551. Since Spenser was born in 1554, they would then be three years apart in age.

It may be significant that prior to Christmas 1578 we find no suggestion that Harvey and Spenser were especially close friends. Prior to 1579, we find no references to Spenser in Harvey's marginalia, though he specifically describes encounters, for example, with Sir Thomas Smith and his son which occurred in 1570–71. For that matter, he could have mentioned 'the new poet' in the marginalia of his Livy or another favoured text, just as he refers to Sir Philip Sidney, Sir Edward Denny, Sir Humphrey Gilbert, and Captain Thomas Smith the younger, to note only a few. In his private *Letter-Book,* Harvey alludes to Spenser (Benevolo) only after the erstwhile sizar had established connections with Philip Sidney and his circle. Particularly in the Latin passages in *Familiar Letters* (1580), the two men trade jokes, and in Spenser's Latin poem there may be hints of sexual intimacy. There are at least two very specific instances in which Harvey could have printed samples of Spenser's verse in his publications in 1577 or 1578, but we find no references to Spenser in those publications.

While Spenser was employed in the household of John Young in London, Harvey continued to pursue his career at Cambridge and to develop an impressive patronage network. Throughout his tenure at the university, Harvey reports that he enjoyed the patronage of Sir Thomas Smith, Elizabeth's principal secretary. Smith, when not in London or out of the country, resided at Theydon Mount, his country estate, or at a residence in Saffron Walden close to the Harvey home. Although Harvey may have made Smith's acquaintance prior to his matriculation at the university, we know that they were actively connected in late 1570 and early in 1571. Harvey received his B.A. in 1570 at Christ Church and was ninth in the Ordo Senioritatis but was not elected a Fellow. Through the influence of Smith, Harvey was elected a Fellow at Pembroke College on 3 November 1570. In 1573, Harvey, looking back on his disappointment at not having been appointed a Fellow at Christ Church, rationalizes that it has turned out for the best: 'Inded ons I suppose verrely Christ Collidg fellowship, whitch I had over great a fansi to, miht have drawn me in to the ministeri, as it hath dun a great mani mo' (164–5). In contrast to Spenser, who may have seriously considered a clerical career, Harvey congratulates himself upon not having been drawn into the 'ministeri'. He aspired to a court appointment and wanted to use his academic talents as a means of winning patronage from great men. Paul Hammer, Lisa Jardine, and Anthony Grafton have documented instances in which scholars, such as Henry Cuffe, formerly a professor of Greek at Oxford, and Gabriel Harvey, University Praelector of Rhetoric at Cambridge, were employed to read classical texts in noble households.[9] In his marginalia, Harvey himself testifies to his access to noblemen and links this access to his knowledge of classical texts.

On 23 April 1574, prior to Spenser's leaving Cambridge in 1574, Harvey was chosen University Praelector of Rhetoric.[10] Spenser had already left Cambridge before Harvey delivered his first set of lectures (later to be entitled *Rhetor* when they were printed) in March 1575 at commencement, and his second course of lectures, *Ciceronianus*, was delivered a year later near the beginning of Easter term in the spring of 1576. Harvey then published *Ciceronianus* in June 1577 and *Rhetor* in November 1577. Both works were printed by Henry Bynneman, who was to print all of Harvey's early publications, and who, significantly, also printed *Familiar Letters* (1580). By publishing his lectures on rhetoric in 1577, Harvey, in the short run, hoped to improve his prospects at Cambridge, but, in the long run, he wanted to show that he, like his mentor Sir Thomas Smith, was qualified for a position at court. This strategy was later to backfire. Direct quotations from *Rhetor* and *Ciceronianus*, Harvey's Latin publications, were used to pillory him in the Latin play *Pedantius*, which was produced in early 1581 in response to the publication of *Familiar Letters* (1580).

Although Harvey's success in winning positions as a reader in noble households suggests that he was able to ingratiate himself with courtiers, his persistent need to promote himself could and did render him tactless. He begins *Rhetor* by drawing unflattering comparisons between his success and the failure of his senior colleagues to draw audiences. After celebrating his own prowess as a lecturer, he deplores the lack of interest in the lectures of Thomas Byng, an outstanding Latinist, and Bartholomew Dodington, Regius Professor of Greek. Harvey's *Rhetor* is dedicated to Bartholomew Clerke of King's College, whose Latin translation of Castiglione's *Courtier* (1571; reprinted in 1577, 1585, 1593, 1603, and 1612) was admired in England and on the Continent.[11] In response to Harvey's dedication, Clerke ironically recommends that Harvey should seek the advice of his senior colleagues and specifically praises Byng. Clerke did his best to counter Harvey's invidious comparison between the crowds attending his lectures and the barren benches to which Byng and Dodington were obliged to lecture, but Clerke's *sprezzatura* was lost on Harvey – who merely reprinted his dedicatee's cautionary words in *Rhetor*!

In spring 1576, Harvey was absent from Cambridge for nearly twenty weeks preceding the Easter term. During this absence, it seems possible that he spent time on the periphery of Leicester House where he may have interacted with Sir Philip Sidney and Daniel Rogers. In *Gratulationes Valdinenses* (1578), he states that he had presented an epigram, presumably in manuscript, to Leicester in 1576 and that it had been widely copied.

Even though *Gratulationes Valdinenses* was not compiled and printed until 1578, the epigram to Leicester is specifically dated 1576 and printed with the rest of the 1578 text.

In 1577 Harvey's prospects suffered a setback because Sir Thomas Smith died on 12 August 1577. In response to Smith's death, Harvey brought out a collection of Latin elegies in his honour entitled *Gabrielis Harveii Valdinatis; Smithus; vel Musarum Lachrymae* (Londini: Henrici Binnemani, 157[7]). In a very simple design each of the muses laments Smith's death. The collection was published again by Henry Bynneman, and it included a dedicatory epistle to the stalwart Puritan Sir Walter Mildmay, Chancellor of the Exchequer and founder of Emmanuel College. Harvey included several poems to John Wood, Smith's nephew, who also surfaces in Harvey's *Letter-Book*. We need to take careful note that no poems written by Edmund Spenser are included in this 1577 collection. In 1577 Harvey had no interest in publicly announcing his 'friendship' with Spenser, an undistinguished member of John Young's London household.

To the degree that Harvey's marginalia are chronologically accurate, we can tentatively assume that he was acquainted with Sir Philip Sidney by the winter of 1577. He recorded in his edition of Livy that he and Sidney had studied the first three books of *Roman History* together prior to Sidney's departure to lead an embassy to the Holy Roman Emperor, the Elector Palatine, and other dignitaries.[12]

Harvey's nemesis – Andrew Perne

At Smith's funeral in 1577, Harvey quarrelled with Andrew Perne, Whitgift's mentor and friend. Reflecting later on the disparity between his ambitions and his achievements at Cambridge, Harvey became convinced that Perne had plotted against him to block his advancement. In *Familiar Letters* (1580), Harvey fiercely attacked Perne as the embodiment of hypocrisy, concluding with a denunciation of him as a liar: 'He often telleth me, he looveth me as himselfe, but out lyar out, thou lyest abhominably in thy throate' (D3v). It is not until *Pierces Supererogation, or A New Prayse of the Old Asse* (1593) that we learn the details of Harvey's quarrel with Perne at Smith's funeral:

> [Perne] once in a scoldes pollicie called me Foxe between iest, and earnest: (it was at the funerall [1577] of the honorable Sir Thomas Smith, where he preached, and where it pleased my Lady Smith, and the coexecutours to bestow certaine rare manuscript bookes vpon me, which he desired):

I aunswered him betweene earnest, & jest, I might haply be a Cubb, as I might be used, but was over young to be a Fox, especially in his presence. (sig. Dd1r, Grosart, 2: 313)

The confrontation over Smith's manuscripts purportedly took place in 1577, but it was not until three years later in 1580, when Harvey was frantically politicking to be appointed University Orator, that Harvey publicly denounced Perne as a hypocrite and another thirteen years passed before he revealed that the quarrel was over Smith's manuscripts.

In 1577, however, Perne had not yet begun to figure as the architect of Harvey's misfortunes. Harvey's principal concern was that his fellowship at Pembroke was scheduled to terminate in November 1578, and so his economic foothold at Cambridge was in jeopardy. He could not be re-elected a Fellow at Pembroke unless he committed himself to studying divinity or succeeded in obtaining a dispensation. He was reluctant to take holy orders, perhaps because of his ambition to secure a position in the government and an appointment at court. Clergymen had not figured prominently in Elizabeth's government prior to Whitgift, and the archbishop's ground-breaking appointment to the Privy Council did not occur until 2 February 1586. A decade earlier in 1577, to Harvey, taking holy orders seemed likely to jeopardize his most cherished ambitions. He was also faced with trying to find a new patron, a well-connected person who could sponsor his career as a courtier and diplomat. In this enterprise, he appears to have enjoyed some success.

There seems to have been a plan to include Harvey in a delegation to a Protestant conference in Schmalkalden in Thuringia scheduled on 7 June 1578. Elizabeth had chosen four deputies to represent England: Laurence Humphrey, John Still, John Hammon, and Daniel Rogers. Of the four deputies selected by Elizabeth for this embassy, John Still is the member of the delegation who is most likely to have been Harvey's sponsor.[13] According to Richard Harvey's *Astrological Discourse* (1583), Gabriel was to have been included:[14] 'Your singular curtesie toward my brother Gabriel, when he should have travailed to Smalcaldie, which curtesie he doth often recognize' (A3r). In the dedication addressed to John Aylmer, Bishop of London, dated 23 January 1581/2, Richard Harvey claims that he has the support of John Young, Bishop of Rochester, and Dr Lewen (A3v) in venturing to publish the *Astrological Discourse*. He also feels comfortable in bringing his discourse to Aylmer's attention because of the bishop's support for the writing of other university men, such as his brother, Gabriel. Richard Harvey inserts an allusion to Gabriel's

Anticosmopolita (A4r), which was entered in the Stationers' Register in 1579, but never appeared in print. To his tract Richard Harvey somewhat gratuitously attaches a 'Compendious Table of Phlebotomie, or bloud-letting'. In the conclusion, he addresses his brother Gabriel and signs himself from Walden on the 6 December 1582. On 9 April 1579 Harvey wrote to Lord Burghley asking him as the chancellor of Cambridge to recommend him as a candidate for the position of Public Orator.[15] A year later, on 14 June 1580, Harvey wrote again ostensibly to thank Burghley for his endorsement.[16]

These letters to Burghley and the dedication to Aylmer suggest that the Harvey brothers and Spenser belonged to distinctly different patronage groups. Richard Harvey's dedication to Bishop John Aylmer in 1583, like Gabriel Harvey's letters to Lord Burghley in 1579 and 1580, argue against Spenser's intimacy with Gabriel Harvey. While Spenser was drafting *Mother Hubberds Tale*, perhaps including an attack on Burghley and polishing the *Shepheardes Calender* with its satire on Aylmer, Harvey was pinning his hopes for preferment on the good graces of the Bishop of London and the Lord Treasurer.

In addition to positioning himself to attract a new patron, Harvey was also intent on keeping his Cambridge fellowship because it represented status and financial security. By appealing to external authorities, such as Leicester, Harvey hoped to circumvent the statutes at Pembroke which required fellows to study divinity after a certain number of years. Faced with mounting pressures, Harvey regarded the visit of the Queen to Cambridge during her 1578 summer progress as a major career opportunity. By showcasing his talents during the progress, he hoped to advertise his eligibility for a court position, attract a replacement for his patron Sir Thomas Smith, and, at the very least, persuade the Earl of Leicester to support the extension of his Pembroke fellowship.

There are indications that Harvey was recognized as a talented Latin orator. His selection as one of the principal debaters during the Queen's 1578 progress testifies to this reputation. It is less clear that his original verse in Latin or English was widely applauded. On Sunday, 27 July 1578, the Vice-Chancellor, Mr Howland of St John's, and the heads of colleges arrived at Audley End to welcome the Queen.[17] Audley End was the property of Thomas Howard, second son of the fourth Duke of Norfolk who had been executed for treason in 1572. Many details are known about the 1578 visit of the Queen to Audley End. Thomas Howard's three uncles (Philip Howard, Earl of Surrey; Charles Howard of Effingham, later naval commander against the Armada; and Henry Howard, later

Earl of Northampton) were present and received perfumed and embroidered gloves; attached were verses punning on their mottoes and crests decorated with their arms. We know specific details about the tokens presented: the Queen received gloves that cost 60s, Burghley's and Leicester's gloves cost 20s each; Thomas Radcliffe, Earl of Sussex and Lord Chamberlain, received a pair of gloves valued at 4s 2d. A Latin oration was delivered by the University Orator, Mr Bridgewater of King's College, who held the position for which Harvey was later to apply.

After Bridgewater's oration, the Queen seems to have retired briefly because it had been a very hot day. The noblemen and Cambridge delegation then moved to Leicester's quarters and held philosophical disputations. The topics concerned *Clementia magis in Principe laudanda quam severitas*, whether mercy or severity was more to be praised in princes, and *Astra non imponunt necessitatem*, whether the stars determine our lives. On the first philosophical topic, Harvey, along with Henry Hawkins (1553-1630), Giles Fletcher (1546-1611), and John Palmer, later Dean of Peterborough (1597-1607), argued the negative, supporting the Machiavellian premise that princes should be feared rather than loved. Of the four men selected to argue the negative, two later served as diplomatic agents abroad, an indication that Harvey's career ambitions in 1578 were not unrealistic. The second topic may not have been debated. Burghley seems to have questioned its propriety because arguing about the stars and fate might lead to discussion of the theological issue, predestination. Burghley limited the length of the speeches by refusing to allow repetition; even so the presentations lasted for over three hours.

Harvey's *Gratulationes Valdinenses* (1578)

Harvey, in addition to participating in these scheduled disputations, on his own initiative presented four handwritten manuscripts of Latin verse to the Queen. We know about this presentation only because it is described at length in Harvey's own publication *Gratulationes Valdinenses* (1578) and because it is referenced by E.K. in the Gloss to Spenser's *Shepheardes Calender* (1579). Harvey's four manuscripts, in supplement to his oral presentation in the disputation, were intended to advertise his knowledge of Latin and so display his qualifications for diplomatic assignments. George Gascoigne, who may have served as a literary model for both Harvey and Spenser, had used a similar strategy three years earlier in the 1575 Woodstock entertainment.[18] When the Queen expressed an interest in reading Gascoigne's Woodstock entertainment, he obligingly produced a polyglot manuscript as evidence of his linguistic talents – a manuscript that he just happened to have ready.[19] Harvey presented three manuscript books to Queen Elizabeth, Leicester, and Burghley, and a fourth was more generally addressed to the Earl of Oxford, Sir Christopher Hatton, and Philip Sidney.

We do not know if any sections of Harvey's manuscripts were orally presented. Some version of the addresses to Elizabeth and Leicester may have been delivered because Harvey later in the printed version emphasizes marks of favour that he received from Elizabeth and Leicester – particularly his being invited to kiss the Queen's hand. It is plausible, however, that Elizabeth may have offered him her hand to kiss at some point in the festivities as a gesture of recognition of his part in the winning disputation on Machiavelli. In *Gratulationes Valdinenses* Harvey is so caught up in dramatizing his feelings about kissing the Queen's hand that it is never made entirely clear why she gave him her hand or when she made this gesture. Nashe claims that he has inside information from witnesses (Nashe, 3: 73) and tells us that Harvey, inspired by the hot breath of an unattractive dance partner, ran headlong to his study and solemnized the occasion in verse:

> and strait knoct me vp together a Poem calde his *Aedes Valdinenses,* in prayse of my L. of *Leycester,* of his kissing the Queenes hand, and of her speech & comparison of him, how he lookt like an Italian: … The bungerliest vearses they were that euer were scande, beeing most of them hought and cut off by the knees out of *Virgill* and other Authors. This is a patterne of one of them, *Wodde, meusque tuusque suusque Britannorumque suorumque,* running through all the Pro-nounes in it. (3: 78).

At least as Nashe later tells the tale, nothing that Harvey did or said at Audley End impeded his career; it was the publication of *Familiar Letters* (1580) that harmed his reputation.

Only one of the four manuscripts, the one addressed to Burghley (BL, Lansdowne MS 120, fols 179–87), seems to have survived. This manuscript has been collated with the text of *Gratulationes Valdinenses* and the collation is printed in the 2014 edition of John Nichols's *The Progresses*.[20] This collation indicates that Harvey added about twenty-four lines including an epigram by Walter Haddon, a friend of Leicester's and Regius Professor of Civil Law at Cambridge, and abbreviated sections relating to Abraham Hartwell and Peter Bizari. The manuscript addressed to Burghley concludes with two efforts by Harvey, *in Effigiem Democriti*, an epigram on a portrait of Democritus, and *in Effigiem Heraciliti*, an epigram on a portrait of Heraclitus, both of which lament the depravity of the age.

Harvey was able to incorporate a diverse selection of works by English and Continental authors because many had already appeared in print.[21] It is useful to note that even in the Burghley tribute Harvey selects English authors who were part of Leicester's circle or who had enjoyed his patronage.[22] We know that Harvey reworked and expanded the manuscript presented to Elizabeth before it was printed because he reported on specific events that had occurred at Audley End. To the printed text Harvey added epigrams labelled as epilogues in the text: 'Pars prima, de Oscula' comments on his being granted the honour of kissing the Queen's hand, and 'Pars Epilogi secunda, De vultu Itali' describes the Queen's allusion to his Italian features.

Since he substantively expanded the manuscript to Elizabeth and added to the manuscript honouring Burghley, it seems likely that all of the manuscripts were expanded for Harvey's printed edition of *Gratulationes Valdinenses*. If so, Harvey had ample opportunity to insert a poem or epigram by Edmund Spenser somewhere in these addresses to Elizabeth, Leicester, Sidney, and other courtiers. In *Smithus* (1577), and even more strikingly in *Gratulationes Valdinenses* (1578), which includes a collection of poems by contemporary poets, Harvey chose to omit any poetry by Edmund Spenser. This omission has to be considered significant for Spenser's biography. In September 1578 Harvey included nothing from the pen of Spenser in *Gratulationes Valdinenses*, but in the spring of 1579 Harvey's name and figure dominate the Epistle and Gloss of the *Shepheardes Calender*.

The Queen's progress continued during August, but Harvey did not rejoin the festivities until September. The Queen probably rode through the town of Bishop's Stortford on the way to Hadham Hall on Saturday, 13 September 1578. Her destination was the home of Henry Capell, who in his early forties had been sheriff of Essex and Hertfordshire. The Capell family also owned property at Rayne in Essex, and Arthur Capell, Henry's son, occupied the Rayne property. Harvey seems to have been acquainted with Arthur, to whom he addresses two letters in his *Letter-Book*. Harvey alludes to himself by his initials and, characteristically, hints at private secrets:

> I assure you and in good faith, Mr. Capell, you shall always finde G.H. the selfe same man that you fownd him by ye fireside in his pore chamber ye night before your departure from Cambridge, when you knowe what secrets and privityes he revealed unto you.[23]

In *Familiar Letters* Harvey situates his discourse about the earthquake in a gentleman's house in Essex – possibly that of Capell, but Arthur Capell is not specifically identified.

At Hadham Hall, Harvey presented the printed *Gratulationes Valdinenses* to the Queen and courtiers; each one of the four printed books has a separate title page. This Latin text deserves more attention than it has received – not only because it illustrates Harvey's ambitions but also because it reveals his lack of social sensitivity. It should be noted, however, that *Gratulationes Valdinenses* has physical resemblances to the *Shepheardes Calender*. Book 1 contains a frontispiece depicting the Queen and three councillors; other books contain the arms of the courtiers being addressed. He also uses epigrams, emblems, and mottoes as well as odes and hymns and other genres as part of his eulogies. One of Harvey's additions to the printed text includes his epilogue memorializing the treasured moment at Audley End in which Elizabeth invited him to kiss her hand:

> Epilogus, de Regiae Manus osculatione; *deque eo, quòd vultum Itali habere, ab excellent*issima Principe diceretur. (B4r, 1–3)
>
> [Epilogue, On The kissing of the royal hand; and on that superb monarch's observation that I had the look of an Italian]
>
> ... *quo verba stupore*
> *Regia concuterent animum: quo numine pectus*
> *Corriperent: pluris*, Quisnam est? *fuit*, Hiccine quaeso
> Ille est? &, Dextram tibi non, Harueie, negabo;
>
> (C2v, 18–21)[24]
>
> [How the Queen's words took possession of my mind and tugged vigorously at my heart. And then her saying, 'Who is this? I want to know who that fellow over there is'. And then, 'Oh Harvey, how could I not extend my right hand to you?'] (*Progresses* (2014), 2: 596; trans., 659)

Recent descriptions of the 1578 progress mention this event because John Nichols included *Gratulationum Valdinensium Libri Quatuor* in his first edition of the *Progresses of Queen Elizabeth* in 1788; he omitted Harvey's and other Latin texts from the second edition in 1823.[25] It is significant for our identification of E.K. and our interpretation of the *Shepheardes Calender* that these events are *not* reported in other sixteenth-century descriptions of the progress. The hand-kissing event is featured only in

Harvey's *Gratulationes Valdinenses* and, significantly, the Gloss to the *September* eclogue of the *Shepheardes Calender*.

We, for example, do not find references to Harvey's having kissed the Queen's hand in Thomas Churchyard's description of the Queen's entertainment in Suffolk and Norfolk or in any other account of this well-recorded progress. Churchyard's account naturally emphasizes the pageants in Norwich which he himself devised. Apparently, a rain storm interrupted the pageantry, and Churchyard converted the 'nimphes of the water' to 'fairies on the land'. As part of a newly devised entertainment, Churchyard, 'appareled like a water sprite, beganne to sounde a timbrell'.[26] After this whimsical event, Churchyard recounts a visit to Lord North where there was an oration delivered by a gentleman from Cambridge. Regarding the visit to Hadham Hall he says:

> From thence to mayster Kapels, where was excellente good cheere and entertaynement. From thence to Hide Hall, where I heard of not greate cheere nor banketing. And then to Mr. Stonard in Essex and then to my Lord of Leycester's house, where the progress ended.[27]

No event featuring Harvey is recorded above during the visit to 'mayster Kapels'. At the conclusion of the progress, Churchyard says that Leicester feasted the Queen and the French ambassador, but that even before their arrival he had entertained a large party at his own table 'using such courtesie unto them for the space of two dayes as was and is worthy of perpetuall memorie' (93). Thus, Harvey's presentation of *Gratulationes Valdinenses* to the Queen and court passed unnoticed in Churchyard's account; significantly, however, it was to be featured only a year later in the Gloss to the *September* eclogue.

In Book 1 of the printed text of *Gratulationes Valdinenses* Harvey also supplies a dialogue between Elizabeth and Leicester concerning his preferment. In 'Pars Epilogi secunda: De vultu Itali' [Second part of the epilogue: of my Italian countenance] (C2v, 25), the Queen asks Leicester if he intends to send Harvey to Italy and France:

> *Protinus et Dominum alloqueris (meminisse iuuabit,*
> *Dum potero meminisse aliquid)* Dic, Hunccine in oras
> Italicas, Francasque tibi transmittere certum est?
> *Certum, inquit Dominus*; benè factum, Iam iam habet ille
> Vultum Itali, faciemque hominis: vix esse Britannum
> Crediderim, potiusque hospes quidam esse videtur.
>
> (C2v, 26–31)

[Then you speak to the Lord [Leicester] (I'll always recall the incident with pleasure, as long as I'm still capable of remembering anything.) 'So, it's your intent to send him to the shores of Italy and France?' 'There is no question about it,' said the Lord. 'It's a good thing, for even now he's got such an Italian look about him that I can hardly believe he's British; he looks more like some visiting dignitary from abroad.']²⁸(*Progresses*, 2: 596; trans., 660)

Harvey uses this dialogue between Leicester and Elizabeth to bring up the international success of his *Smithus; vel Musarum Lachrymae*. He claims that two Italian poets have added his name to their list of choice bards. Harvey, while advertising the international scope of his reputation, disclaims any self-promotion by inserting the parenthetical statement '(data carmina sero / Typographo fuerant)' [the poems were just given to the printer] (C4v, 13–14). He also remarks that 'me quoque dicunt / Vatem pastores' [the shepherds also call me a poet-prophet] (C4v, 30–1), but he insists that he does not believe the shepherds' high opinion of him and observes that it is best to ignore the praises of others and give heed to your inner voice.

Book 2 of *Gratulationes Valdinenses* is dedicated to the Earl of Leicester from whom Harvey hoped to gain preferment, and this is the only book that has received any critical attention. Harvey's comments on Machiavelli and the Medici family have been construed by Thomas Jameson as political commentary on the Alençon–Anjou courtship.²⁹ In his critical analysis, Jameson argues that Harvey wanted his audience to associate Anjou, Elizabeth's suitor and the son of Catherine de' Medici, with Florentine subtlety and to view him as a Machiavel. In fact, Jameson contends that Sidney collaborated with Harvey on this satire on Anjou, because Leicester still hoped to marry the Queen. In support of Jameson's argument, it should be noted that Harvey does include poems – though written by others – that seem to entertain the idea of a marriage between Elizabeth and Leicester.³⁰ We need to keep in mind that less than two weeks later on 21 September 1578 Leicester was to marry Lettice, widow of the Earl of Essex, at Wanstead, where the progress concluded.

Far from earning Harvey an enforced exile, or even an immediate rebuke, Harvey's covert literary venture into matrimonial politics, if there was one, seems to have passed unnoticed. There is, however, an alternative explanation for Harvey's introduction of Machiavelli into *Gratulationes Valdinenses*. Earlier in the progress at Audley End, Harvey was part of the winning oratorical team who had argued the Machiavellian premise that it was better for a prince to be feared than loved. In the printed text of *Gratulationes Valdinenses*, it seems likely that Harvey brought up Machiavelli in order to remind his courtly audience of his victory during the Cambridge-sponsored disputation at Audley End. If so, the introduction of Machiavelli serves the same function as his poem on having been invited to kiss the Queen's hand. The references to Machiavelli remind all and sundry that his side won the Cambridge debate and that the Queen said that he already looked Italian.

We know from Harvey's surviving marginalia that he admired Machiavelli as a thinker, but in Book 2 he gives us the traditional Elizabethan stage view of Machiavelli as the villainous 'Machiavel':

> *Ferrea frons, Orci pectora digna Deo.*
> *Emblema est, semperque fuit: Iuuat ire per altum:*
> *Aut nihil, aut Caesar;noster Alumnus erat.*
> *Nil mediôcre placet: sublimia sola voluto:*
> *Lac pueris cibus est: sanguine vescor ego.*
> (F1r, 6–10)

[An iron countenance, a chest vying in strength with the god of the Dead. My motto is and always has been: shoot for the top: be Caesar or be nobody. He was our favourite son. I never settle for any middling goal; I aim for the heights. Let children suck milk; I dine on blood.] (*Progresses* (2014), 2: 611; trans., 676)

This monologue is followed by a dramatic poem that is entitled 'G. Harueij Mercurius Florentinus, vel Machiavelli [apotheosis in Greek]' [The Florentine Mercury of Gabriel Harvey, or the Apotheosis of Machiavelli], and this insistence upon Harvey's authorship suggests that he devoted special attention to this offering.

In the dramatic poem, Cosimo de' Medici shows Machiavelli's writing to Mercury, and then Mercury and Machiavelli are joined – two bodies but one mind. Jupiter decrees that they are one and the same god. Cosimo de' Medici says that he envies Machiavelli, but this angers Jupiter who decrees that no one is to venture to surpass him. Then everyone sings the *Medicaeorum Hymnus* [Hymn of the Medici] which celebrates the apotheosis:

> *Mercurium peperit Florentia: fallitur orbis:*
> *Qui Macheuallus erat; Mercurius Deus est.*
> (F1v, 22–3)

[Florence has given birth to a Mercury. The world's got it wrong. Who was Machiavelli? He is Mercury, the god.] (Cf. ll. 1–2 of the hymn, *Progresses* (2014), 2: 612; trans., 677)

This new god is not especially honourable since he holds sway over some of Mercury's traditional clients – thieves, tyrants, traitors, turncoats, and assorted deities from hell. Mercury even pays tribute to the goddess Guile, who, linked with Fraud, seems to control power on Earth.

Mercury, now one with Machiavelli, proclaims himself the ruler of the world, but Pallas, the Queen of Britain, objects.

> *Mortales, reliquorum hominum comburite scripta;*
> *Solus ego Reges, Regnaque vestra rego.*
> *Dixit: at excepit Pallas Britannica regna:*
> *Conticuitque Deus, conticuitque Dea.*
>
> (F2r, 21–4)

[Mortals, burn up the writings of everyone else, I'm the only one who rules over your kings and your kingdoms. So, he said, but Pallas exempted Britannic rule. Silent was the god, silent the goddess.] (Cf. *Progresses* (2014), 2: 613; trans., 678)

At the conclusion of the hymn we have an emblem announcing that Mercury is known for his thievery and trickery.

> *Furta, dolique Deos faciunt! Deus ecce vocatur*
> *Mercurius, furtis scilicet, atque dolis.*
>
> (F2r, 26–7)

[Thievery and trickery create gods! Behold a god called Mercury, known for his thievery and trickery.] (Cf. *Progresses* (2014), 2: 613; trans., 678)

Having associated Mercury with thieves and deceit, in an amazing denouement, the emblem is followed by an epigram associating Mercury with Leicester. Harvey tells us that this epigram on the picture of Leicester was written in 1576: 'Epigramma in Effigiem Nobilisimi Comitis Leicestrensis, duobus abhinc annis Londini con-*scriptum; & ex eo tempore à multis descriptuum*' [Epigram to an image of the most noble Earl of Leicester, written two years previously in London, and written down by many men since that time] (F2r).[31]

> *En generosum hominem, pulchrum magis omnibus unum:*
> *En tibi Britannae Nobilitatis Honos,*
> *Quaeris, qui tanti talem genuêre Parentes?*
> *Tres habui Matres; tergeminósque Patres*
> *Prima Venus Mater: Charis altera: tertia Pallas:*
> *Ex Patribus, primas doctus Apollo tulit.*
> *Adde huic Mercurium: Plutum superadde potentem:*
> *Quaere alios Patres, qui minus hosce probas.*
>
> (F2r, 1–2, F2v, 1–6)

[Behold one who is the fairest and most excellent! Before you is the crown of Britain's Nobility. You ask who were the excellent parents who produced such a one? I had three mothers and three fathers. First Mother Venus; second Grace; third Pallas Athena; Of fathers, first learned Apollo; to this add Mercury and then powerful Pluto. / Seek other parentage, you who disapprove of these.] (Cf. *Progresses* (2014), 2: 613; trans., 678)

As the above summary and translation suggest, this epigram celebrates Leicester as the son of Apollo, Mercury, and Pluto. Leicester, as the son of Mercury, would then be linked to Machiavelli. Such a reading is untenable. Harvey cannot have meant to suggest, as his text clearly does, that Leicester owed his parentage to the amalgamated figure of Mercury and Machiavelli. It may be that Harvey hurriedly assembled the text and that he considered specific lines rather than overall structure or that he was so eager to include in *Gratulationes Valdinenses* his epigram from 1576 that he failed to grasp the resulting implications.

Gratulationes Valdinenses (1578) was intended as Harvey's 'signature' work – his *Shepheardes Calender*, but Harvey's text was a more blatant bid for patronage than Spenser's. Inevitably, *Gratulationes Valdinenses* poses for us the problem of how to assess Harvey's talents as a Latin poet and aspiring courtier. He had already published his Cambridge lectures, which testify to his talents as an orator, but the lectures do not speak to his potential as a courtier. In *Gratulationes Valdinenses* he set out to display his mastery of Latin, his potential for handling international relations, and his command of courtly panegyric. Even if Harvey deliberately, or inadvertently, linked Anjou with Machiavelli, that in itself would not be damning; nor is it obvious that an allusion to Leicester's possible marriage with Elizabeth would be disastrous. His marriage to the Countess of Essex may not have been widely known until later in the autumn. An all-important test of a courtier, however, involved knowing how to praise, but to recognize when a compliment had been taken too far, and it is this test that Harvey failed.

Gratulationes Valdinenses concludes with Book 4 in which Harvey addresses encomia to Oxford, Hatton, and Sidney. It is from Book 4 that we learn how to 'read' Harvey as his contemporaries would have 'read' him. Harvey's tribute to Sidney precedes in print Spenser's dedication of the *Shepheardes Calender* to Sidney and has been blandly passed over as one of the first of many celebrations of Sidney as the ideal courtier. Katherine Duncan-Jones, however, has echoed Thomas Nashe in calling attention to the fallacies in this approach to Harvey's tribute to Sidney. Quite superficially, even before the actual text of the poem to Sidney is examined, Harvey made certain social blunders. It is unlikely that Sidney and Oxford would have enjoyed being bracketed together; they were frequently at odds personally and politically.[32] In Sidney's case, Harvey also alludes with approval to Sidney's imminent departure to join the battle for Dutch independence. Elizabeth, however, had not decided if England would intervene in this war. It may have been during this very progress that Sidney learned that the Queen objected to his leaving the court and that she had decided against sending troops to assist the Dutch. From these examples, we should question how sensitive Harvey was to court politics and its effect on foreign policy.

In respect to courtly panegyric, however, we might assume that Harvey would be on very safe grounds; his marginalia indicate that he had experience in reading the classics with aristocrats. Duncan-Jones, however, has argued that Harvey's tribute to Sidney violates Elizabethan norms of social decorum. Calling attention to remarks in which Harvey exaggerates his familiarity with Sidney, '*mihi multis nominibus longe charissimum*' [to me on many accounts by far the dearest] (K3r), she wryly comments that Harvey has gone beyond the parameters of courtly eulogy and is actually suggesting homosexual passion. She adds that Harvey has seriously slipped up by alluding to his liver, conventionally the seat of sexual passion, rather than his heart or soul.[33]

> *Sum Iecur, ex quo te primùm Sidnëie vidi:*
> *Os, oculosque regit, cogit amare Iecur.*
>
> (K4r, 14–15)

[Ever since I first saw you, Sidney, my liver has been burning; my feelings have directed my speech and my sight, my feelings have forced me to love.][34]

Galen, whom Elizabethan medical theory pretty much rubber-stamped, regarded the heart as the seat of the emotions and relegated the liver to the lower status of appetites.

We might regard this quibbling over liver and heart as too subtle to have mattered in an entertainment – were it not that Katherine Duncan-Jones has taken her cue from a contemporary of Harvey's. Her reading of Harvey's text has the support of Thomas Nashe:

> I haue perused vearses of his, written vnder his owne hande to *Sir Philip Sidney*, wherein he courted him as he were another *Cyparissus* or *Ganimede*; the last *Gordian* true loues knot or knitting vp of them is this:
>
> > *Sum iecur ex quo te primùm, Sydnee, vidi,*
> >
> > *Os oculósque regit, cogit amare iecur.*

All liuer am I, Sidney, since I saw thee;
My mouth, eyes, rules it, and to loue doth draw mee.
(Nashe, *Have with You to Saffron-Walden*, ed. McKerrow, 3: 92)

Nashe cites Harvey's Latin and adds his own English translation. If there were not interlinear substance to this 'reading', Nashe would have levelled the charge, but suppressed the direct quotation from *Gratulationes Valdinenses*.

We can only conclude that Harvey was not in full control of his own rhetoric when he ventured into courtly panegyric. In *Gratulationes Valdinenses* his overall intentions are clear. He wanted to emphasize his rapport with prominent courtiers and to advertise his stature in the international community. If the readings of Jameson and Stern are accepted, then he failed to combine eulogy and satire effectively in a maladroit attempt to criticize the Anjou courtship. If, as I have argued, he wanted to remind his audience of his success at Audley End, then his references to Machiavelli and his highlighting of his Italian countenance were intended to prompt Leicester to send him abroad. In either case, his rhetorical design was confused. It was inept for Harvey to conclude Book 2 with a hint that Leicester was Mercury's son, because in the body of the text he had taken great pains to establish that Machiavelli and Mercury were one and the same deity.

It is likely that Harvey was aiming at the techniques that enabled Spenser to offset eulogy with artful touches of irony in the *Aprill* eclogue of the *Shepheardes Calender*, but Harvey, supposing that was his intention, failed to bring it off. Even more damning for Harvey's aspirations to be a courtier were his excesses in his tribute to Sidney. In the *Shepheardes Calender*, Spenser addresses Sidney simply as 'him that is the president / Of noblesse and cheualree' (3–4) in stark contrast to Harvey's testimonial in Book 4 of *Gratulationes Valdinenses* to the overwhelming passions that Sidney has awakened in his liver.

On the very mundane level of getting his fellowship renewed in 1578, Harvey was to fail. On 22 August 1578, after the presentation of Harvey's manuscripts, but before he presented the printed texts of *Gratulationes Valdinenses* to the court, William Fulke, John Young's successor as Master of Pembroke College, wrote a letter requesting that Harvey be allowed to retain his fellowship. Fulke's attempt to get Harvey a dispensation from the statutes requiring study of divinity was carefully worded. He assures the Fellows of his support for Harvey and tells them that 'the Earle of Leycester hath made earnest request for the continuance of Mr.

Harveyes fellowshipp for one yeare'.³⁵ Even the influence brought to bear by mentioning Leicester's name was to no avail; the Fellows denied the request.

Harvey remained hopeful that he could use his academic background as a stepping stone to a position in the government. To further this ambition, he printed *Gratulationes Valdinenses*, a text in which he fashions a portrait of himself as a future envoy to Italy, the protégé of the Earl of Leicester. The contrast between Harvey and Spenser in their early works is instructive: Spenser fashions a persona to conceal his identity and to distance himself from the public; in contrast, Harvey published his private ambitions and advertised any progress that he had made or favours that he had received or might later receive. He congratulated Sidney on being sent to defend the Dutch in the Netherlands – even though Sidney's appointment was not to be forthcoming. He called dramatic attention to his being sent as an envoy to Italy before he was given an assignment by either the Queen or Leicester. He addressed Sidney as his beloved patron, even though Harvey was never to become part of Sidney's inner circle.

Notes

1 Jon A. Quitslund, 'Questionable Evidence in the *Letters* of 1580 between Gabriel Harvey and Edmund Spenser', in *Spenser's Life and the Subject of Biography*, ed. Judith H. Anderson, Donald Cheney, and David A. Richardson (Amherst: University of Massachusetts Press, 1996), 86–7. See also Hadfield, *Life*, 151, who concludes that *Familiar Letters* may have 'kick-started Spenser's career' but ended Harvey's hopes for advancement.

2 Harvey, *Works*, ed. Grosart. 3 vols. Huth Library (London: Hazell, Watson & Viney, Ltd., 1884–5).

3 A complete translation as well as annotated edition of *Gratulationes Valdinenses* is included in the new edition of John Nichols's *The Progresses and Public Processions of Queen Elizabeth I: A New Edition of the Early Modern Sources*, ed. Elizabeth Goldring, Faith Eales, Elizabeth Clarke, and Jayne Elisabeth Archer, 5 vols (Oxford: Oxford University Press, 2014). My research was complete prior to the appearance of this new edition; their Latin text is reprinted from Huntington Library, RB 59268, the text for my citations. Both the Latin text and English translation by Virginia Moul are reprinted in volume 2 of *Progresses* (2014). I, however, use my translations; see also note 27 below. For the reader's convenience, I also cite this edition and translation.

4 It is important to note that EEBO and the earlier University Microfilms reproduced a flawed copy of *Familiar Letters*, missing the leaves F2 and F3..

5 *Familiar Letters*. The full title of *Familiar Letters* is *Three Proper and wittie, familiar Letters.: lately passed betwene two Universitie men: touching the Earthquake in Aprill last, and our English refourmed Versifying. With the Preface of a wellwiller to them both. Two Other very commendable Letters of the same mens writing:*

both touching the foresaid Artificiall Versifying, and certain other Particulars: More lately delivered unto the Printer (London: H. Bynneman, 1580). RB 69544. The Huntington Library, San Marino, CA. This publication contains five, not three, letters. In addition, an early issue of Harvey's *Foure Letters* (1592) was entitled *Three Letters, and certaine sonnets*, but Harvey almost immediately revised and reissued *Three Letters* (1592) as *Foure Letters*; see Francis R. Johnson, 'Gabriel Harvey's *Three Letters*: A First Issue of His *Foure Letters*', *The Library*, Fifth Series (1946), 134–6. In order to avoid the confusion of three, four, and five letters – all entitled *Three Letters* – it makes sense to use the title *Familiar Letters*. Both Nashe and Lyly allude to this text as 'Familiar Epistles'.

6 The *Spenser Variorum* reorganizes the text of *Familiar Letters*, printing the letters in chronological order rather than reproducing the order of the first edition. Spenser's letters, in addition, are separated from Harvey's, whose letters are relegated to an appendix (*The Works of Edmund Spenser: A Variorum Edition*, ed. Edwin Greenlaw, Charles Grosvenor Osgood, Frederick Morgan Padelford, and Ray Heffner, 10 vols (Baltimore: The Johns Hopkins Press, 1949). Textbooks such as *The Renaissance in England: Nondramatic Prose and Verse of the Sixteenth Century*, ed. Hyder E. Rollins and Herschel Baker (Lexington, MA: D.C. Heath & Co., 1954), routinely excerpt the letters.

7 Stern, *Harvey*, 7. Harvey's *ODNB* article by Jason Scott-Warren gives his birthdate as 1552/3, suggesting that he was born between January and March in 1553, but no rationale is given.

8 British Library, Sloane MS 93, fol. 19r. Cited from Harvey, *Letter-Book*, 34.

9 For analysis of secretariats and of scholars reading the classics with aristocrats, see Lisa Jardine and Anthony Grafton, '"Studied for Action": How Gabriel Harvey Read His Livy', *Past and Present*, 129 (1990), 30–78, and Paul Hammer, 'The Uses of Scholarship: The Secretariat of Robert Devereux, c. 1585–1601', *English Historical Review*, 109 (1994), 26–51, and 'The Earl of Essex, Fulke Greville and the Employment of Scholars', *Studies in Philology*, 91 (1994), 167–80.

10 Marginalia on sig. M8r of his Quintilian indicate that he lectured on rhetoric in 1573 before receiving the formal appointment and continued into 1575 (see Stern, *Harvey*, 31).

11 For Harvey's interest in the *Courtier*, see Caroline Ruutz-Rees, 'Some Notes of Gabriel Harvey's in Hoby's Translation of Castiglione's *Courtier* (1561)', *Publications of the Modern Language Association*, 25 (1910), 608–39.

12 Katherine Duncan-Jones, *Sir Philip Sidney, Courtier Poet* (New Haven: Yale University Press, 1991), 117. Duncan-Jones observes that Harvey did not impress Sidney as much as he had hoped 'for he was not included, as he surely would have liked to be, in the very large company assembled ... to travel with Sidney to the Imperial Court' (120).

13 Harvey identifies Still as a possible patron in a letter written to the Earl of Leicester on 24 April 1579, Stern, *Harvey*, 49.

14 Richard Harvey, *Astrological Discourse* (1583), sig. A3r. RB 17109. The Huntington Library. San Marino, CA.

15 Stern, *Harvey*, 53. Harvey dates his letter 'Pridie Idus Aprilis, 1579' in British Library, Lansdowne MS 28, No. 83, but Stern and Moore Smith argue that the letter was written in 1580, claiming that Harvey had forgotten that the calendar had changed on 25 March, but no evidence is cited.

16 British Library, Lansdowne MS 30, No. 57.
17 For a description of the archival evidence relative to the Cambridge delegation, see Zillah Dovey, *An Elizabethan Progress: The Queen's Journey into East Anglia, 1578* (Stroud: Alan Sutton, and Madison, Teaneck: Fairleigh Dickinson Press, 1996), 34. Dovey corrects the date for Harvey's presentation given in Stern, *Gabriel Harvey*, 40.
18 In his *Letter-Book* Harvey alludes three times to Gascoigne's works and puts him next to Chaucer in a catalogue of writers. Harvey composes epigrams on him and an epitaph for him. See Harvey, *Letter-Book*, 69, 85, 100; 134; 55–8, 68–70.
19 For studies of Gascoigne's entertainment, see Gabriel Heaton, *Writing and Reading Royal Entertainments* (Oxford: Oxford University Press, 2010), chapter 1; and Gillian Austen, *The Literary Career of George Gascoigne: Studies in Self Presentation* (Woodbridge: D.S. Brewer, 2008).
20 The 2014 edition of Nichols usefully supplies a full collation of the manuscript addressed to Burghley and the text printed in *Gratulationes Valdinenses*. This collation is attached to the Latin text. All annotations and explanatory notes, however, are attached to the English translation. For the printed edition, Harvey added an epigram by Walter Haddon to the printed text while abbreviating Abraham Hartwell and Peter Bizari and making several other additions and cuts.
21 Thomas Hugh Jameson, '*The Gratulationes Valdinenses* of Gabriel Harvey', unpublished PhD dissertation, Yale University (1938), xxxvii–xxxviii.
22 Eleanor Rosenberg, *Leicester: Patron of Letters* (New York: Columbia University Press, 1955), 325–8. See Rosenberg's important bibliographical comment (328, n, 13) suggesting that additions were made when the book was in production, as we know was the case with *Foure Letters* and *Familiar Letters*.
23 Harvey, *Letter-Book*, 182–3. See also 167–8.
24 I owe the English translations which have verve to my colleague and friend Professor John Mulryan, St Bonaventure University, Allegany, New York. In addition to citing my copy text, Huntington Library, RB 59268, and Mulryan's or my translations, I note for the reader's convenience the pagination of the Latin text and of Virginia Moul's translation in *Progresses* (2014).
25 John Nichols, *The Progresses, and Public Processions, of Queen Elizabeth* (London: Society of Antiquaries, 1788), 2, is frequently cited as a source, but Nichols's source is Harvey's *Gratulationes Valdinenses* which he prints in its entirety. Modern descriptions of the 1578 progress invariably mention Harvey's presentation, but the source is always Nichols or the Gloss to the *Shepheardes Calender*. The Gloss makes it clear that there were two presentations, one of the manuscripts and the other of the printed texts, but the reader of *Gratulationes Valdinenses* might not understand this.
26 Nichols, *Progresses*, 2: 76, on the sudden storm and 86 on the revised entertainment. See also *Progresses* (2014), 2: 739 and 748.
27 Nichols, *Progresses*, 2: 92–3. See also *Progresses* (2014), 2: 751–2.
28 Harvey seems to be trying here for a Vergilian echo: '"Tell me pray, / Is this the man that thou hast fixed to send / To the shores of France and Italy" or "So him to the shores / Of Italy and France you plan to send?" "It is fixed", my lord replied.'
29 Thomas Hugh Jameson, 'The "Machiavellianism" of Gabriel Harvey', *Publications of the Modern Language Association*, 56 (1941), 647–8.

30 Stern, *Harvey*, uses this interpretation of *Gratulationes Valdinenses* to explain why Harvey failed to obtain political advancement (43).
31 As discussed above, this is the epigram that can be used to date Harvey's contact with Leicester House, but it seems to have appeared in print for the first time in *Gratulationes Valdinenses* (1578).
32 Harvey, somewhat quixotically, urges Oxford, who had published poetry, to devote himself to military service in a passage used by Oxfordians to support his authorship of Shakespeare's plays.
33 Duncan-Jones, *Life*, 156. Harvey, *Works*, ed. Grosart, I: xli-xliii, translates only the first section of the tribute to Sidney. Lewis and Short cited 'iecur' as the source for feelings, but Horace, *Epistles*, 1.2.69, seems to associate it with sexual passion.
34 It is worth noting that in the literal translation supplied in *Progresses* (2014), 2: 703, Virginia Moul substitutes heart for liver because she instinctively knows that heart would be the appropriate term even though 'iecur' literally means liver.
35 Harvey, *Letter-Book*, 88.

6

'Minde on honour fixed': Spenser, Sidney, and the early modern chivalric code

Association with the Sidneys may have shaped Spenser's career – as it did those of Lodowick Bryskett and Fulke Greville. It is possible, as suggested by commendatory poems to the *Faerie Queene*, that contact with Sir Philip Sidney led Colin Clout to conceive of himself as an epic poet. There may be at least a hint that Spenser entered the service of the Sidneys and through them had access to Leicester House prior to April 1579. On 24 April 1579, Gabriel Harvey wrote from Trinity Hall, Cambridge, to ask Leicester to offer him 'Doctor Byddles Praebende at Litchfeylde, the Cancelour[ship] very lately falling voyde, by his suddayne discease'.[1] He suggests that John Still, his old tutor, be named the bishop because he is sure that Still will support his candidacy as chancellor. This was an abrupt shift for Harvey, who only months earlier, during the Queen's 1578 progress, had spent money to print *Gratulationes Valdinenses* to persuade Leicester to send him to Italy. It is possible that Spenser's success in becoming Sidney's client prompted Harvey to renew his pleas for promotion – even if the promotion had to be located closer to home. The dedication to the *Shepheardes Calender* was signed on 10 April 1579, just two weeks before Harvey wrote to Leicester shifting the location of his suit for preferment from Italy to England.

Leicester House

Spenser may first have become acquainted with Philip Sidney when Sidney and Greville visited Cambridge in 1571.[2] It is probable that Spenser was introduced to Leicester House through academic connections forged at

Pembroke College. Humphrey Tyndall, the senior Fellow at Pembroke who rode to London to consult with Young on the granting of Harvey's M.A., had become Leicester's chaplain. We know that Tyndall enjoyed Leicester's confidence because it was he who officiated at the Earl's secret marriage to Lettice Knollys, Countess of Essex, on 20 September 1578. Tyndall, like Young and other early patrons of Spenser, belonged to the circle of churchmen who also wielded power in university circles. In 1580, Tyndall succeeded Laurence Chadderton as Master of Queens' College, Cambridge.

In *Gratulationes Valdinenses* Harvey reports that while in London in 1576 he addressed an epigram to Leicester (F2r, 28–30). More specifically, in Harvey's Livy, his marginalia refer to one or more occasions between October 1576 and February 1577 when Harvey read Latin with Sir Philip Sidney.[3] Harvey dates these sessions shortly before Philip left England in February 1577 to lead an embassy to the German Emperor Rudolf II and the Elector Palatine Louis VI. Duncan-Jones warns against taking Harvey's account of his intimacy with Sidney at face value.[4] Allowing for some exaggeration of Harvey's intimacy with Sidney, the references to Sidney in his Livy are precise enough so that we can tentatively assume that he had access to Leicester House by October 1576 and prior to February 1577:

> The courtier Philip Sidney and I had privately discussed these three books of Livy, scrutinizing them so far as we could from all points of view, applying a political analysis, just before his embassy to the emperor Rudolf II. He went to offer him congratulations in the queen's name just after he had been made emperor. Our consideration was chiefly directed at the forms of states, the conditions of persons, and the qualities of actions. We paid little attention to the annotations of Glareanus and others.[5]

Harvey was not part of Sidney's inner circle of acquaintances or he would not have used the telling epithet 'the courtier' as a description of Sidney in his marginalia. This epithet distances Harvey from Sidney and casts doubt on his efforts to portray himself as on terms of easy familiarity with Leicester's nephew.

Though Spenser, too, may have had access to Leicester House by 1577, the extent of Spenser's connections with Leicester himself has sometimes been exaggerated. There is no evidence, for example, that he was ever employed as Leicester's secretary. The Earl's secretaries have been identified, and we have no surviving correspondence in Spenser's hand.[6] Presumably, he received some financial reward from Leicester for his tributes in the

Shepheardes Calender and the *Ruines of Time* – if they were presented to Leicester in manuscript. Had Spenser been employed by Leicester as an agent or messenger who was sent abroad, there should be records of payment for these services, but none has been produced.

Until early 1579 Spenser seems to have been, as he styles himself, the 'Southerne shepheards boye', while he was writing the *Shepheardes Calender*. As an employee in Young's household, and presumably aware of church politics, Spenser himself would have recognized that he was ending any future as a cleric when he published the *Shepheardes Calender* in 1579. We know that he was sensitive to the political climate: he did not publish *Mother Hubberds Tale* until 1591 when the first part of the *Faerie Queene* was already in print – though an early version was probably composed in 1579.[7]

Spenser and the Sidneys

Spenser's dedication of the *Shepheardes Calender* (1579) to Philip Sidney is significant because it seems likely that Spenser would have secured Sidney's permission before printing the dedication. He was sensitive to the awkwardness of dedicating a poem to a person who might disagree with its contents or resent the dedication because it suggested undue familiarity. In *Familiar Letters*, alluding to Stephen Gosson's having dedicated *The Schoole of Abuse* to Sidney, Spenser writes:

> Newe Bookes I heare of none, but only of one, that writing a certaine Booke, called *the Schoole of Abuse*, and dedicating it to Maister Sidney, was for hys labor scorned: if at leaste it be in the goodnesse of that nature to scorne. Suche follie is it, not to regarde aforehande the inclination and qualitie of him to whome wee dedicate oure Bookes. (G3v)[8]

Alluding to Gosson, Spenser says that it would be folly to dedicate a poem to Sidney without permission. The dedication of *Shepheardes Calender* to 'Master Philip Sidney' on the title page suggests that Spenser had shown the poem to Sidney, that Sidney had encouraged him to publish it, and that he had received Sidney's permission to address him as the dedicatee. If we compare Harvey's fulsome language in *Gratulationes Valdinenses* with Spenser's, the very simplicity of his dedication to Sidney argues that they may have been acquainted.

In *Familiar Letters*, Spenser also raises with Harvey his reluctance to impose on his patrons, his fears of seeming encroaching, but in this very passage he makes it clear that he has already been the recipient of financial rewards:

> First, I was minded for a while to have intermitted the uttering of my writings: leaste by over-much cloying their noble eares, I should gather a contempt of my self, or else seeme rather for gaine and commoditie to doe it, for some sweetnesse that I have already tasted. (G3r)

The 'sweenesse' of Philip Sidney's generosity, in fact, is amply documented; he paid for the education of Abraham Fraunce and subsidized the promising logician William Temple.

There is also anecdotal evidence suggesting that Sidney became Spenser's patron.[9] In the 'Commendatory Poems' appended to the *Faerie Queene* (1590), W.L. tells us that it was Sidney who steered Spenser in the direction of the heroic poem that was to become the *Faerie Queene*. In W.L.'s allegorical fiction, Spenser, like Achilles concealed among the women, has disguised himself as a pastoral poet, but Sidney, like Ulysses, recognizes Spenser's poetic destiny: 'heard him sing, and knew his voice'.

> And as *Vlysses* brought faire *Thetis* sonne
> From his retyred life to menage armes:
> So *Spencer* was by *Sidneys* speaches wonne,
> To blaze her fame not fearing future harmes:
> For well he knew, his Muse would soone be tyred
> In her high praise, that all the world admired.
>
> (724)

Like Ralegh, W.L. adroitly compliments the Queen in this commendatory poem. Describing Elizabeth's charms proves beyond Spenser's powers because this task would be too much for human wit, but Spenser, W.L. tells us, is 'excus'd sith *Sidney* thought it fitt'. Sidney is here credited with inspiring Spenser to celebrate Elizabeth in the *Faerie Queene*.

Spenser himself also describes Sidney as his inspiration for the epic in a dedicatory sonnet appended to the *Faerie Queene* (1590). He acknowledges Lord Grey as 'the pillor of my life, / And Patrone of my Muses pupillage', but in the sonnet addressed to Mary Sidney Herbert, Countess of Pembroke, Spenser describes Sidney as the inspiration for his having turned from pastoral to epic, he is the one, 'who first my Muse did lift out of the flore' (734). It is worth noting that these poetic testimonials to Sidney's influence on Spenser were written after Sidney's death when no reward could have been expected. Difficult as it may be to track Spenser's literary debt to Sidney, it seems likely that Spenser felt that Sidney had materially assisted him in finding his way to the *Faerie Queene*.[10]

In the *Familiar Letter* dated 5 October 1579, Spenser identifies himself as writing from Leicester House. This letter was not printed until after 30 June 1580 when *Familiar Letters* was entered in the Stationers' Register, but we should take note that, during the tide of ridicule that engulfed Harvey following the publication of *Familiar Letters*, not one contemporary questioned Spenser's association with either the Sidneys or Leicester House: it was Harvey who was mocked for presuming to claim acquaintance with the nobility and courtiers.

Sir Henry Sidney

Leicester, though the most prominent figure in the political party Spenser came to support, was not necessarily his primary patron. An overlooked but important contact that Spenser would have made in 1579 is Sir Henry Sidney. We are accustomed to attributing to Philip Sidney the star-power of a celebrity; his death fighting for Dutch independence conferred on him the status of a Protestant hero. Even though reports may embroider the facts, Sidney is portrayed as almost saintly in his concern for others. He is depicted as turning aside a cup of water intended for him and insisting that it be used to succour a wounded man.[11] Sir Henry, Philip's father, had as much charisma as his gifted son, but, instead of romantically dying of a wound received on the battlefield, Sir Henry Sidney died harassed by debts and slanderous accusations of financial malfeasance. There is no indication that Sir Henry was especially profligate in handling his own estate; his debts, like those of Lord Grey, were incurred in the Queen's service.

Sir Henry was one of the most competent of Elizabeth's servants: he not only repeatedly served as lord deputy of Ireland but also served as the president of the Council of the Marches in Wales. It is too frequently overlooked that, during most of his life, Sir Henry Sidney was a very important Elizabethan administrator – even if he died while temporarily out of favour. Admittedly Sir Henry was not a courtier in the splendid style of his brother-in-law, Robert Dudley, Earl of Leicester. He was not the Queen's councillor and a recognized statesman in the spirit of William Cecil, Lord Burghley, whom Elizabeth even nicknamed her 'Spirit'. It is unlikely that Sir Henry Sidney had the tact or the combination of diplomacy and devotion that made Leicester the Queen's favourite and Burghley her revered councillor.

Both William Cecil, Lord Burghley, and his son Robert, however, outlived Henry and Philip Sidney by more than a decade. Had Philip lived until 1598, we cannot be sure, but it is possible that Philip, rather than Sir Robert Cecil, would have become the principal secretary in succession to his father-in-law, Sir Francis Walsingham. The Sidneys were more important than their rank or fortunes make them appear. The Cecils built great country houses paid for by the money that they garnered while presiding over the Court of Wards. Henry presided over Ireland and Wales, not making a fortune and even losing some of the resources that he had inherited. Perhaps for that very reason, Sir Henry Sidney embodied the image of the Queen's loyal and trusted servant; he had the reputation of a tested knight and warrior. That Sidney never reaped the rewards of a Burghley or a Leicester may have made his knightly service appear even more noble. Sir Henry served as a paradigm of honour for the next generation, of course for his sons, but also for Fulke Greville, Lodowick Bryskett, and very likely Edmund Spenser.

Sir Henry Sidney was recalled from Ireland in March 1578, but, characteristically, did not leave Ireland until September. He had been given a seat on the Privy Council in 1575, and, when he returned from Ireland, he began to attend meetings in 1579. These Privy Council meetings focused on issues such as the Queen's marriage to Anjou and, increasingly, the threat of an Irish rebellion in the wake of a Spanish invasion. James Fitzmaurice (*ODNB* gives James fitz Maurice Fitzgerald) had landed at Dingle in county Kerry on 18 June 1579 and fortified Dún an Óir at Smerwick harbour. Fitzmaurice's arrival was to ignite the second Desmond rebellion (1579–83). Ireland was unquestionably a painful subject for Henry Sidney. It must have been devastating for him to be present at Privy Council discussions in which the failures of his administration were detailed and analysed. Much that he later wrote about Ireland should be understood as a defensive response to these Privy Council meetings. Certainly, his accounts of bloodthirsty police actions in his *Memoirs* were intended to counter rumours that he had been far too soft in administering the Queen's justice. At the same time, Sidney's obligatory focus on Ireland in 1579 would have prompted him to reminisce about his experiences there. It is likely that Philip Sidney and perhaps Edmund Spenser heard at first hand from Henry himself the stories about his adventures and service which were later recorded in his *Memoirs*.

In estimating the impact that Henry Sidney had on Spenser and on shaping Spenser's perceptions of Ireland, we need to keep in mind that throughout 1579 and possibly even into very early 1580, Henry Sidney thought that he might once again be sent to Ireland as Lord Deputy, or, more agreeably, Lord Lieutenant, the title that his brother-in-law, Thomas Ratcliffe, Earl of Sussex, had enjoyed and that would later be conferred on Essex. Moreover, Sir Henry had stipulated that he would be accompanied by his son Philip, who would be considered his designated successor. According to the Privy Council records of attendance, Sidney attended meetings daily 11–16 March 1579; he attended frequently in May and July.[12] During the months of August, September, and October he faithfully attended meetings at Greenwich, Whitehall, Westminster, Richmond, and the Lord Treasurer's house. In fact, on 6 October 1579, Sir Henry Sidney attended a Privy Council meeting at Greenwich on the day after Spenser signed the letter from Leicester House.

Being a Privy Counsellor and attending Privy Council meetings did not guarantee preferential lodging at court, particularly since the appointment of accommodations was governed by court politics and was at the discretion of the Lord Chamberlain. While the court accommodated approximately one thousand people, not everyone could be given lodgings, and we know from Lady Mary Sidney's correspondence that the Sidneys were not pleased by the accommodations that they were allotted.

> I Thoght good to put you in Remembrance to moue my Lord Chamberlein, in my Lords Name, to have some uther Roome then my Chamber, for my Lord to haue his Resort unto, as he was woont to haue; or ells my Lord wilbe greatly trubled, when he shall haue enny Maters of Dispache: My Lodginge, you see, beinge very lytle, and my sealfe contineway syke, and not able to be mouche out of my Bed. For the Night Tyme, on Roofe, with Gods Grace, shall serue vs; for the Day Tyme the Quen will louke to haue my Chamber always in a Readines, for her Maiesties Cominge thether?[13]

In a follow-up letter, dated Monday, [date and month unclear] 1578 she reiterates her need and that of Sir Henry: 'Hampton Courght I never yet knue so full, as ther wer not spare Rooms in hit, whan hit hath ben thryse better fylled then at this Presenn hit is. But some would be sory, perhaps, my Lord should haue so suer Footinge in the Courght' (272).[14] After mentioning her husband's needs and alluding to her own relationship to the Queen, she makes it clear that she knows the allotment of rooms is political.

Lady Mary's correspondence regarding the difficulty of finding suitable lodging at court is richly suggestive. Hampton Court was approximately fourteen miles from London. The Sidneys would frequently have visited Leicester House in 1579 and possibly even resided there. In addition, they would have resided at Baynard's Castle, the London residence of their daughter, Mary Sidney Herbert, Countess of Pembroke, especially during the three-month period when the Privy Council was meeting daily to debate the Anjou marriage. In addition to becoming acquainted with Sir Henry Sidney in 1579, Spenser would have become acquainted with his later patroness, Mary Sidney Herbert, Countess of Pembroke. We know that Philip accompanied her to Wilton during the period preceding the birth of her first child, and it is not unlikely that Spenser was also her guest. It is a matter of record that Mary Sidney Herbert was later to be one of only two female dedicatees to receive a sonnet in the sequence of 'Dedicatory Sonnets' appended to the 1590 *Faerie Queene*, and this sonnet, significantly, is personal in its details.[15] In the *Complaints* the first of four dedications is addressed to Mary, and it stresses Spenser's relation to Sidney, 'knowing with howe straight bandes of duetie I was tied to him'. Mary Sidney Herbert may also have supplied Spenser with a poetic tribute to be included in *Astrophel*.[16]

Throughout 1579, Sir Henry Sidney was present at Privy Council meetings, but his attendance concluded on 8 February 1580. On this occasion, the Privy Council informed Sidney's Vice-President, who was incidentally John Whitgift, that Sidney would shortly be in Wales to exercise the responsibilities of Lord President.[17] Until approximately February 1580, or a few weeks before, there remained the possibility that Sir Henry would be sent back to Ireland with Philip Sidney as his vice-deputy and heir apparent.

Spenser, like Philip's friends, would have admired Sir Henry Sidney, whom Fulke Greville describes as 'a man of excellent natural wit, large heart, sweet conversation and such a governor as sought not to make an end of the state in himself, but to plant his own ends in the prosperity of his country'.[18] This credit to Sir Henry's selflessness in privileging country over personal prosperity shows how much Greville admired Sir Henry. It may be even more significant, for our purposes, that Sir Henry Sidney was the principal patron of Lodowick Bryskett, who was Spenser's friend and literary confidante during his residence in Ireland. Bryskett, the son of an Italian émigré, was fluent in Italian, and ten years older than Philip Sidney and Edmund Spenser. Bryskett reports that he began his career as a 'scholar' but then became a 'servant', and, significantly, it was Sir Henry Sidney who became his master.[19] Lord Justice Fitzwilliam somewhat disapprovingly wrote to Burghley on 7 April 1571 saying that Molyneux, Clerk of the Council, has left 'a yonge gentleman of my L Deputy's, as the party telleth me, to sarve in his rome. I have not sene a clerk of the concell so do afore this. It is one Bryskett.'[20] Bryskett was recruited as an Irish servitor by Henry Sidney, to whom the young and inexperienced Bryskett owed his position as clerk on the Irish Council. Sir Henry later arranged for Bryskett to accompany Philip on his grand tour beginning in May 1572.[21]

Bryskett owed allegiance to Sir Henry Sidney and was one of Spenser's closest friends in Ireland, but it has been assumed previously that they did not meet each until they were in Ireland. Grey, however, repeatedly asks to have Bryskett sent over in 1581. Lodowick Bryskett, in fact, was in England from June 1579 to February 1581 except for a brief visit to Ireland in spring 1580. It is a virtual certainty that Bryskett would have visited Leicester House and Baynard's Castle to pay his respects to Sir Henry and Philip Sidney, and it is likely that he also visited them at Penshurst and Wilton. Once Spenser became Grey's client, if not before, he would have been interested in meeting Bryskett.

There is ample literary and documentary evidence of a connection between Bryskett and Spenser. The volume published as Spenser's *Astrophel* (1595) contains two elegies by Bryskett, one entered in the Stationers' Register on 22 August 1587, near the time of Sidney's death, and the other probably written specifically to complement Spenser's *Astrophel*.[22] Spenser is also deferred to as knowledgeable about classical virtues and respectfully described as the author of the as yet unpublished *Faerie Queene* in Bryskett's *Discourse of Civill Life*, written in 1581-2, though not published until 1606. Further, in *Amoretti* 33, Spenser offers remarkable evidence of intimacy when he addresses Bryskett by name as 'lodwick' in line 5:

> Great wrong I doe, I can it not deny,
>   to that most sacred Empresse my dear dred,
>   not finishing her Queene of faery,
>   that mote enlarge her liuing prayses dead:
> But lodwick, this of grace to me aread:
>   doe ye not thinck th'accomplishment of it,
>   sufficient worke for one mans simple head,
>   all were it as the rest but rudely writ.

This is the only sonnet in the *Amoretti* in which Spenser addresses a contemporary (omitting those addressed to his wife Elizabeth Boyle). Not only does Spenser allude to Bryskett by name, but the tone of the reference also suggests that Bryskett is his confidante and critic. We know from *Amoretti* 80 that in 1594 Spenser had completed six books of the *Faerie Queene*, but here Spenser credits Bryskett with knowing how much 'taedious toyle' has gone into this accomplishment.

Bryskett also appears as Thestylis in *Colin Clouts Come Home Againe* where he asks Colin Clout to tell him some of the songs sung by Ralegh, Shepherd of the Ocean. Thestylis knows and mourns Sidney, and he is familiar with Spenser's progress on the *Faerie Queene*. In addition to these marks of mutual intellectual respect, we should note that both of Spenser's two civil service offices in Ireland were initially occupied by Bryskett, suggesting that he may have recommended or supported Spenser's candidacy as his successor.[23]

Court humanism versus the early modern chivalric code

To understand the impact that Philip Sidney and his circle had on Edmund Spenser, we need to ask different questions from those posed by Sidney's recent biographers. Katherine Duncan-Jones has supplied us with a provocative literary biography, but she defines her task as cutting through some of the myth-making of earlier generations. Her intention, she explains, is to 'summon him to life, spots and all'. Accordingly, Duncan-Jones informs us that Sidney was pockmarked from a childhood illness and paints him as 'hot-tempered' and 'arrogant' (xii). Alan Stewart tells us that Sidney's reputation as 'England's hero, its shepherd-knight, its greatest courtier poet' was dreamed up by Leicester, 'a master-propagandist', who was interested in excusing his own shortcomings as a military commander (7).[24] According to Stewart, Elizabeth 'belittled' Sidney, forcing him to 'lead a double life: of fame and praise abroad, and of comparative – and deliberate – neglect at home' (7). Neither of these contemporary interpretations of Sidney, however interesting their revisionism may be, tells us what Sidney represented to Spenser.

Spenser's image of Sidney was probably closer to the overstated admiration we find in Shelley's *Adonais* than to modern portraits of him as a pock-marked, arrogant, and ignored aristocrat. In Shelley's words (XLV, 5–7):

> Sidney, as he fought
> And as he fell, and as he lived and loved
> Sublimely mild, a spirit without spot ...

Shelley emphasizes the sublimity of Sidney's 'mildness', and, Spenser, too, appreciates Sidney's 'mildness', surpassing Shelley's praise by labelling it 'goodnesse'. In the already quoted section of *Familiar Letters*, Spenser describes Sidney with the telling phrase – 'if at leaste it be in the goodnesse of that nature to scorne' (G3v). Leicester's propaganda campaign after Sidney's death can have had nothing to do with Spenser's praise of Sidney's kindness. Six years before Sidney's death on a battlefield at Zutphen, Sidney's charm had already captivated Spenser.

Among attempts to describe the ethos of the generation of men who, like Spenser, Sidney, Greville, and others, came of age in the late 1570s and early 1580s, we find F.J. Levy's description of their intellectual milieu as 'court humanism', a 'peculiarly English' version of Italian civic humanism.[25]

> Mulcaster, Ascham, and others ... had propagated a myth of social mobility, of a career open to talents, with 'learning' as the ladder by which the heights might be attained. In effect, the norm they established resolved the old debate of whether the active or the contemplative life were preferable by combining the two, though in such a way as to give the active life priority. (68)

Spenser's cultural context elevated the active over the contemplative life. Mulcaster, his schoolmaster at Merchant Taylors' School, underlines this emphasis upon the active life. Beginning with the premise that the 'commonweal is the measure of every man's being', Mulcaster dismisses the idea that 'pleasure' in 'study' should be an end in itself; pastoral escape, the idyllic retreat Spenser describes in Book VI of the *Faerie Queene*, is not to be an option. Mulcaster concludes that 'such as live to themselves either for pleasure in their study, or to avoid foreign trouble do turn their learning to a private ease, which is the private abuse of a public good'.[26] Learning must be used for the 'publick good'. Spenser never fully internalizes this concept; he honours Rosalind in the *Shepheardes Calender* and elevates his own Rosalind to the status of a muse in Book VI of the *Faerie Queene*. That is not to suggest that Spenser questioned the importance of Gloriana, but he insists upon the primacy of the personal even in the process of paying tribute to the political or 'publick good'.

Levy is certainly correct in stating that Lodowick Bryskett, Edward Denny, Gabriel Harvey, Fulke Greville, Philip Sidney, and Edmund Spenser were fully persuaded that 'learning' was an obligation as well as a privilege. It is less clear that these men – other than Gabriel Harvey and possibly Lodowick Bryskett – would have regarded Sir Thomas Smith as an exemplar of an ideal career path. Smith, by birth lower middle-class, distinguished himself as a scholar, became a professor of civil law at Cambridge. He moved from the university to the court, where he served as ambassador to France. He then became Elizabeth's Principal Secretary, preceding Sir Francis Walsingham, Sidney's father-in-law, in this office. Levy rightly states that Gabriel Harvey was inspired by and attempted to emulate Smith's success. Harvey studied civil law, as had his model, and, in the humanist tradition, aspired to become a courtier and to act as councillor to the Queen. Though Levy is correct in stating that Harvey was motivated by Smith's record, I question that Sidney and Spenser could be described as court humanists or that either man regarded Smith's career path as a model. Levy acknowledges that Philip Sidney's position as one of the ruling elites would have given him advantages not enjoyed by Gabriel Harvey, Lodowick Bryskett, and certainly, Edmund Spenser. Sidney, by virtue of his birth and social status, might have aimed at emulating the careers of his father-in-law, Sir Francis Walsingham and Lord Burghley – and it is even likely that he was being groomed for such a position – but there is evidence that Sidney and Spenser shared an allegiance to a different set of values.

To understand Philip Sidney and the sensibility that produced him, we need to recognize that feudal values and respect for the honour code survived well into the early modern period, especially among military servitors such as Philip's father, Henry.[27] The early modern chivalric code viewed knightly service to the monarch as an idealized military service, a service on the battlefield that reflected the values of honour and loyalty. Leicester, rather than Burghley, became a model for those who subscribed to the early modern chivalric code. In the *Ruines of Time* (1591), Spenser pays tribute to Leicester as 'a mightie Prince':

> It is not long, since these two eyes beheld
> A mightie Prince, of most renowmed race,
> Whom *England* high in count of honour held,
> And greatest ones did sue to gaine his grace;
> Of greatest ones, he greatest in his place,
> Sate in the bosome of his Soueraine,
> And *Right and loyall* did his word maintaine.
> (*Ruines of Time*, 183–9)

It is this image of Leicester as the noblest of Elizabeth's knights whose motto was 'Right and loyall' that inspired Spenser and informed his perceptions of the Sidney circle.[28]

Modern scholars have insufficiently understood this code because they have assumed that only professional soldiers thought of themselves as military servitors. For Sidney, Denny, Greville, and Essex to be a soldier was to be a knight – and not, to use Shakespeare's derisive term, a 'carpet knight'. The early modern chivalric code consisted of a set of unwritten cultural conventions and convictions, which idealized military service, elevating service on the battlefield over jockeying for position at court. Burghley's service, though he may have been morally superior as a man to Leicester, was devalued because he was a 'carpet knight' who made a fortune at court.

Far from subscribing to the values of court humanists, the young Sidney and his friend and soulmate Greville made every effort to flee the court – whenever a suitable escape route beckoned. They fled the court to fight for Dutch independence against Spain and then, intrigued by the challenge of fighting Spanish influence in the New World, Philip Sidney escaped from the court to join Sir Francis Drake in leading an expedition to the New World. In each of these instances, Elizabeth intervened, thwarting Sidney's ambitions; she seems to have deeply valued this son of her loyal servitor, Sir Henry Sidney, and his wife, Mary Dudley Sidney, the devoted friend who had nursed her through smallpox. Elizabeth loved Sidney and frustrated his knightly ambitions, as contemporary reports make clear, because she wanted to preserve the best and brightest of her servants.[29]

It is not surprising that Philip Sidney was attracted to the early modern chivalric code because his father had fulfilled all of its requirements, obligingly serving the Queen, not at court, but in Wales and Ireland. Lord deputies of Ireland were frequently required to act as military servitors to keep the peace. Following in his father's footsteps, Sidney, in turn, became an important exemplar of this honour code for his brother Robert. To Burghley, and to a modern audience, it seems quixotic that Robert Sidney was willing to give up his life for his country, but not to break his pledged word. On 10 December 1595 Robert wrote from Flushing to Burghley, telling him that he could not promise Patrick Seagrave a safe conduct and then violate it once he was inside the town.[30] Of Essex, Paul Hammer has argued that he aspired to follow Sidney and 'sought to win a similarly transcendent knightly renown, which gave added fuel to his martial ambitions'.[31]

In contrast to Sidney and Spenser, Gabriel Harvey and Lodowick Bryskett embraced court humanism and accepted with little difficulty the conventions of the patronage system because it accorded with their values as court humanists. They wrote letters asking for property, but not merely for property; they also ask for offices – opportunities to serve.

These men, like Burghley and his son Robert, wanted to serve the state within the parameters of an established court hierarchy. Harvey's marginalia, for example, show that he was interested in blending self-abasement and flattery:

> Learn from the dog how skilfully to treat a Lord or King. Endure anything in the way of wrongs, and fawn none the less. Visible flattery is abject and unworthy of a gentleman; invisible flattery a matter of skill and suited for men of affairs. (56)[32]

To Sidney, and also to the poet Edmund Spenser, conforming to the values of the court humanist was to 'creepe' and 'crouch' with 'fained face' (*Mother Hubberds Tale*, 727).

Henry Sidney, Ireland, and the early modern chivalric code

From Henry Sidney's memoirs of his service in Ireland, we get a vivid picture of the early modern chivalric code in practice. Even though these memoirs were written when Sidney, disappointed about his prospects of regaining Elizabeth's favour, was despondent about his health and finances, he still portrays Ireland as a medieval land of adventure where feats of chivalry and tests of the honour code are likely to occur. Sidney's narrative also does much to explain the honour code, a culture shared by Elizabethan knights and their Irish counterparts. Like all sixteenth-century English lord deputies, Sidney actively participated in the family feuds of the Anglo-Irish nobility. Rorye Oge O'More was married to the daughter of the Earl of Ormond, Elizabeth's favourite and kinsman, but even so he was declared an outlaw. Rorye was hunted down by a force under the command of the Irish Baron of Upper Ossory, who was an enemy of Ormond's. Sir Henry Sidney's description of this Irish nobleman reads like a passage out of Malory's *Knights of King Arthur*. Sidney describes him as 'my particular sworn brother, and the faithfullest man for the Queen's service for martiall action that ever I found in that country' (188).[33] In addition to celebrating noble knights, Sidney cheerfully recounts all of the destruction he was able to achieve when intervening in a feud between two families:

> I invaded MacMahon's country, preyed, burned, and totally destroyed the same, in revenge of a shamefull murther committed by him in killing a valiant and noble man called the Lord of Louth, and as towardlie a yonge gentleman as ever I knew of the Irishrie, son and heir to Sir Hugh MacGennis, knight, lord and captain of [that] country. (189)

We have to remember that this is Sidney's own account of his conduct. Sir Henry Sidney expected his readers to regard his wholesale slaughter in MacMahon's country, as not merely appropriate but also commendable.

English commentators on late sixteenth-century Ireland frequently describe it as a wild and barbaric society, but in fact there was little difference between the early modern chivalric code of a military servitor like Sir Henry Sidney and those of the Anglo-Irish earls and Gaelic lords. In this unstable social environment, military experience reinforced a warrior ethic that was closer to Malory's honour code than to the sheltered sprezzatura of Castiglione's courtiers. Roger Ascham charged that in Malory's *Knights of King Arthur* 'those be counted the noblest knights that do kill most men without any quarrel and commit foulest adulteries by subtlest shifts', and we, as modern readers, may react, as Ascham did to Malory, when we encounter Sidney's narrative.[34]

The denouement of the MacMahon story is highly significant and epitomizes the behaviour required by the code more effectively than descriptions of it. Sidney's violent reprisals in 'MacMahon's country' prompted MacMahon, wearing a withe around his neck, to surrender himself to Sir William Drury, who had succeeded Sidney. Drury pardoned MacMahon, and Sidney says that he heartily disapproves of his successor's leniency, stoutly claiming that he would have used the withe to hang MacMahon. Perhaps Sidney would have hanged him, but there is room for doubt. MacMahon's action in giving himself up fulfilled the requirements of the warrior's honour code and, confronted by MacMahon's remarkable courage, Sidney might well have pardoned him, just as Drury did. This story could have ended with MacMahon becoming Sidney's sworn brother and loyal servitor. Thomas Churchyard relates precisely this kind of anecdote regarding a confrontation between Sir Humphrey Gilbert and an Irish outlaw. Gilbert offered the outlaw a safe conduct; the outlaw tested him; Gilbert kept his word, and they became sworn brothers.[35] During the late sixteenth and early seventeenth centuries, the values inherent to the chivalric code were being replaced by a culture that defined itself and its enemies by nationality and religion. However barbaric Henry Sidney's memoirs may seem to those who, like Ascham, reject chivalric romance, this code crossed lines of national and religious identity in a way that was to become inconceivable in the eighteenth, nineteenth, and our own centuries.

In the late sixteenth century, a community of honour united the Irish chieftain, old English lord, and English military servitor, all of whom valued giving and keeping their knightly word of honour and fulfilling oaths of friendship and fealty. By our standards it may have been more or less a barbaric brotherhood, but we should recognize that it was more ecumenical than the modern communities defined by religion and national identity that were even then emerging.

The Duellum: Sidney, Oxford, and the tennis court quarrel

Some of what could be described as Sidney's arrogance – or as his biographers label it, adolescent ill-temper – is epitomized in the story of the famous tennis court quarrel between Sidney and Edmund de Vere, seventeenth Earl of Oxford. The quarrel had a specific historical context: the intensely political atmosphere surrounding the negotiations of the French marriage. Fulke Greville, an eyewitness, is conscious of this context and stresses that the quarrel was observed by the French commissioners. For our purposes, the tennis court quarrel is important because of the light it sheds on the idealized honour code, subscribed to by Sidney and his circle. The French commissioners, whom Greville describes as witnesses, may have been part of the Anjou retinue, and, if they were, then the quarrel is likely to have taken place before 27 August when Anjou left for France.[36] In terms of his own narrative, Greville describes the quarrel as occurring after Sidney presented his *A Letter to Queen Elizabeth* advising against the French marriage to the Queen. Greville says that Oxford came to the court when Sidney was playing tennis and demanded that Sidney give up his place. Greville describes the incident as attracting an audience:

> They [French observers] instantly drew all to this tumult: every sort of quarrels sorting well with their humours, especially this; which Sir Philip perceiving, and rising with an inward strength by the prospect of a mighty faction against him, asked my Lord, with a loud voice, that which heard clearly enough before, who, like an echo, that still multiplies by reflections, repeats this epithet of puppy the second time.[37]

Greville's prose is clear at this point: Oxford called Sidney a 'puppy', and Sidney, pretending not to have heard him, succeeded in getting Oxford to repeat the epithet more loudly. We are then told that Philip, 'resolving in one answer to conclude both the attentive hearers, and passionate actor, gave my Lord a Lie, impossible (as he averred) to be retorted; in respect all the world knows, Puppies are gotten by Dogs, and Children by men' (66).[38] Greville's account depicts Sidney as accusing Oxford of lying. After this calculated insult, Sidney expected Oxford to issue a challenge to a duel, but Oxford hesitated long enough for the Privy Council to become aware of the quarrel and to attempt to mend fences.

On 28 August Philip Sidney wrote to Sir Christopher Hatton regarding his quarrel with Oxford, saying that 'howe soever I might have forgeven hym, I should never have forgeven my self, yf I had layne under so proude an injurye, as he would have laide uppon me'.[39] Ralegh, who at this time may have been in Oxford's retinue, reportedly carried the eventual challenge from Oxford to Sidney. Greville reports that Elizabeth decided to make peace and remonstrated with Sidney by pointing out that 'the Gentlemans neglect of the Nobility taught the Peasant to insult upon both' (68). Improbably, but again, as reported by Greville, Sidney then proceeded to lecture Elizabeth on the rule of law and the rights of free men. From this Greville draws the moral that 'there is a latitude for subjects to reserve native, & legall freedom, by paying humble tribute in manner, though not in matter, to them' (69). If Greville's account is even somewhat accurate, we can only assume that Elizabeth was so devoted to Sidney that she allowed him a latitude enjoyed by few privy councillors and fewer courtiers.

Sidney's eagerness to force a quarrel on Oxford underpins the distinction I have drawn between court humanism and the early modern chivalric code. Sidney, as an exemplar of the chivalric code, regarded the duel as essential to the vindication of his honour. His views contrast strongly with the quintessentially humanist perspective we find in Lodowick Bryskett's *A Discourse of Civill Life*. As noted above, internal autobiographical references allow us to situate this translation in 1580–81, when Bryskett was Grey's choice for the position of secretary of Ireland, but Grey was overruled by the Queen and the English Privy Council. Bryskett, in reaction, and evidently with Grey's approval, resigned his position as Clerk of the Irish Council. He then in a proper humanist spirit retired to a cottage on the outskirts of Dublin where he could contemplate the virtues of civil life.

Bryskett frames his translation of Giraldi's *Tre dialoghi della vita civile* as a series of conversations with actual people, some of them government officials, who can be identified, and one of whom is Edmund Spenser. At the end of the first day's conversation, Bryskett launches a humanist critique of the duel, selecting as his spokesman for the duel the military man Captain Thomas Norreys. Norreys, an actual person imported into the fiction and later Spenser's patron and neighbour, describes the duel as 'chalenging and fighting man to man, under the name of *Duellum* which is used now a dayes among souldiers and men of honour' (50).[40]

Bryskett unequivocally denies any classical precedents for this custom, and he insists that no honour can be achieved by the duel even if the duel has been 'devised for some cause of honour' (58). Taking a cue from Plato's hierarchy of values, he states that 'those who respect honour as the end of their actions' are not only 'unworthy to be accounted vertuous men, but deserve blame and reproch' (58). Bryskett had accompanied Sidney on his grand tour a decade before framing this translation, and, in the aristocratic Continental circles they visited, they would have encountered European duels. The humanist Bryskett would have rejected the duel, but that rejection had no impact on Philip Sidney.

Perhaps we could ignore the account of Sidney's attempt to provoke a duel with Oxford, if it were not for the additional evidence we find in his *Defence of the Earl of Leicester*. This work is unique because it survives in its entirety in Sidney's holograph.[41] This text was intended for publication and concludes with a passage that unmistakably challenges the author of *Leicester's Commonwealth* to a duel:

> So again, in any place whereto thou wilt call me, provided that the place be such, as a servant of the Queen's may have free access unto, if I do not, having my life and liberty, prove this upon thee, I am content that this lie I have given thee return to my perpetual infamy. And this which I write, I would send to thine own hands if I knew thee. But I trust it cannot be intended that he should be ignorant of this, printed in London, who knows the very whisperings of the privy chamber ... And from the date of this writing, imprinted and published, I will three months expect thine answer.[42]

Throughout *Defence of the Earl of Leicester*, much to the embarrassment of Sidney's apologists, he puts more effort into defending Leicester's lineage, and thereby his own, than into defending Leicester's virtue. This emphasis, though it seems misplaced to us, may in part be explained by Sidney's allegiance to the early modern chivalric code.[43]

In *Mother Hubberds Tale* (1591), Spenser sets forth his description of the 'rightfull Courtier' (793) and honour serves as a persistent refrain in this description:

> Yet the braue Courtier, in whose beauteous thought
> Regard of honour harbours more than ought
> ...
> He stands on tearmes of honourable minde,
> Ne will be carried with the common winde
> Of Courts inconstant mutabilitie.
>
> (717–23)

Spenser's ideal courtier desires 'noble fame', and in deliberate contrast to the 'Courts inconstant mutabilitie', his mind is all on 'honour fixed'.

> The onely vpshot whereto he doth ayme:
> For all his minde on honour fixed is,
> To which he leuels all his purposis.
>
> (770–2)

Spenser's noble courtier spends his days serving his Prince but does not enrich or promote himself (769–78).

Like Sidney, and others of his generation, Spenser accepted the ideal of an active life, and his acceptance of this ideal predisposed him to align himself with soldier-knights whose deeds in service to Queen and country he would record. Courtiers typically 'creepe' and 'crouche', but the carriage of the ideal courtier is 'vpright' and 'comely':

> He will not creepe, nor crouche with fained face,
> But walkes vpright with comely stedfast pace,
> And vnto all doth yeeld due curtesie.
>
> (727–9)

Sidney chafed at the role of a courtier expected to dance attendance on the Queen when he wanted to lead a great Protestant crusade, and Spenser viewed himself as the author of the epic that would immortalize such heroic actions.

It is no accident that Spenser's dedicatory sonnets to the *Faerie Queene* do not precede but are appended to his epic. He despised the passivity and helplessness of a suitor's position, and, however much he may have aspired to win enduring immortality as a poet and to become England's Vergil, he was unsure of the value of worldly success:

> To speed to day, to be put back to morrow;
> To feed on hope, to pine with feare and sorrow;
> To haue thy Princes grace, yet want her Peeres;
>
> (898–91)

He concludes this indictment of a suitor's life by describing the would-be courtier as fawning and crouching before those who dispense favour.

> To fawne, to crowche, to waite, to ride, to ronne,
> To spend, to giue, to want, to be vndonne.
>
> (905–6)

In contrast to the 'safe assurance' and 'contentment' of 'meane estate' (909), the court is full of 'shadowes vaine' (912).

Personality and temperament are elusive traits, but, in terms of personal inclination, a poet as productive as Spenser arguably was, must have spent an immense amount of time in Mulcaster's despised 'private ease', testing verse forms and reflecting on the construction of his poems. Spenser, even more than Sidney, valued the contemplative and was tempted by 'private' or 'slothful' ease. Major tensions in Spenser's poetry are generated by his preference for the contemplative life in contrast to a prevailing humanist ethos lauding active accomplishment. If Spenser ever came to understand the politics of empire, it never so fully engaged his imagination as did bowers of bliss.

A wonderful anecdote concerning Sidneian patronage of Spenser is reported by the anonymous author of the 'Life of Mr. Edmond Spenser' and included in the 1679 folio of Spenser's collected works. Spenser goes to Leicester House 'furnisht with modest confidence' and canto ix of Book I of the *Faerie Queene*, the canto in which Redcrosse Knight encounters Despair. Then Sidney responds by rewarding Spenser with increasing sums of money – much to his servant's dismay.[44] Neatly wrapping up the anecdote, the author says that Sidney became 'not only his Patron, but his Friend too'.

In an excess of zeal, the author of this anecdote credits Sidney with having obtained a pension for Spenser from the Queen, but, since Sidney had been dead for at least five years when the pension was awarded, we cannot credit this. The entire incident seems to have been apocryphal, but it appears in the first full-scale biography of Spenser. Spenser's sixteenth- and seventeenth-century contemporaries were convinced by anecdotal reports such as these that Spenser was financially indebted to Sidney. Whatever financial support Philip Sidney may have supplied his fellow poet, and it is clear that there was some, he and Sir Henry Sidney influenced Spenser's career. They introduced Spenser, the protégé of Elizabethan churchmen, to the early modern chivalric code, a system of values and conduct that suited his *Faerie Queene*.

Epic poetry, as Spenser was to conceive it, was to be written about the deeds of soldier-knights on a battlefield, not the intrigues of courtiers, who in Shakespeare's memorable words, resemble 'gilded butterflies' and talk of 'court news …Who loses and who wins; who's in, who's out'.[45]

Notes

1 Stern, *Harvey*, 49.
2 *A Sidney Chronology, 1554–1654*, ed. Michael G. Brennan and Noel J. Kinnamon (New York: Palgrave Macmillan, 2003), 30. Although Sidney never formally

matriculated at Cambridge, elegies published at the time of his death suggest that he may have spent time there.
3 Jardine and Grafton, '"Studied for Action"', esp. 37.
4 Duncan-Jones, *Philip Sidney*, 120.
5 Jardine and Grafton, '"Studied for Action"', 36.
6 Arthur Atey was Leicester's secretary from 1572 to 1582, and he was joined by Jean Hotman in 1582. Regarding the absence of documentary evidence, see H.R. Woudhuysen, 'Leicester's Literary Patronage: A Study of the English Court, 1578–1582', D.Phil. thesis, University of Oxford, 1982, 47–9.
7 Blair Worden, *The Sound of Virtue: Philip Sidney's* Arcadia *and Elizabethan Politics* (New Haven: Yale University Press, 1996), 63–5. In his 1591 dedication printed in the *Complaints*, Spenser tells us that *Mother Hubberds Tale* was '*long sithens composed in the raw conceipt of my youth*'.
8 *Familiar Letters* RB 69544, (The Huntington Library, San Marino, CA). Signatures will be cited parenthetically in the text.
9 Discussed in S.K. Heninger, *Sidney and Spenser: The Poet as Maker* (University Park and London: Pennsylvania State University Press, 1989), 10.
10 When the *Faerie Queene* (1590) was published, Spenser prefaced it with a single dedication to the Queen, but then appended dedicatory sonnets addressed to selected aristocrats. For discussion of these poems as a sonnet sequence, see the essay by William Oram, 'Introduction: Spenser's Paratexts', in *The 1590 Faerie Queene: Paratexts and Publishing*, ed, Wayne Erickson, *SLI: Studies in the Literary Imagination*, 38 (2005), vii–xviii.
11 Dominic Baker-Smith, 'Sidney's Death and the Poets', in *Sir Philip Sidney 1586 and the Creation of a Legend*, ed. Jan Van Dorsten, Dominic Baker-Smith, and Arthur Kinney (Leiden: E.J. Brill and Leiden University Press for the Sir Thomas Browne Institute, 1986), 83–103.
12 *Acts of the Privy Council of England*, New Series, ed. John Roche Dasent (London: Eyre and Spottiswood, 1895), 12, 40, 68, 70, 71, 75, 78, 120, 130, 134, 135, 138, 145, 189, 195, 197, 203, 206, 214, 221, 222, 224, 228, 232, 234, 238, 239, 255, 260, 262, 267, 270, 272, 276, 278, 279, 281, 312, 314, 383.
13 *Letters and Memorials of State*, ed. Arthur Collins, 2 vols (London: T. Osborne, 1746), 1: 271. RB 601620. The Huntington Library, San Marino, CA. Lady Mary Sydney to Edmund Molyneux. From Chiswike, 11 October 1578. Sussex, then Lord Chamberlain, was Leicester's enemy.
14 Lady Mary emphasizes that it 'is but for the Day Tyme for his Besines, as indeed hit is for my Brothers Answer of my Stay hear for five or six Dayes' (272). This correspondence with Edmund Molyneux took place in 1578, and Lady Mary's somewhat confusing reference to her stay with 'her Brother' seems to refer to the Earl of Leicester and so may allude to a visit to him in 1578.
15 See Oram, 'Introduction: Spenser's Paratexts', vii–xviii.
16 Pamela Coren, 'Edmund Spenser, Mary Sidney, and the Doleful Lay', *SEL: Studies in English Literature, 1500–1900*, 42 (2002), 25–41. See, also, the persuasive arguments by Margaret Hannay, *Philip's Phoenix* (Oxford: Oxford University Press, 1990), 63–7, and Mary Ellen Lamb, *Gender and Authorship in the Sidney Circle* (Madison: University of Wisconsin Press, 1990), 61–2.
17 Sidney was in Wales by 17 March 1580.

18 *The Prose Works of Fulke Greville, Lord Brooke*, ed. John Gouws (Oxford: Clarendon Press, 1986), 4.
19 Lodowick Bryskett, *A Discourse of Civill Life*, ed. Thomas E. Wright, San Fernando Valley State College Renaissance Editions (Northridge, CA: San Fernando State College, 1970), 15.
20 For Bryskett's life, see Henry R. Plomer and Tom Peete Cross, *The Life and Correspondence of Lodowick Bryskett*, Modern Philology Monographs (Chicago: University of Chicago Press, 1927), 4–6, esp. 4.
21 Bryskett was paid a salary, but Sidney refers to him as 'my friend Bryskett'. See *The Correspondence of Sir Philip Sidney*, ed. Roger Kuin, 2 vols (Oxford: Oxford University Press, 2012), 1: 233.
22 F.B. Trombley, 'Lodowick Bryskett's Elegies on Sidney in Spenser's *Astrophel* Volume', *Review of English Studies*, New Series, 37 (1986), 384–8.
23 Earlier scholarship implies that Bryskett 'gave' offices to Spenser, but it is more likely that he sold his lucrative offices to Spenser at whatever was the market price.
24 For evidence of Elizabeth's appreciations of Sidney, see Steven W. May, 'Sir Philip Sidney and Queen Elizabeth', *English Manuscript Studies, 1100-1700*, Vol. 2, ed. Peter Beal and A.S.G. Edwards (Oxford: Blackwell, 1990), 257–68; and my 'Sidney's Letter to Queen Elizabeth: Text and Context', *Sidney Journal*, 32 (2014), 1–16.
25 F.J. Levy, 'Spenser and Court Humanism', in *Spenser's Life and the Subject of Biography*, ed. Judith H. Anderson, Donald Cheney, and David A. Richardson (Amherst: University of Massachusetts Press, 1996), 65–80, esp. 66.
26 Mulcaster, cited in Levy, 'Spenser and Court Humanism', 66-7.
27 For important discussions of this code, see Brendan Kane, *The Politics and Culture of Honour in Britain and Ireland, 1541-1641* (Cambridge: Cambridge University Press, 2010), chapters 2 and 3. See, also, David J.B. Trim, 'The Art of War: Martial Poetics from Henry Howard to Philip Sidney', in *Oxford Handbook of Tudor Literature, 1485-1603*, ed. Mike Pincome and Cathy Shraunk (Oxford: Oxford University Press, 2009), 587–605.
28 For a history and description of this code, see Mervyn James, 'English Politics and the Concept of Honour, 1485-1642', in *Society, Politics and Culture: Studies in Early Modern England* (Cambridge: Cambridge University Press, 1986), 308–415. In explaining this code, James fails to differentiate professional soldiers, like Sir John Norreys, from the Sidneys. For focus on Sidney as a chivalric and literary figure, see Richard C. McCoy, *The Rites of Knight Hood: The Literature and Politics of Elizabethan Chivalry* (Berkeley: University of California Press, 1989), 55–78.
29 I am aware that Alan Stewart and Katherine Duncan-Jones have questioned Elizabeth's affection for Sidney, but see note 24 above.
30 I am indebted to Rob Stillman for reminding me of the source for this story; see M.V. Hay, *The Life of Robert Sidney, Earl of Leicester, 1563-1626* (Washington, DC: Folger Books, 1984), 127.
31 Cited from Paul Hammer, 'Robert Devereux, 2nd Earl of Essex', *ODNB* (2008).
32 Harvey, *Marginalia*, 56.
33 Herbert Hoare's 'A text for 'Sir Henry Sidney's Memoir of his Government of Ireland, 1583', *Ulster Journal of Archaeology*, First Series, 3 (1855), 33–52, 85–109, 336-57. Ciaran Brady has modernized Hoare's transcription and retitled it *A*

Viceroy's Vindication? Sir Henry Sidney's Memoir of Service in Ireland, 1556–1578 (Cork: Cork University Press, 2002). My citations reflect Hoare's old-spelling transcription, but I have used Brady's pagination for the reader's convenience.

34 Roger Ascham, *The Schoolmaster* (1570), ed. Lawrence V. Ryan, Folger Documents of Tudor and Stuart Civilization (Ithaca: Cornell University Press, 1967), 69.
35 Thomas Churchyard, *A General Rehearsall of Warres, called Churchyardes Choise* (London: J. Kingston for E. White, 1579, Q1r–R1v). RB 56403. The Huntington Library, San Marino, CA.
36 On this chronology, see my 'Sidney's Letter to Queen Elizabeth: Text and Context'..
37 *The Prose Works of Fulke Greville*, ed. Gouws, 39.
38 Allen Nelson and David Harris Sachs decode Sidney's comment as follows: 'I may be a dog (metaphorically speaking), but you are not a man (in any sense of the word)'; or even worse 'Men beget children, but as you live not only apart from your wife, but with boys, you are no man and will beget no male heirs'. See Allen H. Nelson, *Monstrous Adversary* (Liverpool: Liverpool University Press, 2003), 196.
39 BL MS Add. 15981, fol. 31v. Cited from Nelson, *Monstrous Adversary*, 198.
40 Bryskett, *A Discourse of Civill Life*, 50.
41 New York, Pierpont Morgan Library, MS MA 1475, 141.
42 For the standard edition of *Defence of Leicester*, see *Miscellaneous Prose of Sir Philip Sidney*, ed. Katharine Duncan-Jones and Jan Van Dorsten (Oxford: Clarendon Press, 1973), 140–1.
43 On lineage, see James, *Society, Politics and Culture*, 275–8.
44 *A Summary of the Life of Mr. Edmond Spenser* in *Works of ... Mr. Edmond Spenser* (London, 1679), A1–A2.
45 Like Spenser, in *Hamlet* and, of course, *King Lear*, Shakespeare disparages court intrigue, offering jaundiced views of courtiers in the characters Osric and Oswald.

7

Aprill and *November*

The prefatory material to the *Shepheardes Calender* was written prior to 10 April 1579, because it is signed with that date, but the poem was not entered into the Stationers' Register until 5 December 1579. Spenser had ample time to secure Sidney's consent to the dedication and to introduce political commentary into whatever pastoral structure already existed. During these months, England was in tumult over what it would mean politically if Elizabeth of England were to marry a Catholic and heir to the throne of France. Elizabeth's French suitor was twenty-four. In August 1579, Anjou, after a brief delay at Boulogne caused by bad weather, sailed for England, arriving at Greenwich on 17 August. The Queen's forty-sixth birthday was due to be celebrated just three weeks later on 7 September. Whatever her actual sentiments, Elizabeth seems to have conducted herself as if she were in love with her French suitor; she carried Anjou's miniature in her prayer book and wrote a poetic lament when he departed.[1] She may have found Anjou attractive (only the English described him as a frog in 'Froggie went a courting'), and she certainly had reason to be chagrined at Leicester's clandestine marriage only a year before. Her long-time favourite had married her cousin, a younger woman, Lettice Knollys, widow of the first Earl of Essex. Elizabeth's political responsibilities as a monarch, however, are likely to have overshadowed whatever emotions may have figured in her willingness to consider the French match.

The Spanish were intent on boxing England into a corner. They appeared likely to succeed in bringing the Netherlands under their control; Parma had captured Maastricht in June and Michelen in July. Closer to home, in Ireland, the Irish James Fitzmaurice, leading a force partially financed by the papal state in Italy, and, as all English and Irish commentaries emphasize, supplemented by Spanish soldiers, had landed in Munster with the intent of stirring up rebellion. This menacing force was accompanied by a special papal nuncio, the polemicist Nicholas Sanders. To complicate matters, no new Lord Deputy of Ireland had been appointed since the recall and final departure of Sir Henry Sidney in September 1578. William Pelham, the Lord Justice, was acting as Lord Deputy of Ireland, and devastating the Munster countryside, but making no efforts to achieve a political resolution. Particularly because of these threats, it seemed likely that the experienced Sir Henry Sidney might again be sent to Ireland, but he was a brother-in-law to Leicester, whose position as the Queen's favourite had been compromised by his marriage to Lettice, Countess of Essex. In this vexed political context, the Privy Council started considering experienced military commanders as lord deputies of Ireland. In terms of immediate policy, Elizabeth's French alliance offered a means of countering Spanish aggression, enhancing the prestige of England's queen by the alliance, and, perhaps, underlining Leicester's political unimportance.

The Spanish ambassador Mendoza, who seems to have been extremely well informed about the comings and goings of Leicester and the Sidneys, reported in a letter dated 25 August 1579 that a meeting was held by Leicester, his relatives, and friends at Baynard's Castle, the London house of the Earl of Pembroke.

> Leicester, who is in great grief came hither recently, and when he came from his interview with the Queen, his emotion was remarked. A meeting was held on the same night at the earl of Pembroke's house, there being present Lord Sydney and other friends and relatives. They no doubt discussed the matter, and some of them afterwards remarked that Parliament would have something to say as to whether the Queen married or not. The people in general seem to threaten revolution about it.[2]

The reference to 'Lord Sydney' mistakenly elevates Sir Henry Sidney to the peerage, but this error speaks volumes about contemporary estimates of his stature. Duncan-Jones has stated that Edmund Spenser attended this meeting, but, unfortunately, no extant documentation confirms his presence.[3] Philip was certainly present, and it is possible that Spenser accompanied Philip to this meeting. At this point, we appear to have no means of determining when Spenser first came to Leicester House, what he did while he was there, or when and why he departed. The closer the relationship between Spenser and the Sidneys, the less likely they would have been to correspond. All we, in fact, know is that Spenser was at home enough with the Sidneys and Leicester to sign a letter from Leicester House on 5 October 1579.

The French alliance was supported by Sussex and Burghley and opposed by Leicester and Henry Sidney, every one of whom had some say in Irish politics. It is no exaggeration to say that Sir Henry Sidney and his brothers-in-law were dominant figures in Anglo-Irish relations – though Lord Burghley controlled the purse strings. Court politics generally involved a relatively small group of people, all of whom knew each other. In the case of Ireland, the people had familial ties as well as acquaintance. The host of the meeting at Baynard's Castle was Henry Herbert, Earl of Pembroke, Leicester's close friend and the husband of Mary Sidney Herbert, Henry's daughter and Philip's beloved sister; also present were Sir Christopher Hatton, Chancellor of England, and Sir Francis Walsingham, Secretary of State. His daughter Frances Walsingham would marry Philip Sidney in 1583. Through his mother, Lady Mary (Dudley) Sidney, Philip was the heir to both his uncles, Ambrose Dudley, Earl of Warwick, and Robert Dudley, Earl of Leicester. Leicester's marriage in 1578 was a blow to Philip's status, and in June 1581 the birth of Leicester's son and legitimate heir, Robert, Lord Denbigh, ended Sidney's expectations until Denbigh's death in 1584.

Sir Henry Sidney had status largely because of his political offices: Lord Deputy of Ireland and Lord President of the Council of Wales and the Marches. An ongoing feud between Leicester and Sussex, another brother-in-law of Sidney's, a former lord deputy of Ireland, and now Lord Chamberlain, affected every aspect of Irish politics, ranging from the wars among rival Irish earls to manoeuvring at the English court. Recent scholarship has concluded that there was less factionalism on the English Privy Council than had previously been supposed, but this was not true of Ireland. Libels and charges of corruption in Ireland led to the recall of a succession of lord deputies whose careers were undermined by their predecessors and successors.[4]

John Stubbs's *Discoverie of a Gaping Gulf*

John Stubbs's *Discoverie of a Gaping Gulf* appeared in print while Elizabeth was entertaining Anjou, who arrived on 17 August and returned to France on 27 August 1579, near the day of the Baynard's Castle meeting. The full title of the tract indicates its opposition to Anjou's courtship: *The*

Discoverie of a Gaping Gulf Whereinto England is like to be Swallowed by another French Marriage if the Lord forbid not the banns by letting Her Majesty see the sin and punishment thereof (1579).[5] *Discoverie of a Gaping Gulf* was printed on 18 August, and this timing constituted a serious affront to the Queen. The author John Stubbs delivered the tract to the printer around 6 or 7 August 1579 and requested that the printer print one thousand copies, twice the usual print run. Stubbs was a barrister at Lincoln's Inn, and coincidentally the brother-in-law of Thomas Cartwright.

Elizabeth regarded the publication of Stubbs's *Discoverie of a Gaping Gulf* as sedition and thought that Stubbs was egged on by the Puritans. Responding to foreign rumours, she decided that Sir Francis Walsingham, her own Secretary of State, had sponsored Stubbs and so expelled him from court for a few weeks. Sir Christopher Hatton was also excluded from her presence for over a week. When she was advised that she could not charge Stubbs with treason, she decided instead to prosecute him under the 'Act against Seditious Words and Rumours' of 1555. This act had been passed to punish any slander against Philip II of Spain after he had married Elizabeth's sister, Mary. Those convicted of sedition would lose their right hand.

On 27 September 1579, Elizabeth published a royal proclamation in which she accused Stubbs of sedition and dismissed his tract as a 'fardel of false reports, suggestions, and manifest lies forged against a prince of a royal blood, as Monsieur, the French King's brother is'.[6]

> Being lately informed of a lewd, seditious book of late rashly compiled and secretly printed and afterwards seditiously dispersed into sundry corners of the realm, and considering it manifestly containeth ... a heap of slanders and reproaches of the said prince, ... and therewith also seditiously and rebelliously stirring up all estates of Her Majesty's subjects to fear their own utter ruin and change of government, but specially to imprint a present fear in the zealous sort of the alteration of Christian religion by Her Majesty's marriage. (148)

Camden reports that Elizabeth could not be 'persuaded that the author of this book had any other purpose than to bring her into hatred with her subjects and to open a gap to some prodigious innovation'.[7] To prevent an insurrection, Elizabeth and her ministers launched a campaign to ensure that the clergy would support the proclamation.

William Page, who may have been charged with distributing the tract throughout the realm, had sent fifty copies to Sir Richard Grenville, also a Member of Parliament in Cornwall, requesting that Grenville should circulate the copies among his friends. Stubbs the author, Singleton, the printer/publisher, and Page were arrested. Elizabeth ordered that all copies of Stubbs's book be seized and destroyed. After the convictions of the author, printer, and bookseller, Elizabeth pardoned the printer Singleton, perhaps because of his age, but, even though the French ambassador and Anjou himself asked her to show mercy, she insisted that the sentence be carried out on Stubbs and Page. Two lawyers, James Dalton and Robert Monson, protested against the sentence on the grounds that the statute under which they were prosecuted had expired with Mary's death. They were also imprisoned.

On 3 November Stubbs was punished by the loss of his right hand. We do not know if Spenser or Sidney was present when the sentence was carried out in the marketplace in Westminster, but both John Stow and William Camden witnessed these events. Camden reports with chilling detail:[8]

> Hereby had *Stubbs* and *Page* theire right handes cutte off with a Cleaver, driuen through the wrist by the force of a beetle [mallet], vpon a scaffold in the marketplace at Westminster. The Printer was pardoned. I remember (being there present) that when *Stubbs*, hauing his right hand cutt off, put off his hatt with his left, and sayd with a loud voyce, 'God saue the Queene'; the Multitude standing about was deeply silent. (Bbv)

To explain this silence, Camden says that it may have been prompted by 'horror of this new and vnwonted punishment', or 'out of pitty' for the man of 'honest and vnblameable report', or out of 'hatred of the marriage, which most men presaged would lead to the overthrow of Religion'.

Although we do not know if Spenser was present when the sentence was carried out, there is some evidence that the savagery of the punishment haunted him as it did Camden. Years later, Spenser evokes the image of a mutilated poet in Book V of the *Faerie Queene*. As Arthur and Sir Artegall approach Queen Mercilla's presence chamber, they see:

> Some one, whose tongue was for his trespasse vyle
> Nayld to a post, adiudged so by law:
> For that therewith he falsely did reuyle,
> And foule blaspheme that Queene for forged guyle,
> Both with bold speaches, which he blazed had,
> And with lewd poems, which he did complyle;
> For the bold title of a Poet bad
> He on himselfe had ta'en, and rayling rymes had sprad.
>
> (V.ix.25)

The tongue of the poet Bonfont ('well of good words') has been nailed to a post just outside the Queen's presence chamber. The name 'Bonfont' has been crossed through and rewritten as 'Malfont'. By the time that

Spenser wrote Book V of the *Faerie Queene*, he was even more sceptical about courtly favour than when he wrote the *Shepheardes Calender* and *Mother Hubberds Tale*. Depending upon the politics of the day, Bonfont, presumably a favoured court poet, could become Malfont and have his tongue nailed to a post.

The possibility of such reprisals did not deter Spenser from publishing the *Shepheardes Calender* – though he seems to have had second thoughts about making public his early version of *Mother Hubberds Tale*.[9] Only a little more than a month after Stubbs had lost his hand, the *Shepheardes Calender* was entered in the Stationers' Register by Hugh Singleton, the very printer who had printed Stubbs's *Discoverie of a Gaping Gulf*.[10] The selection of Singleton may not by itself indicate that Spenser was a Puritan, but in 1579 he had the courage to associate himself publicly with a Puritan printer who had very narrowly escaped having his hand cut off.

Courtly panegyric

Spenser's *Aprill* eclogue can be compared with Harvey's *Gratulationes Valdinenses* because both are panegyrics intended to honour and praise Queen Elizabeth, but, not surprisingly, Spenser is the better poet. He is fully in control of his classical models and mythological trappings while Harvey makes the reader uncomfortable when he dwells on his passionate exhilaration at kissing the Queen's hand. Spenser is deft in using the Niobe myth to counter his own adulation of the Queen while Harvey is heavy-handed when he attempts to weave allusions to Machiavelli and Mercury into his treatment of Leicester's lineage. Neither man, in balance, seems fully in command of courtly panegyric. Harvey's timing is at fault: he endorses a marriage between Elizabeth and Leicester during the progress of 1578, a week or so before on the very same progress Leicester was to marry the Countess of Essex. Also, his tribute to Sidney 'Sum Iecur ... cogit amare Iecur' (*Gratulationes*, K4, 14–15) passes the bounds of good taste. Spenser, however, either misunderstands what is required from courtly panegyric or, it is possible, deliberately criticizes Elizabeth for her lack of martial leadership. In his *October* eclogue, Spenser associates the pastoral with Elizabeth and 'plesance' and the epic with Leicester and 'warres' (59).

Even if Spenser had yet to conceive of Elizabeth as Britomart, he did not need to elevate Leicester over her. In *October*, Piers calls out to Cuddie to abandon the pastoral and '[T]urne thee to those, that weld the awful crowne' (40). We are then shown that soldiers lack military experience:

we are given images of knights whose 'woundlesse armour rusts, / And helmes unbruzed wexen dayly browne' (42–3). The knights of 'fayre *Elisa*' may lack the inspiration of epic poetry – but they also seem to require male leadership to perform their martial duties.

> Whither thou list in fayre *Elisa* rest,
> Or if thee please in bigger notes to sing,
> Aduaunce the worthy whome shee loueth best.
> (45–7)

Spenser's allegiance to Leicester is plainly announced in the next line: 'That first the white beare to the stake did bring' (48). To be sure that there is no confusion about this allusion, E.K.'s Gloss tells us that this 'worthy' is 'the most honorable and renowmed the Erle of Leycester, whom by his cognisance … rather then by his name he bewrayeth' (134). Again, we have an ironic Spenserian aside in the Gloss: 'being not likely that the names of noble princes be known to country clowne'.

At first it seems possible that Spenser's poetic muse may inspire the 'doubted Knights' with some of the commitment to Queen and country that he values in the 'worthy whom shee loueth best' (47). Piers, however, thinks that Leicester is a subject requiring the poet's muse to sing in 'bigger notes' than when he praises 'fayre *Elisa*'. Spenser had nothing whatsoever to gain by elevating Leicester over Elizabeth, particularly in 1579 when no one knew if his recent marriage would jeopardize his position as royal favourite. Piers states that after the 'stubborne stroke of stronger stounds' (49) has subsided, then he may be able to think of 'loue and lustihead' and possibly produce a 'carrol lowde' or a 'Myllers rownde' for 'fayre *Elisa*'. Though the events at Tilbury, in which Elizabeth, clad in armour, rallied her troops, were in the future, Spenser did not have to relegate her to a 'carrol' or 'rownde'. No poet aspiring to a position at court would have been likely to make this error. From this passage in the *Shepheardes Calender*, we can conclude that, in December 1579, Spenser, like Sidney, supported war in the Netherlands against Spain, and perhaps had yet to conceive of Elizabeth as an integral figure in an epic poem, as she was later to become in the *Faerie Queene*.

Aprill and the cult of Elizabeth

Spenser's *Aprill* affords an early example of the mythology that grew up around the Virgin Queen. Beginning with Frances A. Yates's influential analysis of Elizabethan iconography, we have recognized that there was a cult of Elizabeth and understood that poems, such as Spenser's *Aprill* eclogue, were related to that cult.[11] Early studies of the mythology surrounding Elizabeth, however, paid little attention to chronology and so used symbolism that did not develop until the 1580s and 1590s to explain *Aprill*, a poem printed in 1579. Spenser's '*Aprill* eclogue' preceded many of the magnificent visual treatments of Elizabeth. There might conceivably be parallels between *Shepheardes Calender* and the earliest of the 'Sieve' portraits dating from 1579, but the more famous 'Sieve' portraits were not painted until 1580–83; the 'Ermine' dates from 1585, the 'Armada' from 1588, and the 'Ditchley' from 1592.[12] The celebrated 'Rainbow' portrait of Elizabeth dates from 1600 and may owe some of its imagery to Sir John Davies's *Hymnes to Astraea* (1599).[13] The popular mythologies depicting Elizabeth as equal to the classical Augustus, the imperial Constantine, and even the Protestant equivalent to the Virgin Mary were not literary commonplaces when Edmund Spenser's *Shepheardes Calender* appeared in print. Spenser's *Aprill* is not an early version of the cult of Elizabeth, but a brilliant critique of that cult written just as it was beginning to develop.

In consequence, iconographic details in portraits of Elizabeth in the 1580s and 1590s are not the context for Spenser's eulogy; the immediate context for Spenser's fourth eclogue is the celebration of the birth of Augustus in Vergil's *Fourth Eclogue*. It has not been sufficiently recognized, however, that the Vergilian echoes in Spenser's *Aprill* point away from, not towards, Elizabeth as a saintly and imperial figure. Because Vergil's *Fourth Eclogue* was interpreted as prophesying the birth of Christ, it facilitated the allegorical treatments of later Christian commentators. Spenser is fully aware of this amalgamation of classical and Christian sources and features it throughout the *Shepheardes Calender*. His innovation is in using this symbolism to eulogize the Queen and then to undercut his own eulogy.

The decidedly pagan, pastoral deity Pan is used to signify God the Father and Christ. It is Pan's union with the nymph Syrinx that produces a 'daughter without spot' (50):

> Of fayre *Elisa* be your siluer song,
>   that blessed wight:
> The flowre of Virgins, may shee florish long,
>   In princely plight
> For shee is *Syrinx* daughter without spotte,

> Which *Pan* the shepheards God of her begot:
> So sprong her grace
> Of heauenly race,
> No mortall blemishe may her blotte.
>
> (46–54)

This assertion of Elizabeth's divinity is unequivocal: she is '*Syrinx* daughter without spotte', and her immortality is also suggested: 'No mortall blemishe may her blotte'. This adulation of Elizabeth is further commented upon by E.K.'s Gloss in which we are told that Pan is not only Henry VIII, but also 'Christ himselfe':

> So that by Pan is here meant the most famous and victorious King, her highness Father, late of worthy memorye K. Henry the eyght. And by that name, oftymes (as heareafter appeareth) be noted kings and mighty Potentates: And in some place Christ himselfe, who is the verye Pan and god of Shepheardes. (68)

Elizabeth, like the Virgin Mary, is 'without spotte', and she is the lineal descendant of the white roses of York and the red roses of Lancaster; she is the Tudor rose.

Though it has been suggested by some that it was imprudent for Spenser to identify Elizabeth with the Virgin Mary at the very point in time that she seemed likely to relinquish her virginity and marry Anjou, this is not the way that Spenser formulates his tribute to Elizabeth.[14] Later on in the cult of Elizabeth, virginity is associated with imperial power because Elizabeth is figured as Astraea, the just maid. In *Aprill*, there is no indication whatsoever that Elizabeth's *virginity* is what makes her royal; in fact, we are explicitly told that it is her lineage, her dynastic blood-line, that guarantees her sovereignty. In fact, as Helen Hackett has argued, details in *Aprill* seem to keep open the idea of a married Elizabeth.[15] When the shepherds' daughters bring the flowery garlands to deck Elisa, we are told:

> Strowe me the ground with Daffadowndillies,
> And Cowslips, and Kingcups, and loued Lillies:
> The pretie Pawnce,
> And the Cheuisaunce,
> Shall match with the fayre flowre Delice.
>
> (140–4)

The phrase 'match with the fayre flowre Delice' may allude to the fleur de lys, the regal crest of France; this allusion seems particularly likely because the phrasing 'match with the fayre flowre Delice' (144) might well serve as a compliment to Elizabeth on her 'match' or her forthcoming nuptials. E.K.'s Gloss singles out 'fayre flowre Delice' for commentary. He says that the '[f]lore delice' has been mistakenly understood as flower of light, but instead should be termed the flower of sensuality – not an approving glance at the French match (70). In this instance, the text says one thing and the Gloss another, complicating our perception of Spenser's intentions.

Framing the pastoral

Calling attention to the emphasis on Colin's suffering in the Argument to *Aprill*, Louis Montrose sees Spenser as paralleling himself with Colin, the adoring shepherd, and views his poem as a tribute to his queen.[16] Spenser's subtlety, however, is suggested by his use of the dialogue frame. By framing the eclogue with Colin's unhappiness over his unrequited love of Rosalind, Spenser undercuts any suggestion that Colin's unhappiness over Rosalind is lessened by the vision of Elizabeth. The political does not trump the personal, and that is as true in the *Shepheardes Calender* as it is later in the *Faerie Queene*. The converse is true. The frame mediates against the panegyric force of the eclogue. Thenot, like Spenser's audience, is listening to Hobbinol sing Colin's song, a symbolic inset of what is happening in the *Shepheardes Calender* as a whole. We, the audience, are distanced from the celebration of Elizabeth's virtues. Colin remains grief-stricken as Hobbinol sings Colin's song. Colin's talents and his psychological state, not Elizabeth's virtues, command our attention at the beginning and conclusion of the eclogue.

Reading Spenser's allusions

In an attempt to explain Spenser's linking of pagan and Christian images, James E. Phillips called attention to what he describes as Spenser's 'syncrestic religious imagery' and argued that from neo-Platonic sources, such as Philippe Duplessis-Mornay, Giordano Bruno, and others, both Spenser and Sidney imbibed a philosophy that preached the unity of all religions with Christianity – the oneness of the true religion.[17] Spenser is not working as a neo-Platonist; he does not believe that the classical and Christian are 'one and the same', as a neo-Platonist would. A better term for describing his technique, particularly in the *Shepheardes Calender*, would be polyvalence because it allows for choice on the author's part and for the conflation of images with many different meanings. For example, Spenser and his readers know that Henry VIII is not Jesus Christ – even though both are Pan. Viewed from this perspective, Spenser's approach seems more like that of Pico della Mirandola in the *Oration on the Dignity of Man* where Pico consciously sets out to reconcile Plato and Aristotle. Pico knows that Plato and Aristotle's views are dissimilar, but he wants to reconcile their positions. Like Pico, Spenser is consciously selecting and reconciling ostensibly contrary entities and doctrines; this is distinct from neo-Platonism.

Spenser frequently associates classical places with Christian places, not because they refer to the very same mountain or garden but because they are referring to the same type of place. Pan in the *Shepheardes Calender* is the pastoral god of classical antiquity; he is Henry VIII, and he is Jesus Christ. This polyvalent interpretation, influenced perhaps by typological reading, is basic to Spenser's allegorical method and is also illustrated by passages in the *Faerie Queene*. Spenser links the mountains of Sinai, Olivet, and Parnassus in his description of the Mount of Contemplation (I. x. 53–4), and then the gardens and bowers in Book II range from Mount Ida to Mount Parnassus and culminate in Eden (II.x.57).

This polyvalence, more frequently associated with the *Faerie Queene*, also informs the symbolic structure of the *Shepheardes Calender*. In *Maye*, Piers contemplates the reckoning that Pan will exact: 'When great Pan account of shepeherdes shall aske' (54). In the Gloss, E.K. supplies a lengthy and learned justification for identifying 'Great Pan' with the deity:

> 'Great Pan is Christ, the very God of all shepheards, which calleth himselfe the greate and good shepherd. The name is most rightly (me thinkes) applied to him, for Pan signifieth all or omnipotent, which is onely the Lord Iesus' (p. 82).

In *June*, Hobbinol '[t]hat Paradise has found, which *Adam* lost' (10). E.K. also offers a geography lesson detailing the exact location of this paradise and comments as follows:

> 'A Paradise in Greeke signifieth a Garden of pleasure, or place of delights. So, he compareth the soile, wherin Hobbinol made his abode, to th'earthly Paradise, in scripture called Eden; wherein Adam in his first creation was placed' (p. 91).

Returning to the precise wording of the text of the eclogue, in this paradise Pan kisses the 'christall faces' of the nine muses. Colin, however, insists on 'pyping lowe in shade of lowly groue' (71) and playing 'to please' himself (73). Colin does not want, as Pan did, to challenge Phoebus and risk disgrace (65–70). In these instances, the text does not require us to identify Pan as Christ.

Later, in the *Julye* eclogue, Morrell tells Thomalin not to blame 'holy hylles' because they are sacred to the saint:

> S. Michels mount who does not know
>   that wardes the Westerne coste?
> And of S. Brigets bowre I trow,
>   all Kent can rightly boaste:

From Kent, we move to Mount Parnassus:

> And they that con of Muses skill,
>   sayne most what, that they dwell
> (As goteheards wont) vpon a hill,
>   beside a learned well.
> And wonned not the great God *Pan*
>   vpon mount *Oliuet*
> Feeding the blessed flocke of *Dan*,
>   which dyd himselfe beget?
>
>   (41–52)

Spenser is not suggesting that these are the same mountains, ranging from 'St Michels' on the 'Westerne' coste to 'S. Brigets bowre' in 'Kent' to Mount Parnassus where the muses dwell near 'a learned well' and 'Oliuet' where (41–53) Pan 'wonned'. These mountains are not one sacred place; they are all types of what we should consider polyvalent 'holy hylles' (38). Likewise, Pan, Christ, and Henry VIII are not the same individual, but are types of a polyvalent figure.

In *Aprill*, as we observed above, Pan is 'the shepheards God' (51), but as E.K. insists: 'K. Henry the eyght ... noted kings and mighty Potentates ... in some place Christ himselfe, who is the verye Pan and god of Shepheardes' (p. 68) Pan (now identified with Henry VIII) is the father of Elizabeth, who, like the Virgin Mary, is without spot. The point is that Pan can be Christ and, however outrageous that may seem, he can also be Henry VIII. Spenser's text, as we see in this and other instances, does not expect us to limit ourselves to one meaning for an allusion. He comfortably links, equates, and conflates Hebraic, Christian, and classical allusions, and he quite explicitly and daringly folds political allusions into this mix. Rather than tying Spenser's aesthetic technique to a philosophical system, such as neo-Platonism, we might consider that the habit of reading typologically made it easy for Spenser and his readers to accept polyvalent symbolism in instances in which our more literal reading habits may lead us to see contradiction.

Spenser's habitual use of images as allusions that invite multiple readings also supplies him with a means of ironically undercutting or commenting upon his own symbolic suggestions. In *Aprill* Spenser depicts the poet as singing the praises of Elizabeth as the 'flowre of Virgins' and then he uses another set of allusions to convict the poet of blasphemy. At lines 73 to 85 in *Aprill*, Hobbinol compares Elisa with Phoebus Apollo, the sun, and with Cynthia, the moon, and, predictably, finds that she outshines the sun and the moon. He then abruptly shifts from this panegyric stance, in which the poet sings the praises of Elizabeth as the 'flowre of Virgins', and alludes to Niobe, thus introducing an allusion which serves to undercut his own comparison of Elizabeth with the Virgin Mary and to convict the poet of blasphemy:

> But I will not match her with *Latonaes* seede,
> Such follie great sorow to *Niobe* did breede.
> Now she is a stone,
> And makes dayly mone,
> Warning all other to take heede.
>
> (86–90)

Niobe, Queen of Phrygia, served as a famous exemplum of the need for humility. She praised the beauty of her fourteen children, seven sons and seven daughters, boasting of her own fertility and rating the charms of her offspring higher than those of Apollo and Diana. She told her subjects to stop worshipping Latona, and this presumption so angered Latona, the mother of Phoebus Apollo and Cynthia Diana, that she ordered her heavenly children to kill all of Niobe's children. Niobe, endlessly weeping for her lost children, was turned into a stone fountain. E.K. underlines this interpretation by equating the poet and Niobe:

> The vnfortunate Niobe being sore dismayed, and lamenting out of measure, was feigned of the Poetes, to be turned into a stone vpon the sepulchre of her children. For which cause the shepherd sayth, he will not compare her to them, for feare of like misfortune. (70).

The shepherd-poet will not compare Elizabeth with Apollo or Diana for fear of being turned into a stone fountain; however, he has compared Elizabeth with the Virgin Mary, saying that no 'mortall blemishe may her blotte' and even suggested her immortality. In doing so, the shepherd-poet suggests that he has blasphemed as much as or more than the hapless Niobe.

Among the interpretations of the Niobe allusion suggested by critics, we find the following. Helen Hackett interprets the allusion to Niobe as an indication that the poet 'wishes to avoid bringing down a curse of childlessness and sterility upon Elizabeth' (107). If this were E.K.'s intention, then we would have to identify Elizabeth with Niobe, a figure of pride, who presumes to compare herself with the gods and to boast of her own fruitfulness. Louis Montrose tries to account for this crux by suggesting an analogy between Niobe and the poet in which 'Colin constructs his relationship to Elisa as that of parent and child', but Spenser had access to many myths concerning parents and children and this reading evades the problem of why Spenser introduces Niobe into his eulogy of Elizabeth.[18] Yet another critic, Robert Lane, explores what he terms the self-referential power of the *Aprill* eclogue and argues that the poet-narrator is questioning Elizabeth's royal rhetoric.[19] Pointing to the poet's position apart from the circle around the royal figure in the accompanying woodcut, Lane suggests that the poet can objectively comment on the adulation offered by the court. This interpretation of the poet's isolation from the adoring court may also be occurring, but Lane does not account for the allusion to Niobe and its implications. Spenser is leading us in a direction not anticipated by his commentators.

Spenser's allusion to Niobe, supplemented by E.K.'s commentary, invites us to question the propriety of equating Henry VIII with Christ and Elizabeth with the Virgin Mary. This is a prime example of Spenser's irony, of his willingness to offer panegyric praise and then undercut that very praise. The poet explicitly tells us that he will 'not match her [Elizabeth] with *Latonaes* seede', Diana and Apollo, because of the sorrow it brought to Niobe. He does not want to commit Niobe's blasphemy and be turned into a stone, but he introduces this allusion to comment ironically on his own description of Elizabeth as the Virgin Mary and of Henry VIII as Pan (Christ). The *Shepheardes Calender* may have been instrumental in introducing the cult of Elizabeth, but it may also be the only example of a text in which this cult is treated ironically.

By linking his poet-narrator to Niobe, Spenser suggests that it is blasphemy to laud Elizabeth as the Virgin Mary. This should not surprise us because he later adds details to the *Faerie Queene* which comment ironically on the Elizabethan court (I.iv.8). He makes Lucifera the ruler of the House of Pride, but she is not just a queen, she is a 'mayden queene' (I.iv.8). Highlighting the connotations of vanity, Pride could be depicted as a woman carrying a mirror, but in iconography, even when the ruler of the House of Pride is a female ruler, she is never explicitly described as a 'mayden queene', nor is she described as being served by the 'six sage Counsellours': Idleness, Gluttony, Lechery, Avarice, Envy, Wrath.

Vergilian echoes

As a number of critics have observed, appending the Gloss to Spenser's *Shepheardes Calender* enhanced its claim to being a learned text by lending it the appearance of annotated copies of Vergil. Because Spenser is consciously imitating Vergil and inviting his readers to make comparisons with Vergil's eclogues, we need to be aware that his omissions – what he leaves out – may be as significant as the elements he selects for emphasis. Vergil's *Fourth Eclogue*, Spenser's model, served as an important source for Astraean symbolism. In addition to foretelling the birth of a child who will bring back the Golden Age of peace and plenty, Vergil uses Astraea's return to Earth as a sign that the Golden Age is to resume: Astraea, the just maid, honoured in the heavens as the constellation Virgo, returns to earth. Vergil repeats 'iam' to emphasize the implications of Astraea's return:

> Ultima Cumaei venit *iam* carminis aetas;
> magnus ab integro saeclorum nascitur ordo.
> *iam* redit et Virgo, redeunt Saturnia regna;
> *iam* nova progenies caelo demittitur alto.
> (italics mine, 4–7)[20]

[*Now* is come the last age of the song of Cumae; the great line of the centuries begins anew. *Now* the Virgin returns, the reign of Saturn returns; *now* a new generation descends from heaven on high.]

The return of Astraea also heralds the reign of Apollo ('tuus iam regnat Apollo', 10), the god of poets.

Spenser's model, Vergil's *Fourth Eclogue*, afforded him an opportunity to associate Elizabeth with the return of the Golden Age. Our expectations that Spenser will do just that are so strong that more than a few commentators have claimed that he does attribute Roman virtues to Elizabeth and that he does celebrate her reign as the return of the Golden Age. Spenser, however, rejects this association. In any of the likely eclogues of the *Shepheardes Calender*, *Aprill*, *September*, or *November*, we find no references to Astraea, the just maid who ushered in the Golden Age of classical antiquity. Though we might expect Spenser to bring up Astraea, the heavenly virgin who came to Earth under the sign Virgo, the very month of Elizabeth's birth, he ignores this possible tribute. Astraea is not part of Spenser's symbolism in the *Shepheardes Calender* because Spenser does not want to affirm that Elizabeth has ushered in a golden age. He, like Philip Sidney, wanted to support the Netherlands, and he was dismayed by the Anjou courtship. Spenser, unquestionably, knew Vergil's *Fourth Eclogue* extremely well, and to understand his position we need to recognize that his exclusion of the Astraean symbolism from the *Aprill* eclogue was deliberate. He concedes only that Elizabeth is a peaceful ruler and adds gratuitous condescension by emphasizing her gender ('Such for a Princesse bene principall', *Aprill*, 126).

Aprill and *November*

The crosscurrents and parallels established in the design of the *Shepheardes Calender* reveal and conceal Spenser's political allegiance. Elizabeth's accession day was 17 November, and it was celebrated even more dramatically than her birthday by the court. It is no accident that in the *Shepheardes Calender* November, traditionally the month celebrating Elizabeth's accession to the throne of England, becomes the month of her death. The names given to Elizabeth in the *Shepheardes Calender* are Eliza, Elisa (*Aprill*), and Dido (*November*). Spenser plays on the association of the name Elissa with Dido. As Paul McLane has pointed out, in Surrey's popular translation of Book IV of the *Aeneid*, we find the following summary of what will follow: '*The occasion of the love betwene Elissa the Quene of Cartage, after called Dido, and the Troian lord Aeneas, briefly gathered out of Virgyl*'.[21] Dido was a name given to Elissa and used interchangeably with it in Elizabethan accounts of the tragic encounter between the empire-builder Aeneas and the Queen of Carthage.

In the Argument to *November* we are told that the eleventh eclogue will mourn the death of '*some mayden of greate bloud*'. E.K. says that '*personage is secrete, and to me altogether vnknowne, albe of him selfe I often required the same*' (138). E.K. has no idea who the 'mayden of greate bloud' may be, but adds that he was curious enough to ask the author her name. Then in lines 37–8 Thenot introduces references to a 'great shepheard':

> For deade is Dido, dead alas and drent,
> Dido the greate shepehearde his daughter sheene.

In the Gloss to line 38, E.K. teasingly tells us that the father of the 'mayden of greate bloud' is 'some man of high degree, and not as some vainely suppose God Pan' (145). In case the reader may not recall that the great god Pan is both Christ and Henry VIII, we are told that the 'great shepheard' is not 'God Pan', i.e., Christ, leaving the possibility that he may indeed be Henry VIII. Casting the Queen's horoscope or discussing her death was dangerous, and so this by-play is handled with the utmost delicacy. To be sure that the political level is kept solidly in view, E.K. also tells us that the 'mayden of greate bloud' is not Rosalind because 'he speaketh soone after of her also'. Colin does not later speak of his mistress; Rosalind does not appear in *November*.

The verse form and the structure of the *November* eclogue associate it with *Aprill*. Both eclogues begin with dialogues; in *Aprill* the dialogue between Hobbinol and Thenot introduces a song written by Colin Clout (though in this case sung by Hobbinol). *November* begins with a dialogue between Colin Clout and Thenot, but in *November* it is Colin himself who delivers the magnificent elegy that celebrates Dido, who 'for beauties prayse and plesaunce had no pere' (94). She never scorned the 'simple shepheards swaine', but instead fed him on 'curds and clouted Creame' (99–100). It is of particular interest that Dido has given some favour to Colin Clout, 'als *Colin cloute* she would not once disdayne' (101). It seems possible, even likely, that under the Sidneys' auspices, Spenser enjoyed some royal attention before his 1589 visit to the court with Ralegh, but this occasion has yet to be documented.

In *Aprill*, the 'Ladyes of the lake' are led by the nympth Chloris who bears a 'Coronall' of 'Oliue braunches' (120–3). Likewise, in November the 'water Nymphs' that used to sing and dance with Dido 'and for her girlond Oliue braunches beare' (143–5), now advance with 'balefull boughes of Cypres' (145). The muses who used to wear 'greene bayes' now bring 'bitter Eldre braunches seare' (147); even the Fates mourn Dido's untimely death. The triumphant celebration of Elisa has become the funeral dirge for noble Dido, the 'mayden of greate bloud', who has just died. The likelihood that these poems have political implications has long been entertained. In an early effort to recover their topical meanings, Paul E. McLane suggested that Elisa in *Aprill* and Dido in *November* represented two sides of Spenser's view of his virgin queen.[22] Exploring and adding to McLane's hypothesis, Annabel Patterson approached *Aprill* and *November* as 'two views of the English cultural situation, with the more somber one, given the circumstances of 1579, prevailing'.[23] Richard McCabe comments that the 'choice of the name Dido, recalling the unfortunate Vergilian queen who destroyed herself for love of a foreign prince, suggests an allusion to the proposed match with Alençon, an event which, according to Sir Philip Sidney, would accomplish "the manifest death" of the Queen's "estate'".[24] Spenser's polyvalence in the *Shepheardes Calender* makes it unnecessary to select one meaning; all of these suggestions have merit.

The play on Elizabeth as Elisa–Dido is reinforced by the structure of *Aprill*, the eclogue linked with *November*. *Aprill* begins and concludes with a frame in which Thenot and Hobbinol lament Colin's unhappiness over love. To demonstrate Colin's talents as a poet, Hobbinol sings a song written by Colin in praise of Queen Elizabeth. The panegyric to Elizabeth is followed by Latin emblems from the *Aeneid* in which Aeneas meets his mother Venus, addresses her as an unknown virgin, but then recognizes that she must be a goddess. April, traditionally, is the month sacred to Venus, and the concluding mottoes link Elizabeth with Venus, the goddess of love and beauty. The emblems and gloss to *Aprill* explicitly identify Elizabeth with Venus: 'Elisa is no whit inferiour to the Maiestie of her, of whome that Poete so boldly pronounced, O dea certe' (71).

Venus, however, was also the mother of Aeneas, the empire builder. These allusions to Venus glance at England's future. In 1579, viewing the breach between Elizabeth and Leicester over his marriage and her courtship by Anjou as politically dangerous, Spenser suggests possible resolutions in the linked eclogues, *Aprill* and *November*: Elizabeth, like Venus, can marry Anjou or some other suitor and produce a son who will become an empire builder; alternatively, she can foster the already married Leicester, the hero and empire builder who may fulfil England's imperial mission. Or, as shadowed in *November*, Elizabeth, like Dido in the *Aeneid*, jealous of her lover, can destroy herself and harm the body politic. Spenser's specific political position on the marriage question is left ambiguous, but the *Februarie* and *March* eclogues suggest that he opposed the French match.

In *Aprill*, his version of Vergil's fourth eclogue, Spenser summoned up the image of Elizabeth as an Astraea who was to usher in the Golden Age of Augustus, and then turns away from the identification of Elizabeth as Astraea. In so doing, he underlines the alternative shadowed in the *November* eclogue. This pastoral elegy for Dido also functions as Spenser's comment on Vergil's fifth eclogue, the elegy for Julius Caesar. This elegiac connection suggests the possibility that Elizabeth, like Julius Caesar, will die without ensuring the stability of her state, that her death, like Caesar's, will lead to civil war. November, the month of Elizabeth's accession to the throne, becomes in the *Shepheardes Calender* the month of her death. The *November* eclogue, instead of commemorating Elizabeth's triumphant accession to the throne on 17 November, becomes a beautiful, but mournful, dirge.

Notes

1. For Elizabeth's poem to Anjou, see Bodleian, Ashmolean MS 781, fol. 142.
2. *CSP, Spanish, 1568-1579*, 693. Mendoza thinks that Sidney belongs to the peerage.
3. Duncan-Jones, *Sir Philip Sidney*, on Spenser and the meeting at Baynard's Castle, 162.
4. I use the terms 'faction' and 'party' interchangeably to represent a group with common political and religious interests; in the case of the Sidneys and Ireland, the common interests were reinforced by kinship ties. For an analysis and descriptive historiography of the controversy over factions, see Simon Adams, 'Favourites and Factions at the Elizabethan Court', in *The Tudor Monarchy*, ed. John Guy (London and New York: Arnold and St Martin's Press, 1997), 253-74. For a sceptical view of terminology, see Natalie Mears, 'Courts, Courtiers, and Culture in Tudor England', *The Historical Journal*, 46 (2003), 703-22.
5. *John Stubbs's Gaping Gulf with Letters and Other Relevant Documents*, ed. Lloyd E. Berry (Charlottesville, VA: Folger Shakespeare Library by University of Virginia Press, 1968), xlvii–xlix, and Duncan-Jones, *Sidney*, 162. All references to the *Gaping Gulf*, the Queen's proclamation, and Lord Henry Howard's 'Answer to the *Gaping Gulf*' will be to Berry's edition.
6. STC 23400. For the Queen's Proclamation, see Berry, ed., *Gaping Gulf*, 147–52, esp. 148.
7. Camden, *The Historie of the Most Renowned and Victorious Princesse Elizabeth … Composed by Way of Annals* (London: Printed for Benjamin Fisher, 1630), Bbr (Book 3: 9).
8. Camden, Latin edn, 379ff; cf. 1625 English edn, III: 16, and 1635 edn, 239 (italics mine).
9. I agree with Blair Worden that the serendipity of an ambassador named Simier is too much of a coincidence and so accept the existence of an early manuscript of *Mother Hubberds Tale*, but, because of variants in extant manuscripts, I am not persuaded by arguments that we can deduce the contents and structure of the 1579 text from what was eventually published in 1591.
10. For Spenser's printer, see H.J. Byrom, 'Edmund Spenser's First Printer, Hugh Singleton', *The Library*, Fourth Series, 14 (1933), 121–56. On 29 October 1580 he assigned his rights to John Harrison the younger, who had the 1581 second edition printed by Thomas East.
11. Frances A. Yates, 'Queen Elizabeth as Astraea', *Journal of the Warburg and Courtauld Institutes*, 10 (1947), 69–70. Helen Hackett addresses the problem of offering a chronology of Elizabeth's iconography in *Virgin Mother, Maiden Queen: Elizabeth I and the Cult of the Virgin Mary* (New York: St Martin's Press, 1995). The specific chronological and historical context is not identified in articles by Louis Adrian Montrose in '"The "perfecte paterne of a Poete": The Poetics of Courtship in *The Shepheardes Calender*', *Texas Studies in Literature and Language*, 21, No. 1 (Spring 1979), 34–67; '"Eliza, Queene of shepheardes," and the Pastoral of Power', *English Literary Renaissance*, 10 (1980), 153–82, esp. 168; 'The Elizabethan Subject and the Spenserian Text', in *Literary Theory / Renaissance Texts*, ed. Patricia Parker and David Quint (Baltimore: Johns Hopkins University Press, 1986), 907–46. For a persuasive discussion of Italianate precedents, see S.K. Heninger, Jr, 'The Typographical Layout of Spenser's *Shepheardes Calender*', in

Word and Visual Imagination, ed. Karl Josef Holtgen and Peter M. Daly (Erlangen: University of Erlangen Press, 1988), 33–71. See also Ruth Samson Luborsky, 'The Allusive Presentation of *The Shepheardes Calender*', *Spenser Studies*, 1 (1980), 29–67.

12 For a history of Elizabeth's portraits, see Roy Strong, *Gloriana: The Portraits of Queen Elizabeth I* (Wisbech: Thames and Hudson, 1987), esp. 71–9.
13 Strong, *Gloriana*, 157–61.
14 For a study that also addresses the ambiguity I find in *Aprill*, see David Norbrook, *Poetry and Politics in the English Renaissance* (1984; rev. ed. Oxford: Oxford University Press, 2002), 53–81, esp. 76–81. Unlike Montrose and to some degree Norbrook, I do not think that, at this stage of his career, Spenser thought that he was creating a public image for his monarch, particularly in *Aprill*.
15 Hackett, *Virgin Mother, Maiden Queen*, 106. For the alternative, see Lyn Staley Johnson, *The Shepheardes Calender: An Introduction* (University Park, PA: The Pennsylvania University Press, 1990), who argues that Spenser praises Elizabeth as a bride or celestial Venus, 'whose virgin state engendered peace and plenty' (170). According to Johnson's reading, this praise acts as a veil for Spenser's advice not to marry Anjou: he is assuring her that she needs neither husband nor child to assure her 'immortality and her country's stability' (170).
16 Montrose, 'Eliza, Queene of Shepheardes, and the Pastoral of Power', 153–82. See also Catherine Bates, *The Rhetoric of Courtship in Elizabethan Language and Literature* (Cambridge: Cambridge University Press, 1992).
17 James E. Phillips, 'Spenser's Syncretistic Religious Imagery', *English Literary History*, 36 (1969), 110–30.
18 Montrose, 'The Elizabethan Subject and the Spenserian Text', 320–3; 337.
19 Robert Lane, *Shepheards Devises: Edmund Spenser's Shepheardes Calender and the Institutions of Elizabethan Society* (Athens: University of Georgia Press, 1993): 'The self-referential quality of April's eclogue declares the poet's implication in matrices of power and the representational system integral to them but also affirms his capacity for critical reflection on those relations and that system' (21).
20 Virgil, ed. H. Rushton Fairclough. 2 vols. Loeb Classical Library, 1: 28.
21 Cited from Paul E. McLane, *Spenser's Shepheardes Calender: A Study in Elizabethan Allegory* (Notre Dame: Notre Dame University Press, 1961), 52.
22 McLane, *Spenser's Shepheardes Calender*, 28–9.
23 Annabel Patterson, *Pastoral and Ideology: Virgil to Valéry* (Berkeley: University of California Press, 1987), 121–2.
24 Richard McCabe, '"Little booke: thy selfe present": The Politics of Presentation in *The Shepheardes Calender*', in H. Erskine-Hill and R.A. McCabe, eds *Presenting Poetry: Composition, Publication, Reception* (Cambridge: Cambridge University Press, 1995), 15–40.

8

Puzzling identities: From E.K. to Roffy's 'boye' to Rosalind

The eclogues of the *Shepheardes Calender* are prefaced by a discussion of the calendar in which a well-read E.K. determines that the calendar traditionally begins in March, but then undercuts this learned conclusion by stating that this particular calendar will begin in January. E.K., self-proclaimed author of the Gloss, prefaces his epistle on the calendar with a dedication lauding the work of 'the most excellent and learned ... Orator and Poete, Mayster Gabriell Haruey' (25). E.K. also offers a preface containing the 'generall argument of the whole booke' followed by woodcuts, arguments, eclogues, emblems, and glosses which comment on the eclogues. In the Gloss, we find definitions of dialect words, explanations of classical allusions, suggestive hints that names and events may contain topical allusions to contemporary people or issues, but the Gloss is inconsistent – sometimes elucidating and sometimes obfuscating the author's intentions. Because the author of the Gloss professes not to know what the author intends, the authors of the eclogues and of the Gloss are depicted as two separate people.

The identity of E.K. has been and is a crux in scholarship on Spenser, and one that I hope that this chapter will assist in resolving by proving that Gabriel Harvey had to be involved in constructing the Gloss of the *Shepheardes Calender*. As things stand, the E.K. of the *Shepheardes Calender* has been variously understood to be a real-life Edward Kirke, some other contemporary of Harvey and Spenser with the appropriate initials, Harvey using the initials E.K., or Spenser disguising himself as E.K.[1] Those who take the initials literally have frequently identified E.K. as Edward Kirke (1553–1613), a colleague of Spenser's at Pembroke.[2]

Critics who think that Spenser authored every aspect of the poem have argued that Spenser is E.K. and that he acts as both author and critic.[3] If we take the view that Spenser was responsible for the passages in which E.K. celebrates 'Immerito' as the new poet who rivals Theocritus, Vergil, and Petrarch, then, as David Shore has pointed out, we have to imagine a Spenser who is self-congratulatory. This kind of self-promotion would conflict with Spenser's persona as Immerito.

If it can be demonstrated that Spenser consulted with Harvey on a number of details, then Harvey must be recognized as Spenser's collaborator. In that case, the questions shift from querying if Harvey was involved to asking how much he was involved and what roles he played.

Gabriel Harvey as E.K.: Spenser's collaborator on *Shepheardes Calender*

Substantive evidence from Harvey's biography indicates that he collaborated with Spenser. In the *Shepheardes Calender* there are personal allusions to people and events that only Harvey would have known. As we know, Sir Thomas Smith was Harvey's neighbour and principal patron before his death in 1577; Smith, on the other hand, is unlikely to have been personally known to Spenser, who is conspicuously absent from *Smithus*, Harvey's commemoration of his patron. It is thus significant that E.K. alludes to an unpublished manuscript belonging to Sir Thomas Smith in the Gloss to line 10 of the *Januarie* eclogue of *Shepheardes Calender*.

> couthe) commeth of the verbe Conne, that is, to know or to haue skill. As well interpreteth the same the worthy Sir Tho. Smitth in his booke of gouernment: wherof I haue a perfect copie in wryting, lent me by his kinseman, and my verye singular good freend, M. Gabriel Haruey: as also of some other his most graue and excellent wrytings (38).

The Gloss states that Gabriel Harvey has a copy of Smith's manuscript (which would have dated from around 1565). From later references in the Harvey–Nashe controversy, we know that Harvey quarrelled with Andrew Perne at Sir Thomas Smith's funeral in 1577 over a manuscript and that Harvey ended up in possession of it. It is useful to note that Smith's manuscript 'booke of gouernment' was not printed until 1581, two years after the *Shepheardes Calender* was in print. E.K. states that he owns a manuscript of Smith's, which was conveniently loaned to him by Gabriel Harvey. Harvey does not print his description of wresting

Smith's manuscript away from Andrew Perne for fourteen years, when he publishes *Pierces Supererogation* (1593). The chronological facts indicate that Harvey participated in crafting this allusion to Smith's manuscript. In 1579, Harvey was the only source for this addition to his library. It should also be noted that this allusion to Smith is irrelevant to the themes in the eclogues of the *Shepheardes Calender*, but highly relevant to E.K.'s campaign to advertise the 'excellent and learned both Orator and Poete, Mayster Gabriell Harvey'.

Nashe later mocks the allusion to Harvey in the Gloss to the *Shepheardes Calender* as Smiths's 'kinseman and verye singular good freend' (p. 38).

> Onely hee tells a foolish twittle twattle boasting tale (amidst his impudent brazen-fac'd defamation of *Doctor Perne*,) of the Funerall of his kinsman, *Sir Thomas Smith* (which word *kinsman* I wondered he causd not to be set in great capitall letters,) and how in those Obsequies he was a chiefe Mourner. (Nashe, 3: 58)

Suggesting that Harvey was an inveterate name-dropper, Nashe undercuts his claim of kinship with Sir Thomas Smith. We should take note that Smith is glossed in the *Shepheardes Calender* and alluded to in *Familiar Letters* – even though there is no evidence that Spenser was himself acquainted with him.

There are other biographical references demonstrating that Harvey had to be involved in preparing E.K.'s commentary. Specific details of the bibliographical history of Harvey's *Gratulationes Valdinenses* are known *only* because the Gloss to the *Shepheardes Calender* calls attention to the sequencing of Harvey's bids for patronage during the Progress of 1578. Spenser could not have known the exact sequence of events unless Harvey explained it to him. Further, there is no reason why Spenser would have wanted to rehearse this story in minute detail in the Gloss to the *September* eclogue. This is what occurred. In July, Harvey presented the manuscripts of *Gratulationes Valdinenses* to the Queen at Audley End, Essex. In September, on the second occasion, Harvey presented the printed copies of *Gratulationes Valdinenses* to the Queen and court at Capel House in Hertfordshire – six weeks after the manuscripts were first presented. These events are detailed in the Gloss to the *September* eclogue:

> Whose especiall good freend Hobbinol sayth he is, or more rightly Mayster Gabriel Harvey: of whose speciall commendation, aswell in Poetrye as Rhetorike and other choyce learning, we haue lately had a sufficient tryall in diuerse his workes, but specially in his *Musarum Lachrymae*, and his

> late *Gratulationum Valdinensium* which boke in the progresse at Audley in Essex, he dedicated in writing vnto her Maiestie. afterward presenting the same in print vnto her Highnesse at the worshipfull Maister Capells in Hertfordshire. (*September*, 176, p. 126)

Only Harvey would have known and wanted publicly to rehearse the sequencing that included his first dedicating a handwritten text to the Queen and then later presenting her with a printed text which included poems on events occurring at Audley End, that is, his having kissed the Queen's hand and being told that he already looked Italian. Even the printed text of *Gratulationes Valdinenses* (1578) does not make this sequencing entirely clear. In 1579 the only testimony regarding the precise ordering of these events is found in the Gloss to the *September* eclogue.

Over a decade later, Thomas Nashe recognized how much of his ambition Harvey had revealed in *Gratulationes Valdinenses*. In *Strange Newes* (1592), he supplies an alternative narrative of Harvey's preferment:

> Ile tell you a merry ieast. The time was when this *Timothie Tiptoes* made a Latine Oration to her Maiestie. Her Highnes as shee is vnto all her subiects most gratious; so to schollers she is more louing and affable than any Prince vnder heauen. In which respect, of her owne vertue and not his desert, it pleased hir so to humble the height of hir iudgement, as to grace him a little whiles he was pronouncing, by these or such termes. *Tis a good pretie fellow, a lookes like an Italian*; and after hee had concluded to call him to kisse her royall hand. (Nashe, 1: 276–7)

A reader of *Gratulationes Valdinenses* (1578) would not have known that there were two presentations, but Nashe was an admirer of Spenser's and a student of the *Shepheardes Calender*, and so he duly acknowledges the sequence of events that is explained and rehearsed in the *September* eclogue:

> Herevppon hee goes home to his studie, all intraunced, and writes a whole volume of Verses; first, *De vultu Itali*, of the countenance of the Italian; and then *De osculo manus*, of his kissing the Queenes hande. Which two Latin Poems he publisht in a booke of his cald *Ædes Valdinenses*, proclaiming there by (as it were to England Fraunce, Italie, and Spaine) what fauour hee was in with her Maiestie. (1: 277)

Nashe warns that no nobleman should encourage Harvey because he is likely to publish the event: 'Lette all Noblemen take heede how they giue this *Thraso* the least becke or countenance, for if they bestowe but halfe a glaunce on him, hele straight put it verie solemnly in print and make it ten times more than it is' (1: 276).

Later, in the second part of *Familiar Letters*, entitled *Two Other, very commendable Letters, of the same mens writing*, Spenser is portrayed as writing a two-part letter, the first part dated 5 October 1579 from Leicester House and the second part on 23 October 1579 from Westminster. In the first section of the letter, Spenser discusses the publication of *Shepheardes Calender* and alludes specifically to Harvey's 'fine Addition' of a Gloss:

> The selfe former Title stil liketh me well ynough, and *your fine Addition no lesse*. If these, and the like doubtes, maye be of importaunce in your seeming, to frustrate any parte of your aduice, I beeseeche you, without the leaste selfe loue of your own purpose, councell me for the beste. (II.1, G3r-v, italics mine)

Spenser's reference to Harvey's 'fine Addition' could refer to the 'Epistle' at the beginning or the 'Gloss' at the end, or both, that is, to the front matter and the Gloss.

E.K. also describes himself as adding to the *Shepheardes Calender*: 'Hereunto haue I added a certain Glosse or scholion for thexposition of old wordes and harder phrases: which maner of glosing and commenting, well I wote, wil seeme straunge and rare in our tongue' (29). While the Gloss supplies information that at times seems to parody scholarship, at others it tantalizes the reader with hints of secrets that cannot be reported.

It required unusual subterfuge and more than a little self-congratulation on Harvey's part to write a dedication to himself, so much so that his authorship would seem improbable – if Harvey's revealing marginalia and his *Letter-Book* had not survived. In these texts, Harvey drafts letters and writes notes testing various strategies for self-promotion, and one of his preferred techniques is to applaud his achievements in the third person. In his *Letter-Book* Harvey uses initials and writes in the third person to describe a 'garden communication or dialogue in Cambridge betweene Master G H and his cumpanye at a Midsummer Commencement' (fol. 51b, p. 95). Harvey then switches to the first person and says the following: 'I am so loth, my good masters, to depryve you of any thinge that I can possibly communicate with you of this autors dooinge in whom nothinge is vulgar but ether in respecte of the manner or matter' (95). Later in the same general discourse the first-person narrator obtains Harvey's permission to copy a 'wise and ingenious Latin epigramme … in effecte conteyninge the argumente of his curragious and warly[k]e apostrophe to my lorde of Oxenforde in his fourth booke *Gratuationum*

Valdinensium' (99). Harvey's *Letter-Book* contains numerous examples of his writing tributes to himself in the third person or using a fictional narrator to sing the praises of G H.

S.K. Heninger, Jr, in addition, has offered persuasive evidence that Gabriel Harvey collaborated with Spenser on designing the physical appearance of the text and has concluded that Harvey was responsible for the typographical layout imitating the format of the Sansovino edition of Sannazaro's *Arcadia*.[4] I am persuaded by Heninger's arguments that Harvey was Spenser's collaborator, but I think that Spenser, as author, exercised full editorial control over the textual production of the *Shepheardes Calender*.[5] Stylistically, the Gloss seems to be the work of Gabriel Harvey, but Immerito, exercising ironic distance, stands behind this commentary. Spenser's distance allows him to parody the very idea of a Gloss by glossing inconsequential words, such as 'neighbour towne' (p. 38) and to turn Harvey's pedantic remarks, some probably reported verbatim, into a counterpoint to the colloquial language of the shepherds.

The interchanges between Spenser and Harvey (Immerito and E.K.) in the *Shepheardes Calender*, at their best, generate a wonderful self-parody. The literary genealogy of Immerito furnishes just such an ironic sequence. E.K. engages in some serious name-dropping: Vergil and Chaucer, Marot and Skelton. In the Gloss to the *Januarie* eclogue of the *Shepheardes Calender*, we are given a literary source for Spenser's name, John Skelton's *Boke of Colin Clout* (1530), a satire of church and state. The *Shepheardes Calender* contains religious and political satire and so resembles Skelton in theme and genre. Both Spenser and Harvey admired Skelton, and Harvey experimented with his distinctive verse form, *skeltonics*, in his *Letter-Book*:[6]

> Our most sumptuous and floorishinge cities
> Ar like dissonant and iarring dittyes,
> Good and badd,
> Merry and sadd, sober and madd,
> Ar there to be hadd;
> Ritche and pore
> Of ether great store
> Lordes and potentates,
> Vassals and runnegates,
> Gentlemen and lawyers,
> Coblers and colliers. (p. 117)

Although Harvey paid Skelton the compliment of serious imitation, in the Gloss to the *Shepheardes Calender* it is Colin Clout, not Hobbinol, who is associated with Skelton. E.K. also tells us that Colin is a name borrowed from the Protestant French poet Clement Marot, who substantively influenced the *December* eclogue.[7] Nothing, however, is meant to be straightforward. We are also informed that Immerito has adopted Colin Clout as a pseudonym to keep his identity secret, much as Vergil used the name Tityrus (*Januarie*, Gloss, 1). Colin Clout, however, will use the Vergilian name Tityrus to refer, not to Vergil but to Chaucer, Colin's English mentor. After E.K. recites this elaborate system of literary cross-references, E.K.'s pretentious literary genealogy is deflated when Spenser identifies himself simply as Colin Clout. This is one example of the irony created when we juxtapose the text with the scholarly pretensions of the Gloss.

The same parade of learned allusions is offered by E.K. in his explanation of why the *Shepheardes Calender* is organized with the year beginning in January. He acknowledges that it is 'wel known, and stoutely mainteyned with strong reasons of the learned that the yeare beginneth in March' (33). The explanation includes the opinions of old astrologers, Christian philosophers, Julius Caesar, Romulus (a ten-month year), and the Egyptians who began the year with September. After summoning up all of these authorities and historical precedents, E.K. dismisses them with the comment that 'our Authour ... thinketh it fittest according to the simplicitie of commen vnderstanding, to begin with Ianuarie' (34). Because of decorum, E.K. tells us, shepherds should not undertake a matter of 'so deepe insight' or of 'doubtful iudgment' (34). Intellectual puffery is undercut by a simple appeal to verisimilitude sanctified as decorum.

In summary, we know that Harvey collaborated with Spenser. No contemporary printed or manuscript source exists for the biographical details about Harvey that we find in E.K.'s Gloss. E.K. uses words such as 'yonkerly', a favourite of Harvey's, and he employs Harvey's characteristically learned construction of the possessive, for instance 'the name of a shepheard in Marot his Aeglogue'. If we rule out Harvey's collaboration, we would face the dilemma of having to account for a Gloss that systematically imitates Harvey's diction and syntax, a task within Spenser's capacity, but unmotivated. On the other hand, the Gloss seems to further Spenser's authorial intentions, going so far as to hint at topicality when there may be none or insisting on the author's good intentions at points when topicality is intended. It is Spenser and Spenser alone who could have orchestrated the relationship between E.K.'s Gloss and the poem. There is even bibliographical evidence that Spenser edited the poem after

Harvey supplied whatever additions and annotations which he gave Spenser. E.K. supplies Glosses in *Julye* and *September* on material that was later cut from the poem.[8]

Dedication of the *Shepheardes Calender*

Spenser probably did not publish the *Shepheardes Calender* immediately upon completing it; there was an interval of eight months between the date of the dedication and its entrance into the Stationers' Register. At some point, Spenser seems to have changed the dedicatee from the Earl of Leicester to Philip Sidney, perhaps because Sidney contributed to the cost of printing the *Shepheardes Calender*. Harvey was quite comfortable with the role of a suitor, and in 1578 asked Leicester to further the renewal of his fellowship at Cambridge and in 1579 and 1580 requested support from Burghley, University Chancellor, in gaining the position of University Orator. In contrast, Spenser seems to have been reticent about imposing on 'noble eares'.[9] He appears to have had misgivings about dedicating the *Shepheardes Calender* to the Earl of Leicester, whom he suggests may be too grand a personage for him to adopt as a dedicatee; he reveals this diffidence in a letter addressed to Harvey and printed in *Familiar Letters* (1580): 'Suche [contempt] mighte I happily incurre, entituling My Slomber, and the other Pamphlets vnto his honor. I meant them rather to Maister Dyer' (G3v-G4r).[10]

William A. Ringler, Jr, in a useful article on the terms of address, 'honor' and 'worship', points out that 'honor' is used to address a nobleman or equivalent and that 'worship' is used to address a knight or gentleman.[11] He argues that Spenser originally intended to address *Shepheardes Calender* to Leicester whom he describes as 'his honor' in the proem, 'Goe little booke'. Ringler notes the precision with which these terms are used in *Familiar Letters*. Referring to his employment by a 'Lorde', Spenser says that he will devote himself 'to his Honours service' and then reports that 'gentle M. Sidney, I thanke his good Worship', has asked for news about Harvey. In the *Shepheardes Calender* Spenser sends his poem to the 'president / Of noblesse and of Chevalree', a compliment that could have served for either Leicester or Sidney, but fails to revise the address to a lord, 'his honor' ('To His Booke', 11) to 'his worship' when he shifts the dedication to Sidney. E.K.'s Epistle punctiliously observes the distinction and says that Immerito 'dedicated it to the Noble and worthy Gentleman, the right worshipfull Ma. Phi. Sidney, a special favourer and maintainer of all kind of learning' (193–5).

The anonymity of Roffy's boy

Immerito's studied anonymity has puzzled biographers and critics. There does not seem to be an easy explanation for why Spenser concealed his authorship of the *Shepheardes Calender*, but a partial explanation may lie in his desire to spare Bishop John Young the embarrassment of having his former protégé publish anti-clerical satire and an attack on Bishop Aylmer. Unfortunately, we as yet know very little about clerical politics or about Spenser's relationship with Young. It may be relevant that Philip Sidney, for example, lived for a time in the house of Bishop Thomas Cooper (Thomalin), Bishop Aylmer's antagonist in *Julye*. In his *Defence of Poetry*, Sidney praises the *Mirrour of Magistrates*, the 'Earle of Surries Liricks', and the '*Shepheardes Kalender*', but he does not identify Spenser as the author of the *Shepheardes Calender*.[12] Since we know from *Familiar Letters* that Spenser was acquainted with the Sidney circle, and since the so-called stigma of print does not prevent Sidney from identifying Surrey by name, his decision to treat the *Shepheardes Calender* as anonymous is likely to have been motivated by Spenser's request.[13] Alternatively, we would have to assume that Sidney did not know that Spenser was the author of the *Shepheardes Calender*, even though it was dedicated to him and even though Spenser believed in securing permission for dedications in advance. It is more likely that Sidney knew that Spenser was the author of the *Shepheardes Calender*, but also knew that Spenser wished to conceal his identity.

In the *Shepheardes Calender* there are teasing internal references to Colin Clout as 'Roffy's boy', but an overview of the poem's reception suggests that Spenser's authorship may not have been widely known outside of the Cambridge circles to which Harvey belonged. We now know that Spenser was the author of the *Shepheardes Calender* and regard it as a landmark publication in early Elizabethan verse, but Spenser's self-presentation is singularly oblique. He is not identified as the author on the title page; the text is inscribed by 'Immerito' and dedicated to Sidney on a plain page that has no frontispiece. Although the Epistle about the calendar and the Gloss on the text may make the *Shepheardes Calender* appear a learned publication, the title page itself is not especially impressive. Immerito also makes a point of calling attention to the anonymity of his poem:

> Goe little booke: thy selfe present,
> As child whose parent is vnkent:
>
> (1–2)

In contrast to Immerito's anonymous 'little booke', in E.K.'s Epistle Sidney is identified as the dedicatee and as a 'speciall fauourer and maintainer of all kind of learning' (30).

The name Gabriel Harvey, however, dominates the front matter and the Gloss to *Shepheardes Calender*; even the dedication to Sidney is overshadowed by a long and very fulsome dedicatory address to Gabriel Harvey. At times E.K. appears to be more in charge of the presentation than Immerito; it is he who 'commendeth the lyking of this his labour, and the patronage of the new Poete' to Harvey (25). Are we to consider the *Shepheardes Calender* the work of Immerito or of E.K.'s featured dedicatee, that extraordinary orator and poet Gabriel Harvey?[14] E.K. signs the dedicatory Epistle and takes credit for the Gloss: 'Here unto haue I added a certain Gloss'. It is not until the publication of *Familiar Letters* (1580) that Spenser is publicly acknowledged to be the author of *Shepheardes Calender*, and in this same publication Harvey is suggestively identified as the author of a 'certain Gloss'.

Reception of *Shepheardes Calender*

A sampling of Spenser's contemporaries seems to have been unaware that he was the 'unkent' Immerito. Contemporary references to the anonymity of the author of the *Shepheardes Calender*, however, are suggestive because one of them comes from a person engaged in supplying a history of English poets and identifying important contributors to literary achievement in English. As noted above, these contemporary references, taken together, suggest that Spenser may have remained relatively anonymous outside Cambridge and Sidney circles prior to the publication of the *Faerie Queene*. Eight years after the publication of *Shepheardes Calender*, the poet and soldier George Whetstone, or his printer, seems to have thought that Sidney was the author, rather than the dedicatee, of Spenser's 1579 pastoral. Whetstone, a friend of Gascoigne's, dedicated his commemorative tribute to Ambrose Dudley, Earl of Warwick, and to 'those who would be like vnto him' (A4v) (Sidney). Emphasizing that Sidney was not 'a Carpet knight' (B2v) who gloried in his garments, Whetstone identifies him as an author of substantial merit.[15] He seems informed about Sidney's literary achievements; three years prior to the publication of the *Arcadia*, he describes the unpublished text as 'unmacht for sweete deuise: / Where skill doth iudge, is held in Soueraigne price' (B2v):

> What else he wrote, his will was to suppresse,
> But yet the darke, a Dyamond cannot drowne:
> What be his workes, the finest wittes doe gesse,

The Shepheards notes, that haue so sweete a sounde.
With Lawrel Bowghes, his healme, long since haue crownd
And not alone, in Poesie he did passe:
But eu'ry way, a learned Knight he was.

In a marginal notation to the left of the above stanza, Whetstone (or perhaps his printer) has written the following:

> The last sheppards calenders
> the reputed worke of
> S. Phil. Sydney a worke
> of deepe learning, iudgment & witte
> disguised in Shep Rules.

To illustrate Sidney's learning, Whetstone next alludes to his translation of *De la vérité de la religion Chrestienne* by Philippe Duplessis-Mornay and marginally notes that at Sidney's request, the translation was to be completed by Arthur Golding (B3r). The mistaken attribution of the *Shepheardes Calender* to Sidney may help to explain the poem's popularity: Sidney was a national hero after his early death.

Whetstone's mistaken attribution to Sidney is not the only indication that Spenser's authorship was not widely known. The *Art of English Poesy* (1589), now attributed to George Puttenham, alludes to the *Shepheardes Calender*, but this author also seems unaware that Spenser is the author of the *Shepheardes Calender*: 'For eglogue and pastorall Poesy, Sir *Philip Sydney* and Maister *Chalenner,* and that other Gentleman who wrate the late shepheardes Callender'.[16] William Webbe, author of *Discourse of English Poetrie* (1586), knows that Spenser is the author of the *Shepheardes Calender*, but his commentary demonstrates as much or more admiration for Gabriel Harvey as for Edmund Spenser. Webbe says that he has reserved a special place for 'one, who, if not only, yet in my iudgement principally, deserueth the title of the rightest English Poet that euer I read, that is, the Author of the *Sheepeheardes Kalender,* intituled to the woorthy Gentleman Master Phillip Sydney: whether it was Master *Sp* or what rare Scholler in Pembrooke Hall soeuer because himself and his freendes, for what respect I knowe not, would not reueale it ... sorry I am that I can not find none other with whom I might couple him in this Catalogue in his rare gyft of Poetry: although one there is'.[17]

The one exception turns out to be Gabriel Harvey, who is now occupied with 'grauer studies' (245). Webbe's *Discourse* shows that he has read *Familiar Letters* and indeed that may be why he is aware that Spenser is the author of the *Shepheardes Calender.* Webbe, however, couples Spenser with Harvey and seems to regard Harvey as the authority on metrics and poetics, a conclusion that might have been drawn from a very literal reading of *Familiar Letters* and a cursory reading of the verse in *Shepheardes Calender.*

Homosexuality in *Shepheardes Calender*

The obvious homoerotic allusions in the *Shepheardes Calender* also argue for Harvey's collaboration with Spenser. If Harvey in no way collaborated with Spenser in writing the *Shepheardes Calender,* then it is difficult to dismiss the hints about Hobbinol's love for Colin Clout as recondite humour or 'good fun'. If Harvey was not a party to the jokes about homosexual love, then they were cruel – classical parody or not.

In the *Januarie* eclogue, Colin's unhappy romance with the mysterious Rosalind is juxtaposed with Hobbinol's unrequited love for Colin.[18] It is well to remember that Harvey was still pursuing an academic career at Cambridge in 1579. The Gloss carries the hint of homoeroticism further and insinuates connections between Harvey (Hobbinol) and pederasty. If Spenser alone were responsible for the Gloss, then we would have to suppose that these references to pederasty were inserted without Harvey's knowledge. Colin describes the homoerotic relationship as follows:

> It is not *Hobbinol,* wherefore I plaine,
> Albee my loue he seeke with dayly suit:
> His clownish gifts and curtsies I disdaine,
> His kiddes, his cracknelles, and his early fruit.
> Ah foolish *Hobbinol,* thy gyfts bene vayne:
> *Colin* them giues to *Rosalind* againe.
>
> (55–60)

Hobbinol is enamored of Colin Clout, but Colin remains securely heterosexual and gives the presents he receives from his male admirer to Rosalind, his hard-hearted Petrarchan mistress.

Hobbinol's unrequited love for the male Colin Clout has a classical precedent in Vergil – just as Colin's unrequited love for his mistress Rosalind has a precedent in Petrarch. Vergil's *Second Eclogue* was taught in every Elizabethan grammar school, and it relates the story of the rustic Corydon and his rejection by the boy Alexis. Corydon gives gifts to Alexis, but Alexis scornfully rejects them. It is customary to dismiss the hint of a romance between Hobbinol and Colin by nodding in the direction of a Vergilian precedent.[19] The Gloss to the *Januarie* eclogue, however, teasingly claims that the poem contains not only 'hidden meanings' but even allusions to real people. In fact, Hobbinol, the man in love with Colin, is pointedly identified as Spenser's real-life friend, Gabriel Harvey. We are told that Hobbinol 'is a fained country name, whereby, it being so commune and vsuall, seemeth to be hidden the person of some his very speciall and most familiar freend, whom he entirely and extraordinarily beloued, as peraduenture shall be more largely declared hereafter' (*Januarie*, line 59, p. 39).

Because Harvey is identified as Hobbinol and the Gloss insists on a homoerotic attachment to Spenser on Harvey's part, Harvey is likely to have had genuine latitude in his composition of this section of E.K.'s Gloss. It is one thing to say that Hobbinol gives Colin gifts and that Colin then gives them to Rosalind, but quite another to bring up pederasty in an exposition of this gift exchange. In his Gloss, E.K. comments, 'In thys place seemeth to be some sauour of disorderly loue, which the learned call paederestie'. E.K. then begins to expound the grounds for legitimizing love between men and elevating homosexual affection over romantic love between a woman and a man:

> For who that hath red Plato his dialogue called Alcybiades, Xenophon and Maximus Tyrius of Socrates opinions may easily perceiue, that such loue is muche to be alowed and liked of, specially so meant, as Socrates vsed it: who sayth, that in deede he loued Alcybiades extremely, yet not Alcybiades person, but hys soule, which is Alcibiades owne selfe (39).

After associating pederasty with Platonic love, E.K. then dismisses heterosexual love because he thinks that it easily degenerates into lust: 'And so is paederastice much to be praeferred before gynerastice, that is the loue whiche enflameth men with lust toward woman kind' (39). After Hobbinol links Platonic love with love between men and elevates it over heterosexual love, he then acknowledges that there are authorities who take a more critical view of homosexuality:

> But yet let no man thinke, that herein I stand with Lucian or hys deuelish disciple Vnico Aretino, in defence of execrable and horrible sinnes of forbidden and vnlawful fleshlinesse. Whose abominable error is fully confuted of Perionius, and others. (p. 39)

E.K. seems aware that, although some commentators on Plato may have allegorized pederasty as Platonic love, many in his own culture are not sanguine about love between men and boys. It may also be useful to note that E.K. has shifted the discussion from homosexuality to pederasty, a shift that is problematical.

The humanist Erasmus was alarmed by the homosexual content in Virgil's *Second Eclogue* and left detailed instructions on how to deal with it. He says nothing about spiritual pederasty; instead (and every teacher knows and values this technique), he encourages the instructor to distract students by talking about other things in the text.[20] It is important to remember that Gabriel Harvey was a university don. The entire episode and the commentary on it are troublesome as well as potentially humorous. Harvey, who hoped to use his career at Cambridge to become a courtier, however, needs to be in on the joke.[21]

Rosalind, Spenser, and Harvey

If the five epistles in *Familiar Letters* are arranged chronologically, there are the following references to a person whom Spenser loves (figuratively, 'Rosalind'), and perhaps Machabyas (Maccabaeus) Chylde whom Spenser is generally supposed to have married on 27 October 1579. The resulting story-line indicates that Colin may have died of unrequited love, but that Edmund married the woman whom he loved. Harvey is at his most attractive in this personal interchange and seems to enjoy his persona as the sceptic about love. It is also interesting that Spenser's sweetheart seems to be involved in the interchange and has written a letter to Harvey.

First, Spenser to Harvey, 15–16 October 1579 with an enclosed Latin poem dated 5 October 1579. Spenser states that he was reluctant to dedicate the *Shepheardes Calender* to an august personage because it was 'made in Honour of a priuate Personage vnknowne' (Rosalind, G3r). In his Latin poem Spenser contrasts Harvey's pursuit of the highest honours with his own willingness to yield himself to love. 'Nor, by your leave, may you, the Great Cato of our age, win the sacred name of honoured poet, however nobly you sing or however lofty be your song, unless you yield yourself to folly – the world is so full of fools!'[22]

Second, Harvey to Spenser, 23 October 1579: Harvey turns to Latin for personal comments and scolds Spenser for living in the service of Cupid. He says that Ovid's *Art of Love* was renamed the 'Art of Lying' and adds that he will never stop berating Spenser until he has rid him of this 'yonkerly, and womanly' humour (J1v).

Third, Spenser to Harvey, 2 April 1580: again, using Latin for his personal references, Spenser assures Harvey that his sweetheart ('Meum Corculum') commends herself to Harvey and wonders why he has not answered her letter. Let Harvey beware lest his neglect become a capital offence for him in her eyes as it surely will be for Spenser himself (A4r–v).

Fourth, Harvey's letter to Spenser dated 23 April 1580: Harvey compliments Spenser by borrowing an epithet from Rosalind:

> and perhappes it will aduaunce the wynges of your Imagination a degree higher: at the least if any thing can be added to the loftinesse of his conceite, whom gentle *Mistresse Rosalinde*, once reported to haue all the *Intelligences* at commaundement, and an other time, Christened her, *Segnior Pegaso*. (E1v–E2)

This passage playfully suggests that '*Mistresse Rosalinde*' – though indifferent to Colin Clout – has a warm appreciation of Edmund Spenser. At this letter's conclusion, Harvey again turns to Latin for his personal comments:

> *Sed amàbo te, ad Corculi tui delicatissimas Literas, propediem, quam potero, accuratissimè: tot interim illam exquisitissimis salutibus, atque salutationibus impertiens, quot habet in Capitulo, capillos semiaureos, semiargenteos, semigemmeos. Quid quaeris?* (G1r)
>
> [But blessings on you! I shall reply to your sweetheart's letter in the very first day I can with care. Meanwhile convey to her as many exquisite greetings and salutations as she has hairs, half-gold, half silver, half gemmy on her little head.]

Harvey, after promising an immediate reply to the charming letter from Spenser's sweetheart, salutes her with as many warm wishes as she has hairs on her head. Significantly, he adds a salutation to her as Spenser's wife.

> *Per tuam Venerem altera Rosalindula est: eamque non alter, sed idem ille (tua, ut ante, bona cum gratia), copiosè amat Hobbinolus. O mea Domina Immerito, mea bellisima Collina Clouta, multo plus plurimùm salue, atque vale.* (G1r)
>
> [By your own Venus, she is another little Rosalind: and not another, but the very same old Hobbinol loves her (as before, with your kind leave) with all his heart. O my lady Immerito, my most beautiful Collina Clouta, good-better-best-bye, and farewell.]

Identifying himself as Hobbinol, Harvey assures 'my lady Immerito, my most beautiful Collina Clouta' that – with Spenser's leave – he indeed loves her. This banter depicts Harvey as a friend of Spenser's wife as well as of Spenser.

Douglas Hamer seems to have been the first to suggest that Harvey's reference to Spenser's sweetheart was an allusion to his first wife, and he made this suggestion prior to the discovery of a possible marriage record.[23] This identification has been elaborated more recently by Andrew Hadfield, who, I think, satisfactorily settles the question of Rosalind's identity. Hadfield identifies Machabyas Chylde as Rosalind in the *Shepheardes Calender* and Elizabeth Boyle, Spenser's second wife, as Rosalind in *Colin Clouts Come Home Againe* with some deferential nods in the direction of Queen Elizabeth in the *Faerie Queene*.[24] This identification of Machabyas Chylde as Rosalind locates Spenser's sweetheart in London and makes it even more likely that, after leaving Pembroke College in 1574, Spenser was employed in London by John Young.

Notes

1. For a recent article summarizing and commenting on earlier discussions, see D. Allen Carroll, 'The Meaning of E.K.', *Spenser Studies*, 20 (2005), 169–82.
2. Grosart thought that E.K. was Edward Kirke, who entered Pembroke in 1571 as a sizar and then moved to Caius College where he graduated B.A. in 1575 and M.A. in 1578. He took holy orders and became rector at Risby in Suffolk on 26 May 1580.
3. For an argument that Spenser is E.K., see Louise Schleiner, 'Spenser's "E.K." as Edmund Kent (Kenned/ of Kent): Kyth (Couth), Kissed, and Kunning-Conning', *English Literary Renaissance*, 20 (1990), 374–407; more generally, see David R. Shore's excellent summary article in the *Spenser Encyclopedia*, 231; for background, see Evelyn Tribble, 'Glozing the Gap: Authority, Glossing Traditions and *The Shepheardes Calender*', *Criticism*, 34 (1992), 155–72.
4. S.K. Heninger Jr, 'The Typographical Layout of Spenser's *Shepheardes Calender*', in *Word and Visual Imagination*, ed. Karl Josef Holtgen and Peter M. Daly (Erlangen: University of Erlangen Press, 1988), 45–51.
5. As Michael McCanles suggested in 'The *Shepheardes Calender* as Document and Monument', *Studies in English Literature*, 22 (1982), 2: 'It is part of the fiction of *The Shepheardes Calender* that E.K.'s glosses and commentary are not part of the fiction'.
6. Skelton describes skeltonics as follows: 'For though my ryme be ragged, / Tattered and iagged, / Rudeley rayne beaten, / Rusty and moughte eaten, / If ye take well therwith, / It hath in it some pyth' (53–8).
7. The name Colin may be borrowed from Marot's *De Madame Loyse de Savoye*. For discussion of French influences, see Anne Lake Prescott, *French Poets and the English Renaissance: Studies in Fame and Transformation* (New Haven: Yale University Press, 1978).
8. Jack Stillinger, 'A Note on the Printing of E.K.'s Glosses', *Studies in Bibliography*, 14 (1961), 203–5.
9. For the view that these passages could have antagonized Leicester, see Hadfield, *Life*, 149, 127–8.
10. While Spenser never seems to have considered Dyer as a dedicatee, there is evidence in his *Letter-Book* that Harvey did, suggesting that this passage may be Harvey's interpolation.

11 William A. Ringler, Jr, 'Spenser, Shakespeare, Honor, and Worship', *Renaissance News*, 14 (1961), 159–61.
12 Sir Philip Sidney, *Defence of Poetry*, in *Miscellaneous Prose of Sir Philip Sidney*, ed. Katherine Duncan-Jones and Jan Van Dorsten (Oxford: Clarendon Press, 1973), 112.
13 For sceptical views of the stigma of print, see Steven W. May, 'Tudor Aristocrats and the Mythical Stigma of Print', *Renaissance Papers*, 10 (1980), 11–18, and my 'Manuscript Culture Revisited', *Sidney Journal*, 17 (1999), 19–30.
14 For E.K.'s role in obfuscating interpretation, see Sherri Gellar, 'You Can't Tell a Book by Its Contents: (Mis)Interpretation in/of Spenser's *The Shepheardes Calender*', *Spenser Studies*, 13 (1999), 21–55.
15 George Whetstone, *Sir Phillip Sidney, his honorable life, his valiant death, and true virtues* (London: Thomas Cadman, 1587), A3v. RB 14643. The printer seems to have been more than a silent partner because he prints a separate dedication to the Earl of Warwick.
16 *Elizabethan Critical Essays*, ed. G. Gregory Smith, 2 vols (Oxford: Clarendon Press, 1904), 1: 65.
17 *Elizabethan Critical Essays*, ed. Smith, 1: 245.
18 For more discussion, see Jonathan Goldberg, *Sodometries: Renaissance Texts, Modern Sexualities* (Stanford: Stanford University Press, 1992), and 'Colin to Hobbinol: Spenser's *Familiar Letters*', *South Atlantic Quarterly*, 88 (1989), 107–26. See also Bruce R. Smith, *Homosexual Desire in Shakespeare's England* (1991; Chicago: University of Chicago Press, rev. ed.1994).
19 For background on Spenser and Vergil, see David Wilson-Okamura, 'Problems in the Virgilian Career', *Spenser Studies*, 26 (2011), 1–30.
20 For analysis, see Margaret Tudeau-Clayton, *Jonson, Shakespeare and Early Modern Virgil* (Cambridge: Cambridge University Press, 2006), 73.
21 Harvey is very clearly satirized as heterosexual by Thomas Nashe, who describes him as maladroit in his pursuit of women, and also by the authors of *Pedantius*, who portray him as in love, but fault him for addressing academic poems to his mistress.
22 McCabe, Spenser, *Shorter Poems*, 577. I use this translation to supplement my own as well as one provided by John A. Quitslund.
23 Douglas Hamer, 'Spenser's Marriage', *Review of English Studies*, 7 (1931), 271–90. On the discovery of a likely marriage record, see Mark Eccles, 'Spenser's First Marriage', *Times Literary Supplement*, 31 December 1931, 1053.
24 Andrew Hadfield, 'Spenser's Rosalind', *Modern Language Review*, 104, No. 4 (2009), 935–46.

9

Familiar Letters (1580)

Two men, Gabriel Harvey and Thomas Nashe, are in a position to determine what we think of Edmund Spenser – his personality and his standing with his contemporaries. For the most part, Harvey's portrait of Spenser as his admiring disciple has been accepted. Even though Nashe questions these views of Spenser, Harvey, and their correspondence, he has been ignored. The text and authorship of *Familiar Letters*, however, are crucial to our understanding of the early Spenser.

Text of *Familiar Letters* (1580)

Familiar Letters appeared as a quarto volume with a title page advertising its themes as 'the Earthquake in Aprill last, and our English refourmed Versifying'. In the first set of three letters, the first letter is by Spenser and the next two are by Harvey. These three letters are dated from 2 April to 23 April 1580; the second set is dated from 5 October to 23 October 1579. Scholars consulting the *Spenser Variorum* or Grosart's edition of Harvey are looking at a very different text from the original 1580 publication. Grosart and the editors of the *Spenser Variorum* ignore the format of the actual text, reorganize the letters into chronological order, and discuss them according to this imposed chronology rather than in the order in which they were printed. This 'reordering' gives Spenser's Latin poem *Ad Ornatissimum virum, multis iamdiu nominibus clarissimum, G.H. Immerito sui, mox in Gallias nauigaturi* a prominence that it was not accorded in the original text.

Spenserian editors have been reluctant to acknowledge that, in every substantive respect, Harvey is the principal author of *Familiar Letters*. The book contains 20,277 words. Thomas Nashe accused Harvey of having written 'Well-Willer's Preface' (545 words) and even offers the testimony of the compositor. Including 'Well-Willer's Preface', Harvey's total word count is 16,844 or 83 per cent; excluding the Preface, Harvey's word count is 16,299 or 80 per cent. Spenser's word count is 3,433 or 17 per cent. Spenser's letters serve largely as the frame and justification for Gabriel Harvey's rhetorical display.

The following outline suggests the organization, some of the main topics, and relative length of the items included in *Familiar Letters*: this outline also identifies the format I will use in referring to these texts.

PART I: Letters 1–3. 2 April 1580 – 23 April 1580

Well-Willer's 'Preface' dated 19 June 1580 (545 words). The correspondence is introduced by a preface claiming that the correspondence was copied out 'at Immeritos handes' and lauding Harvey's contributions to the text (A2r).

I.1. Spenser's letter to Harvey from Westminster, 2 April 1580 (1,043 words). This letter serves as an introduction to Harvey's discourse on the earthquake that will occur four days later and to his lecture on quantitative verse. Spenser's letter is internally dated 2 April 1580, but a reference to the earthquake occurring on 6 April has been inserted into the text. The text was thus edited, presumably by Harvey, but the date given for the letter in its entirety was not corrected.

I.2. Harvey's letter to Spenser from Saffron Walden, 7 April 1580 (7,477 words). Harvey offers a discourse on the 6 April earthquake. The earthquake occurred near Easter, making it susceptible to interpretation as an omen of God, and it inspired Abraham Fleming, Thomas Churchyard, and a number of Harvey's contemporaries to commemorate it with pamphlets and ballads. Harvey's discourse on the earthquake also includes criticism of the state of learning at Cambridge and a bitter invective on Andrew Perne, the first of several attacks in subsequent publications.

I.3. Harvey's second letter to Spenser from Saffron Walden, 23 April 1580 (6,220 words). Harvey delivers a lecture on quantitative verse, presumably to set Immerito straight on English prosody. There are allusions to Spenser's service with Bishop John Young and to his marriage, which may have occurred over six months earlier on 27 October 1579. This letter may contain a satire on the Earl of Oxford entitled *Speculum Tuscanismi* and concludes *Nosti manum & stylum*.

The above letter dated 23 April 1580 is followed by a separate title page announcing the addition of *Two Other Very Commendable Letters, of the Same Mens Writing*. The letters in the second set were reportedly written in October 1579 at the height of the controversy over the French match. We are given no explanation of why the letters written in spring 1580 are printed before the letters written in autumn 1579.

Part II: Letters 1–2. 5 October 1579 – 23 October 1579

II.1. This letter of Spenser's is his major contribution to *Familiar Letters*. His letter to Harvey is written partly from Leicester House on 5 October 1579 and partly from Westminster and 'Mystresse Kerkes' on 15–16 October 1579 (2,390 words). This letter includes Spenser's *Iambicum Trimetrum* and his Latin poem *Ad Ornatissimum virum, multis iamdiu nominibus clarissimum, G.H. Immerito sui, mox in Gallias nauigaturi*. In the poem Spenser portrays himself as vulnerable to love in contrast to Harvey, who is willing to sacrifice the sweets of life to his ambition to succeed as a public figure. At line 111 the reference to 'Edmundus' is a clue to Spenser's identity. This passage may have erotic undertones. On 16 October 1579, Immerito is preparing for a trip abroad in his 'Honours service'; according to life records, Spenser was to marry his first wife eleven days later on 27 October 1579.

II.2. Harvey's reply from Trinity Hall, Cambridge, 23 October 1579 (2,602 words). Harvey disputes the desirability of following Drant's ('your gorbellied master's') rules for quantitative verse. He mentions the possibility that he may be resident for a year or two in Italy and doubts that Spenser will go overseas in the next week or the following week.

As is clear from this outline, the sets of letters were printed in reverse chronological order. If, in fact, the letters dated 1579 in the second section are omitted, *Familiar Letters* has little or no relevance to Edmund Spenser.

Printing the 1580 letters first emphasizes Harvey's 7 April letter on the earthquake, and this departure from chronology also made it possible to introduce Harvey as an authority on verse and versification in the third letter of the first set. It is extremely significant that both of the topics featured in Harvey's 1580 letters are also emphasized on the title page of *Familiar Letters*, where the subject matter is identified as 'the earthquake in Aprill last' and 'our English reformed versifying'. Bibliographical facts thus reinforce the textual evidence that the letters were deliberately arranged in reverse chronological order to heighten the impact of Harvey's work.

Harvey had a specific objective in printing *Familiar Letters*; he wanted to display and advertise his rhetorical talents as a means of securing the position of University Orator at Cambridge. To stress his appearance of disinterest, he embellished a fiction that he had already rehearsed in his *Letter-Book*, that is, that someone without his knowledge had printed his work. In the text of *Familiar Letters*, we are told that it was Edmund Spenser who copied out the correspondence for a 'faithfull friende' of Well-willer's who was then responsible for handing the letters to the printer. This story changes in Harvey's *Foure Letters* (1592). Virginia Stern, Harvey's sympathetic biographer, however, accepts Harvey's version of the story at face value and offers the following hypothetical scenario: She notes that E.K. in the *Shepheardes Calender* had urged Harvey to 'pluck out of the hateful darknesse, those so many English poemes of yours, which lye hid, and bring them forth to eternall light' (*Epistle*, 30–1). She then speculates that E.K. and Spenser approached Spenser's printer, Hugh Singleton, but this effort to print the correspondence with Spenser's printer fell through and so Spenser, 'in the spring of 1580, approached Harvey's printer, Henry Bynneman, with the timely earthquake letter and Harvey's letter and poems related to the new quantitative verse' (61). This is her explanation of how *Familiar Letters* came to be printed in 1580 by Harvey's printer, but there is evidence in Harvey's *Letter-Book* and his other publications that Harvey himself was responsible for publishing the correspondence.

In *Familiar Letters*, Harvey addresses Spenser as 'Signor Immerito', using the Italian 'Signor' perhaps to allude to a mission to Italy that Spenser would like to take, has taken, or may undertake at some time in the future.[1] The epithet 'Immerito' is the name that Spenser applies to himself in 'To His Book', the proem that introduces the *Shepheardes Calender*, and this pseudonym, like that of Colin Clout, emphasizes his unworthiness. In his *Letter-Book*, Harvey offers to explain his use of the name Immerito for Spenser, but characteristically says that it must be kept secret: 'And heare will I take occasion to shewe you a peece of a letter that I lately receyvid from Courte written by a frende of mine, that since a certayn chaunce befallen unto him, a secrett not to be revealid, calleth himself Immerito'.[2] In the Epistle to the *Shepheardes Calender* and in *Familiar Letters*, we find extravagant praise of Master Gabriel Harvey in contrast to the portrayal of Spenser as his subordinate.

Agency, authorship, and audience

Most assumptions about the personality and ambitions of the early Spenser are based on *Familiar Letters*. For this reason, its biographical importance would be difficult to overstate. Jon Quitslund and, later, Andrew Hadfield reached a consensus that, to cite Quitslund first, the letters were aimed at catching the attention of 'those in positions of authority who recognized the utility of university-trained eloquence and the value of men who could already claim to be well connected' (87).[3] Hadfield elaborates as follows:

> The correspondence can be read to indicate that the writers are for hire to a prospective patron, showcasing their skills as letter writers whose achievements go beyond anything contained in one of the many letter-writing manuals freely available at the time.[4] (Hadfield, *Life*, 151)

Since Harvey wrote 80 to 83 per cent of the text (Spenser only 17 per cent), it may be an overstatement to conclude that Spenser was involved in 'the planning and production of the volume' (149).

In fact, the audience of *Familiar Letters* does not seem to be 'those in positions of authority' or 'prospective patrons'. The text of *Familiar Letters* lauds Harvey's achievements and relegates Spenser to a subsidiary role because it is designed to promote Harvey's candidacy for the position of University Orator at Cambridge. If we look closely at this text, Well-Willer introduces the correspondence by saying that Spenser's prose is promising and that it gives some hope of 'good mettall in the Author' (A2r). Well-Willer then proceeds to laud Harvey's unpublished letters, assuring us that he has 'written manye of the same stampe bothe to Courtiers and others, and some of them discoursing vppon matter of great weight and importance, wherein he is said, to be fully as sufficient and hable, as in *these schollerly pointes of Learning*' [italics mine].

The point clearly made is that *Familiar Letters* is intended as a scholarly production, 'these schollerly pointes of learning', that is, the science of earthquakes and prosody, in contrast to works of 'great weight and importance' which might attract an audience of courtiers, diplomats, or non-academic patrons. In short, this text is intended to address Harvey's academic audience, who, in contrast to courtiers or those in authority, might be interested in 'schollerly pointes of learning'. In a passage that Thomas Nashe accuses Harvey of writing, Well-Willer goes on to celebrate Harvey's contributions, as 'twoo of the rarest and finest Treaties, as wel for ingenious deuising, as also for signifcant vttering, & cleanly conueying of his matter, that euer I read in this Tongue' (A2r).

The conclusion that Spenser participated in planning and producing *Familiar Letters* is crucial to our understanding of the early Spenser, and so it is useful to review arguments that these letters should be considered Harvey's, not Spenser's, publication. *Familiar Letters* has received, paradoxically, too little and too much attention. The *Spenser Variorum* illustrates the desire to minimize the importance of *Familiar Letters*: Spenser's letters are reordered by date and Harvey's letters are relegated to an appendix. On the other hand, the correspondence has been embraced by those eager to enlarge Spenser's canon, most of whom treat the correspondence as if it had been printed and authorized by Edmund Spenser. To illustrate this approach, the printed version of the *Short Title Catalogue* (1976) lists the correspondence entirely under Spenser's name and merely cross-lists the publication under Harvey.[5] Gabriel Harvey, however, is the principal author of *Familiar Letters* and, from the perspective of more than one of Harvey's contemporaries, its editor.[6] The attribution of this correspondence to Spenser, rather than Harvey, has contributed to the misconception that Spenser was a carbon copy of Harvey and that he, like Harvey, aspired to a career at court and was prone to self-advertisement. Spenser, however, as will be demonstrated below in the discussion of personal circumstances, had already achieved preferment before *Familiar Letters* was entered in the Stationers' Register on 30 June 1580.

There is evidence, including, first, the printer, second, contemporary critique by Nashe, third, style, fourth, related passages from Harvey's *Letter-Book*, and, fifth, personal circumstances of the two men, to question the practice of considering Spenser to be a co-author of *Familiar Letters*. The printer of *Familiar Letters*, significantly, was Henry Bynneman, and Bynneman had previously printed four works by Harvey. He had printed Harvey's lectures on rhetoric, *Rhetor* (November 1577) and *Ciceronianus* (June 1577), and he had printed the memorial to Sir Thomas Smith, *Smithus; vel Musarum Lachrymae* (January 1578) and *Gratulationes Valdinenses* (September 1578), describing the Queen's progress to Cambridge. Bynneman, however, had never published or printed anything by Spenser, nor was he ever to do so. Spenser's

Shepheardes Calender was printed by Hugh Singleton and then re-entered to James Harrison in a very short period of time. From the perspective of the author's relationship to the printer, Harvey's relationship to Bynneman should be considered the authorizing relationship for this publication.

Nashe on the authorship question

Familiar Letters is preceded by a Preface addressed to the 'CURTEOUS BUYER' by a 'Welwiller of the two Authours'. Though no one has previously called attention to this, I think it relevant that in his *Letter-Book* Harvey creates a figure named Benvolio, that is, 'well willer'. In *Familiar Letters*, Well-Willer tells us that he became aware of the letters through a 'faithfull friende', 'who with muche entreaty had procured the copying of them oute, at *Immeritos* [Spenser's] handes' (A2r). Even though Spenser is pointedly implicated in preparing the letters for the press, Well-Willer dismisses the first letter by Spenser as promising, a letter that gives some hope of 'good mettall in the Author' (A2r). Well-Willer then gets down to business and in the lavish tone of E.K.'s Epistle to the *Shepheardes Calender* extols the extraordinary genius of Gabriel Harvey: 'But shewe me, or Immerito, two Englyshe Letters in Printe, in all pointes equall to the other twoo, both for the matter it selfe, and also for the manner of handling, and saye, wee neuer sawe good Englishe Letter in our liues' (A2r). Well-Willer also strikes a familiar note by telling us that Harvey has many unpublished letters that are literary masterpieces: 'And yet I am credibly certified ... that himselfe hathe written manye of the same stampe bothe to Courtiers and others, and some of them discoursing vppon matter of great waight and importance' (A2r). After these tributes to Harvey, Well-Willer concludes by expressing some reservation about the idea of publishing 'familiar' letters, stating that the letters might be more 'curious' if the two men had published the letters themselves, but then assures the reader that the authors were not 'priuy to the Publication' (A2v).

Spenser's contemporary Thomas Nashe was convinced that Harvey, not Spenser, was responsible for the publication of *Familiar Letters*. In 1592 he published a reply to Harvey's *Familiar Letters* and a detailed answer to Harvey's *Foure Letters*. Nashe's reply is printed as the wonderfully titled *Strange Newes, of the intercepting certaine Letters, a Conuoy of Verses, as they were going Priuilie to victuall the Lowe Countries*. Although

Nashe is at some pains to respond to Harvey's mean-spirited portrayal of Robert Greene on his deathbed, he also supplies a new explanation of why Spenser is called Immerito:

> Signior Immerito (so called because *he was and is his friend* vndeseruedly) was counterfeitly brought in to play a part in this his Enterlude of Epistles that was hist at, thinking his very name (as the name of *Ned Allen* on the common stage) was able to make an ill matter good. (Nashe, 1: 295–6)

Nashe accuses Harvey of having written Well-Willer's Preface 'To the Curteovs Buyer', and unequivocally rejects the notion that Spenser had anything to do with publishing the letters:

> I durst on my credit vndertake, *Spencer* was no way priuie to the committing of them to the print. Committing I may well call it, for in my opinion G.H. should not haue reapt so much discredite by beeing committed to Newgate, as by committing that misbeleeuing prose to the Presse. (Nashe, I:296)

Nashe thinks that Harvey wrote the exorbitant praise of his own style, which he quotes verbatim from Well-Willer's Preface and then comments:

> but for an Author to renounce his Christendome to write in his owne commendation, to refuse the name which his Godfathers and Godmothers gaue him in his baptisme and call himselfe *a welwiller to both the writers*, when hee is the onely writer himself.[7] (1: 296)

If there were any possibility that Spenser, rather than Harvey, authored Well-Willer's Preface, then Harvey should have been able to prove that Nashe was wrong, and it seems likely that he would have done so publicly. All of the players in what Nashe describes as this 'interlude' were alive and well in London in 1592–93 – except Spenser, who was probably in Ireland. Nashe also hints suggestively that Harvey has edited what finally appeared as *Familiar Letters* to enhance the impact of his own work.

Harvey's style

In his Preface, Well-Willer uses precisely Harvey's syntax and diction when he compliments the 'Author' for using his 'pleasaunte, and witty Talente with so muche discretion and with so little harme, contrarye to the veine of moste, which haue thys singular conceyted grace in writing'

(A2r–v). The phrase 'singular conceyted grace' offers an apt description of the effect that Harvey is seeking. He is accustomed to expressing himself in Latin, a language governed by a case grammar. His syntax makes use of numerous complicated interpolated clauses that work efficiently in Latin, but less effectively in English.

> A moste excellent sounde Iudgement in my conceit: and ful wel beseeming so Honorable and admirable a Witte, as out of Question, *Picus Mirandula* had: who being yet scarcely thirty yeres of age, for his singularitie in al kind of knowleege, as wel diuine and prophane, was in Italy and France, as *Paulus Iouius* reporteth, surnamed *Phoenix*, as the odde, and in effecte the onely singular learned man of Europe. (I.2, D1r–v)

Except for a few colloquial expressions, such as his fondness for 'yonkerly', Harvey's diction is Latinate. Because he is consciously seeking for a 'conceited' effect, he is consistently verbose, supplying alternative wordings for the same statement.

Turning to a somewhat more vexed stylistic question, did Harvey edit Spenser's letters? The answer has to be yes because Spenser's first letter is dated 2 April 1580, but there is an internal allusion to an earthquake which will occur on 6 April, four days later. As observed above, I assume that Harvey edited the letter, inserting the reference to the earthquake, but neglected to correct the letter's date. There are other passages in letters attributed to Spenser that seem to contradict his persona as Immerito or to connect thematically more with Harvey than Spenser.

Spenserians have coined the term 'lost works' to deal with the unpublished works discussed in *Familiar Letters*, in *Shepheardes Calender*, and in the printer's note to the *Complaints*. The idea of numerous 'lost' or unpublished works, however, seems to originate with Harvey, whose *Anticosmopolita* was entered in the Stationers' Register on 30 June 1579, but never printed. E.K. mentions *Anticosmopolita* in the Gloss to *September* of the *Shepheardes Calender*, where he tells us that Hobbinol, 'more rightly Mayster Gabriel Haruey', is the author of numerous unpublished works:

> most rare and very notable writings, partely vnder vnknown Tytles, partly vnder counterfayt names, as hys *Tyrannomastix*, his Ode Natalitia, his *Rameidos*, and especially that parte of *Philomusus*, his diuine *Anticosmopolita*, and diuers other of lyke importance. (*September*, p. 176)

Anticosmopolita is also mentioned in *Familiar Letters*, but, even though it was entered in the Stationers' Register prior to the entering of the *Shepheardes Calender*, this text never seems to have seen the light of day.

Harvey's references to these and other unpublished works were not just a youthful pose. Almost twenty years later, in a letter to Sir Robert Cecil on 8 May 1598, he lists his 'sundry royall Cantos (nigh as much in quantitie, as Ariosto) in celebration of her Maiesties most prosperous and in truth glorious gouernement' and also of 'manie other Traicts and Discourses, sum in Latin, sum in Inglish, sum in verse according to the occasion, but much more in prose'.[8] As a climax to this description of his many unpublished works, he tells Cecil: 'I speak it not anyway to boste (that loath the follie of any such vanity) but to certifie ye truth. For I can in one year publish more, then anie Inglishman hath hitherto dun' (I: xxvii).

In the Postscripte to Spenser's 2 April 1580 letter, we find references to 'Dreames' which may possibly allude to *A Theatre for Worldlings* or to the 'Visions' later appearing in *Complaints*. Still, the repetitive antithesis of 'amende the best, nor reprehende the worst' is more characteristic of Harvey's style than Spenser's.

> Postscripte
> I take best my *Dreames* shoulde come forth alone, being grown by meanes of the Glosse (running continually in maner of a Paraphrase) full as great as my *Calendar*. Therin be some things excellently, and many things wittily discoursed of *E.K.* and the Pictures so singularly set forth, and purtrayed, as if *Michael Angelo* were there, he could (I think) nor amende the best, nor reprehende the worst. I know you woulde lyke them passing wel. (I.1, A4v)

It is also uncharacteristic of Immerito, Spenser's modest persona, to assert that his work includes 'Pictures so singularly set forth' that 'Michael Angelo' could not improve upon them. This kind of hyperbole bears the hallmark of Master G.H.

Unfortunately, stylistic evidence can never be conclusive; only the recovery of holograph evidence would be decisive. Fortunately, it seems likely that Harvey was so confident of his rhetorical ability that his emendation of Spenser's texts may have been minimal. These stylistic considerations, combined with bibliographical facts, such as the date and publisher, suggest that the texts included in *Familiar Letters* should be critically revisited.[9]

Harvey and the epistolary genre

As discussed in Chapter 5 above, we know that Harvey practised writing letters for publication because these stylistic experiments have survived in MS Sloane 93, the collection described as Harvey's *Letter-Book*.[10] The *Letter-Book* contains material related to *Familiar Letters* and supplies a few passages that appear with minimal revision in the 1580 publication. In a strict sense, this collection is a notebook as well as a copybook of letters that may have been sent. And, in this collection, Harvey repeatedly rehearses a scenario in which Spenser (Immerito or Benevolio) publishes Harvey's work without his permission. For example, in a letter addressed to Signor Benevolio (a rough translation of 'Well-Willer'), Harvey carries on about his chagrin when his work is published without his permission:

> Behoulde what millions of thankes I recounte unto you, and behoulde how highly I esteeme of your good Mastershipps overbarish and excessive curtesy, first in publishing abroad in prynte to the use or rather abuse of others, and now in bestowing uppon myselfe a misshapin illfavorid freshe copy of my precious poems, as it were a pigg of myne owne sowe ... It is Italian curtesye to give a man leave to bee his own carver ... What greater and more odious infamye for on of my standinge in the Universitye and profession abroad then to be reckonid in the Beaderoule of Inglish Rimers ... Canst thou tell me or doist thou nowe begin to imagin with thyselfe what a wunderfull and exceedinge displeasure thou and thy Prynter have wroughte me? (58–60)

Later, in what may be a section of the *Letter-Book* focused on dissuading Spenser from valuing the vernacular, Harvey addresses Spenser in full as both 'Immerito' and 'Benevolio': 'Il Magnifico Segnior Immerito, Benivolo' (66) and repeats the accusation that Spenser has published his work without his permission:

> And canst thou tell me nowe, or doist thou at the last begin to imagin with thy selfe what a wonderfull and exceeding displeasure thou and thy prynter have wroughte me, and howe peremptorily ye have preiudishd my good name for ever in thrustinge me thus on the stage to make tryall of my extemporall faculty, and to play Wylsons or Tarletons parte. (67)

In these fictional scenarios, Harvey visits and revisits a situation in which Spenser–Immerito–Benevolio and his 'printer' publish Harvey's works without his permission – roughly the circumstances in which Well-Willer tells us that *Familiar Letters* came to be made public.

Harvey may not have intended to harm Spenser by publishing *Familiar Letters* (1580) and, in fact, may have thought that he was promoting him.

Spenser, who probably understood Harvey and his motivation, may have appreciated the irony of what happened after the publication. Even a very cursory reading of Harvey's *Letter-Book* makes it clear that Harvey thought that his contributions to *Familiar Letters* were likely to be an immense success. Just a little more than a month after *Familiar Letters* was entered in the Stationers' Register, we know from Harvey's *Letter-Book* that he was planning a follow-up publication. Telling psychological evidence is found on folio 48v where he revised the precise title page that he planned to use for this follow-up publication.

The title page for this projected publication was originally dated 1 March 1580 but was revised to read 1 August 1580. Harvey made this revision subsequent to his delivery of *Familiar Letters* to Henry Bynneman on 30 June 1580. The dedicatee of this second publication is to be 'Maister Edwarde Diar, / In a manner oure onlye Inglish Poett. / In honour of rare Qualityes, / And noble vertues. / *Quodvultdeus* Benevolo' (89). This work is commended by J.W. (possibly John Wood, nephew of Sir Thomas Smith) and described as an 'Edition of his frendes / Verlayes: togither with certayne other / Of his poeticall devises; / And in steade of A Dedicatorie Epistle, / Praesentith himself, and the uttermost / Of his habilitye and value / To his good worshippes / Curtuous, and favorable likinge'. This first of August, 1580.[11] Harvey's revised title page in his *Letter-Book* demonstrates the strength of his investment in *Familiar Letters*, and the timing of the revision reveals his conviction that the publication would be a success.

Personal circumstances

In 1580, faced with the possible defeat of his campaign to become University Orator, Harvey seems to have rushed *Familiar Letters* into print to demonstrate his rhetorical prowess, but he seriously misjudged the impact that his rhetorical *tour de force* was to have on his Cambridge audience. In this strange and confused publication, Harvey attempted to call attention to his talents, and, as Nashe and other contemporaries recognized, Spenser was included in *Familiar Letters* principally to enhance Harvey's prestige.

By early 1580, but more likely before his marriage in October 1579, Spenser had become the client of the fourteenth Lord Grey, who had previously acted as the patron of the poet George Gascoigne. Grey would have known that the position of Lord Deputy of Ireland was not a sinecure and that he would need a hard-working, and above all loyal, personal secretary. And Grey, like anyone else, would have wanted to make sure that Spenser had those qualities well in advance of departing for Ireland.

Two passages in *Familiar Letters* seem to place Spenser in Grey's service at least as early as October 1579. Critics have assumed that all references to a lord or noble patron in the Harvey–Spenser correspondence must refer to the Earl of Leicester, but these passages relate more to Grey's circumstances than to those of Leicester in 1579 and 1580. In a letter dated 5 October 1579, Spenser writes:

> I beseeche you by all your Curtesies, and Graces, let me be answered, ere I goe: which will be (I hope, I feare, I thinke) the next weeke, if I can be dispatched of my Lorde. I goe thither, as sent by him, and maintained most [sic] what of him: and there am to employ my time, my body, my minde, to his Honours seruice. (II.1, H2v)

Scholars have too readily assumed that these are allusions to a mission to France or Italy which Spenser undertook in Leicester's service, but it is more likely that he is referring to a trip or trips across the Irish Sea for Lord Grey. On 23 October 1579 Harvey replied that he would wager all the books in his library 'that you shall not, I saye, bee gone over Sea, for al your saying, neither the next, nor the next week' (J1v). Grey had an old and honourable title, and he, like Leicester, was a peer and so would have been addressed as his 'Honour'. This reference to his 'Honours seruice' may refer to Grey, who we know employed Spenser, or to Leicester, who may conceivably have employed him – though this employment has never been documented.

In the same letter on 23 October 1579, Harvey addresses Spenser as 'Il Pellegrino', the traveller, and tells Spenser that he is preparing a lecture for his 'Lord'. In a passage that seems unambiguous, Harvey specifically mentions that Spenser's 'Lord' has received 'credite and preferment', but Leicester had received no recent preferment in October 1579. His marriage to Lettice, Countess of Essex, was still fresh in Elizabeth's mind, and she was actively involved in negotiating the French match and working out a proclamation that would threaten reprisals against any public opposition. The next passage almost certainly alludes to Grey's anticipated appointment as Lord Deputy:

> And, thinke you I will leaue my *Il Pellegrino* so? No I trowe. My Lords Honor, the expectation of his friendes, his owne credite and preferment, tell me, he muste haue a moste speciall care, and good regarde of employing his trauaile to the best. (II.2, J1v)

Commentators with one notable exception have merely assumed that Harvey must be discussing a trip undertaken by Spenser for Leicester.[12]

Some passages in *Familiar Letters* make sense *only* if we assume that Spenser and Harvey are discussing Lord Grey. In this same letter dated 23 October 1579 from Trinity Hall, Harvey includes a long passage discussing a lecture on Homer's Ulysses and Virgil's Aeneas that Harvey is planning to deliver to Spenser's patron:

> And therfore I am studying all this fortnight, to reade him suche a Lecture in *Homers Odysses*, and *Virgils Æneads*, that I dare undertake he shall not neede any further instruction, in *Maister Turlers Trauayler*, or *Maister Zuingers Methodus Apodemica*: but in his whole trauaile abroad, and euer after at home, shall shewe himselfe a verie liuelye and absolute picture of *Ulysses* and *Æneas*. (II.2, J1v–J2r)

These light-hearted allusions are appropriate to Grey, who, like Ulysses, will explore foreign places, and, like Aeneas, will be occupied with empire building in Ireland. In the same section, Harvey hopes that Spenser's patron will have the guidance of Minerva and Venus and so have the 'the pollitique head, and wise gouernement of the one: and the amiable behauiour, and gratious courtesie of the other: the two verye principall, and moste singular Companions, of a right Trauailer' (J2r).

These comments could apply to Leicester only if we ignore chronology. Five or six years later, in 1585, Leicester was to set out for the Netherlands, but these comments are irrelevant to Leicester's circumstances in 1579. This letter was supposedly written on 23 October 1579, and it cannot have been written after 1580 when *Familiar Letters* was printed. Harvey's references to Leicester as either Ulysses or Aeneas would be singularly irrelevant to Leicester's circumstances in October 1579 at the height of the controversy over Elizabeth's marriage to Anjou and at least five years before he is sent to the Netherlands.

Chronology: Spenser's preferment

Although Grey did not receive the official letter of appointment as Lord Deputy of Ireland until 15 July 1580, his appointment as Lord Deputy had been under consideration well before October 1579, the ostensible date of the first instalment of *Familiar Letters*. In determining the chronology of events, we have to examine rumours in official sources as well as official documents, particularly the suppositions and reports circulating among interested parties in Ireland. Also, when Grey temporizes about accepting the appointment or suggests that Elizabeth has changed her mind, we should assume that terms are being negotiated. The official letter would confirm an agreement that was reached much earlier.

There is evidence which supports the dates we are given in *Familiar Letters*. In Ireland, a number of officials continued to agitate for the return of Sir Henry Sidney; others supported the appointment of Sir William Pelham, Lord Justice, as Lord Deputy, but they were all aware of the possibility of Grey's receiving the appointment. Rumours about Grey circulated in Ireland weeks, perhaps months, before November 1579 when Irish officials began to write to members of the English Privy Council expressing their approval of Grey's appointment. Grey, of course, would have had to begin the process of organizing his expedition and providing supplies for his recruits well before June 1580 when *Familiar Letters* was entered in the Stationers' Register.

As early as 6 November 1579 Walsingham had written to Sir Nicholas Malby that Grey was being considered for the position of Lord Deputy.[13] By 28 November 1579, William Pelham, Lord Justice of Ireland, himself a possible candidate for the position of Lord Deputy, thought that it was politic to write to Walsingham that Grey would be a good choice.[14] Prior to February 1580, we know that it had been decided not to reappoint Sir Henry Sidney as Lord Deputy and send Philip as his deputy. We know this because on 8 February 1580 the Privy Council wrote to John Whitgift, then Bishop of Worcester and Sir Henry Sidney's deputy in Wales, saying that he should expect Sidney to arrive shortly. We also know that in early spring 1580 Lodowick Bryskett, who had been in England from June 1579 and was to remain there until January or February 1581, made a brief visit to Ireland.

It has seemed probable that Spenser preceded Grey to Ireland because a substantial salary payment of over £29 was made to Spenser on 20 September 1580 shortly after Grey arrived.[15] No one pays in advance, and this handsome payment is likely to have covered Spenser's service in Ireland prior to Grey's arrival. Since working this out, it has come to my attention that Nicholas Canny also thinks it likely that Spenser preceded Grey to Ireland. Canny outlines a scheme developed early in 1580 by Sir Henry Wallop, Sir Edward Waterhouse, and Sir William Pelham to deliver various counties in Munster, the estate of Viscount Barry, and the entire county of Kerry to members of the Leicester faction at the English court.[16] Fulke Greville was already in Ireland in early 1580, having sailed as captain of the *Foresight* to guard the Irish coast against the expected Spanish invasion. Pelham and Waterhouse conveyed Greville, who seems to have acted as the emissary of Leicester and Walsingham, by boat along the full length of the Shannon estuary from the ocean mouth at Mount Brandon to Limerick city so that he could see the Desmond estates that were likely to be forfeit to the Crown. Canny thinks it very likely that Spenser accompanied Greville on this trip. Citing *Faerie Queene*, IV.iii.27, he comments that only a first-hand acquaintance with this remarkable view could account for the vividness of Spenser's description of the collision between the river Shannon in full flood and the rising 'tide that comes from th' Ocean mayne'. Working independently, Canny and I have reached the same conclusion. My rationale for supporting an early trip to Ireland on Spenser's part involves the large sum that Grey paid Spenser after his arrival in 1580 and a lease. We know that some time in the spring of 1580 Spenser went to Ireland on Grey's business because during this visit he found time to locate a property in New Abbey that he wanted to lease for his family. The lease was dated the same day as Grey's orders.

Returning to the general issue of dating Grey's appointment, we know that at the very latest by 7 April 1580 Arthur Lord Grey's appointment as Lord Deputy had been discussed with Leicester's support.[17] Then, on 22 May 1580 Philip Sidney, who had known for at least three months that he and his father would not be returning to Ireland, wrote to Edward Denny and in his letter alludes to Grey's appointment as an accomplished fact: 'And very willingly doe I beare the preferringe of the noble Lord Gray, since so I preferre him to my selfe, as I will [be *crossed out*] ever be most glad to doe him service with affectionate honor, which truly I am but to very fewe' (2: 980). Sidney's statement 'to doe him service with affectionate honor' should not be glibly discounted as mere courtesy. He adds that he regards Grey with an esteem that he reserves 'to very fewe'. This warm assessment of Lord Grey, particularly in the preferment of him before Sidney's own father, is a significant tribute. In the next passage, Sidney seems eager to ensure that Denny will remain loyal to Grey even if his friend Denny might have preferred Sidney to be named Lord Deputy:

> And if you should doe otherwise in steade of thankinge you I should [doute *inserted*] you might in like sorte dispence with your selfe to sett me behinde some other of lesse bothe acqueitance & worthe. Honour him therefore still, and as you match me with him, for therein will I matche my selfe with you.[18]

Grey seems to have had a talent for enlisting the allegiance of idealistic young men; Lodowick Bryskett, Denny, Sidney, and Edmund Spenser respected him.[19]

Sidney then discusses a method of reading and recommends 'Sacroboscus Sphaere' to Denny:

> it shall be necessary for you to exercise your hande in setting downe what you reed, as in descriptions of battaillons, camps, and marches with some practise of Arithmetike, which sportingly you may exercise ... For historicall maters, I woold wish you before you began to reed a little of Sacroboscus Sphaere, & the Geography of some moderne writer, wherof there are many & is a very easy and delightful studdy. (982–3)

Virginia Stern has pointed out that Harvey wrote exactly Sidney's phrase, 'sportingly' around 1580 in his copy of Sacrobosco. On the title page of his Sacrobosco, Harvey wrote 'Arte, et virtute, 1580' and on sig. aiir: 'Sacrobosco, & Valerius, Sir Philip Sidneis two bookes for the Spheare. Bie him specially commended to the Earle of Essex, Sir Edward Dennie, & divers gentlemen of the Court. To be read with diligent studie, but sportingly, as he termed it' (79, n. 102). Stern thinks that when Harvey writes 'To be read with diligent studie, but sportingly, as he termed it', he is echoing a conversation with Sidney. It is perhaps more likely that Sidney's letter to Denny, like his letter of advice about travel addressed to his brother, circulated in manuscript.[20]

At the conclusion of the letter to Denny, Sidney comments that he has gone on much too long, but sends his regards to a person who 'hath my Lord Grayes company' and may be in Ireland or about to embark for Ireland: 'have I spent more lynes then I thought to have done words. but good will carries mee on this impudence to wish my councell to him, *that* (to say nothing of your selfe) hath my Lord Grayes company' (2: 985). James Osborn thought that this was an allusion to Spenser, but Duncan-Jones and others have been sceptical because it has been assumed that Spenser and Grey met just a week or so before Grey left for Ireland.[21]

Such a chronology is improbable for a number of reasons. It is predicated upon the notion that Leicester or the 'government' told Grey to hire Spenser. Lord Grey offered Spenser the position of serving as his personal secretary – just as Essex and Mountjoy were to select Henry Wotton and Fynes Morrison as their secretaries. Further, it is logical that Grey would have offered him the position of personal secretary only *after* he had tested Spenser's competence and loyalty. The position of Lord Deputy of Ireland was hardly a sinecure, and Grey could have ill afforded a disloyal or unreliable secretary. Given this revised chronology, it is likely that Osborn was correct and that Sidney is alluding to Spenser in this letter to Denny. This veiled reference to Spenser, like Sidney's allusion to Spenser in the *Defence of Poetry*, respects Spenser's desire for anonymity. Sidney's allusion to Spenser, however, accounts for why Harvey came to echo Sidney in marginalia in his copy of Sacrobosco. Since we know that Harvey and Spenser corresponded in 1579–80, Harvey is likely to have obtained a copy of Sidney's letter to Denny from Spenser and then made notes about it in his copy of Sacrobosco.

Sidney's reference to 'this impudence to wish my councell to him' has been interpreted as an allusion to class, which would rule out Spenser. Sidney, however, was willing to fight a duel with the higher-ranked Earl of Oxford over pushing him off a tennis court; he is unlikely to have been deferentially referring to someone with superior social status. It is more likely that Sidney was quick to recognize and to acknowledge the genius of Edmund Spenser. Whatever modern literary assessments of Sidney and Spenser may be, in terms of what Spenser had already achieved as a writer in 1580, it would have been appropriate for Sidney to defer to Spenser in May 1580. In 1580, from the perspective of Spenser's literary accomplishments, it could indeed be considered 'impudent' for Sidney to counsel Spenser, author of the *Shepheardes Calender*, as well as sections of the *Faerie Queene* and parts of *Mother Hubberds Tale*, on what books to read and how to read them. The author of the *Defence of Poetry* would not be likely to agree with Gabriel Harvey that the sections of the *Faerie Queene* existing in 1580 could be dismissed by saying that '*Hobgoblin*' has 'runne away with the Garland from Apollo'.

In addition, at least one document has survived which shows that Spenser preceded Grey to Ireland. Early in the *Calendar of Fiants* for Elizabeth's reign under 1580, we find a reference to a lease to New Abbey in County Kildare near Dublin, which was granted to Spenser under commission:

> Lease under commission 15 July to Ed. Spenser, gent.; of the site of the house of Friars called the New Abbey, co. Kildare, with the appurtenances; also an old waste town adjoining & its appurtenances, in the queen's disposition by the rebellion of James Eustace. To hold for 21 years. Rent £3.[22]

The circumstances are unclear, and the relevant documents, as will become a consistent refrain moving forward, were destroyed in the 1922 fire in the Irish Public Record Office, but this lease has exactly the same date as the official commission empowering Grey to serve as Lord Deputy. An Irish fiant resembles an English warrant; it serves as a record of an order to have the grant officially enrolled on the patent rolls, and, though I should specify that the patent for New Abbey was not officially enrolled until 24 August 1582, the lack of an official patent does not mean that Spenser could not have occupied New Abbey as soon as he arrived in Ireland. Nothing was official until a patent was enrolled, however, and this fact will later require us to revise estimates regarding Spenser's ownership of various properties.

Grey had received his instructions by mid-July, but he did not arrive in Dublin until 12 August 1580 aboard the *Handmaid*. In July and August 1580, even if Spenser returned to England to assist in arrangements to victual the army or to transport his wife, he would have been occupied with organizing the expedition and unlikely to have had the time – let alone *any* motivation – to collaborate with Harvey on the publication of *Familiar Letters*. Even if we ignore the chronology outlined above, in the summer of 1580 Spenser needed to impress his patron with his discretion and could not have afforded to engage in literary antics with a college friend. In June 1580, Harvey, on the other hand, was eager to establish his credentials as a rhetorician worthy of appointment as Public Orator at Cambridge.

Familiar Letters (1580) and *Foure Letters* (1592)

It was not until he published *Foure Letters* (1592) that Harvey revealed his motivation for having published *Familiar Letters* (1580). The 1580 publication with its discussion of learned topics, such as the science of earthquakes and academic prosody, was prompted by his ambition to become University Orator at Cambridge. Among the surviving documents that shed light on Harvey's campaign, we find correspondence with Lord Burghley. On 9 April 1579 Harvey wrote to Lord Burghley asking him for a recommendation for the post of University Orator.[23] Six months later, on 25 October 1579, Richard Bridgewater, then University Orator of Cambridge, wrote to Burghley announcing his resignation and saying that he would have submitted it earlier except that '*owing to the importunate ambition of certain persons who are contending about it, as though it were a matter of life and death*', he had withheld his formal resignation (p. 35). In 1579 Harvey was of those 'ambitious' people who were 'contending' as though the appointment were 'a matter of life and death'. At some point in this process, Harvey become convinced that Andrew Perne had done something to derail his campaign. On 14 June 1580, Harvey again wrote to Burghley to thank him for his recommendation and to remind him of his ambition to become University Orator.[24] Five days later, on 19 June 1580, Well-Willer's Preface was dated, and two weeks later, on 30 June 1580, *Familiar Letters* was entered in the Stationers' Register.[25]

The final decision about the position of University Orator was not reached until nearly nine months later in March 1581, when Anthony Wingfield received the appointment which Harvey coveted. No one, least of all Harvey, would have conceded failure eight months earlier. In fact, it is likely that Harvey wrote his 1580 letter of thanks to Burghley because he hoped that his letter to the chancellor would prompt Burghley to intervene more dramatically. This is precisely the kind of strategy that he had successfully used some years earlier to get John Young to intervene in the controversy over the award of his master's degree at Pembroke College. His tactlessness in disparaging the state of learning at Cambridge, even though he hoped to be named University Orator, is in keeping with earlier missteps. He was insensitive in *Rhetor* when he contrasted his own popularity as a lecturer with the 'barren benches' to which his senior colleagues were obliged to lecture.

Pedantius

Familiar Letters did not work the magic that Harvey had hoped. Just one month before the University Orator was appointed, on 6 February 1581 the Latin play *Pedantius* was produced at Trinity College, Cambridge, next to Trinity Hall, where Gabriel Harvey resided. The play is now attributed to Edward Forsett, the likely scribe of Caius MS 62.[26] Nashe was later to say that the author was Anthony Wingfield, probably because it was Wingfield who defeated Harvey for the position as University Orator. In this Latin play, Harvey is depicted as Pedantius, a self-important rhetorician who owns a magnificent library, filled with volumes which he has painstakingly annotated. Nashe says that the producers of the play used Harvey's own gown as a costume, but, even without this touch, the references to Harvey's library and its annotated contents make the portrait unmistakable. Although Pedantius preens himself on his intellect, his knowledge of Cicero is exposed as deriving from Nizolius's *Thesaurus Ciceronianus*, a well-known Ciceronian phrase book. In addition to satire on his pedantry, Pedantius is portrayed as socially ambitious and eager to cut a figure as a dandy – even though he cannot pay his tailor. He has read Castiglione's *Il Cortegiano* and considers himself a courtier, statesman, and personage of importance. He is wooing Lydia, to whom he unsuitably declaims Ciceronian tags.

G.C. Moore Smith, the early editor of the Latin text, demonstrated that many of the pronouncements of Pedantius are directly quoted from Harvey's published lectures on rhetoric, *Smithus*, and *Gratulationes Valdinenses*.²⁷ *Pedantius*, for example, contains a direct quotation from *Familiar Letters*, 'Nosti manum & stylum' (I.3, G1r), the phrase concluding the first instalment of *Familiar Letters*. This phrase appears in Act V, scene 3 of *Pedantius*. At least a decade *before* Nashe ridiculed *Gratulationum Valdinensium Libri Quatuor*, we find the familiar references to Harvey's Italian-looking countenance, 'vultu Itali' and to his satire 'Speculum Tuscanismi', both given in italics. After his wooing has been foiled, Pedantius says that he will write a tragedy on his unhappy love and entitle it *Lachrymae Musarum*, a reference to the subtitle of *Smithus* and to Harvey's conceit of depicting the muses as weeping at the loss of Sir Thomas Smith. By the conclusion of the play, Pedantius is reduced to such financial straits that he may have to sell his fabulous library. This is a clear hit at Harvey whose library, with its marginalia, has become an important tool for scholars interested in sixteenth-century reading practices. This is not brutal satire, but, as Sir John Harington aptly commented, the play is full of 'harmeles myrth'.²⁸

By 6 February 1581 Spenser had been in Ireland for months, maybe a year, depending upon when he permanently left for Ireland. There was no particular reason for Cambridge wits to include Spenser in this satiric play even if they, unlike Nashe, accepted 'Well-Willer's' improbable claim that Spenser was responsible for copying out *Familiar Letters*. It is important to emphasize that in *Pedantius* we do not find explicit quotes from the *Shepheardes Calender* or allusions to Spenser as its author. In contrast, as noted above, there are specific textual allusions that are quoted directly from Harvey's works.

Perhaps most memorably, in Act II, scene iii *of Pedantius*, we find the phrase '*cogit amare iecur*' quoted directly from Harvey's eulogy to Sidney in *Gratulationes Valdinenses*. This quotation, as discussed in Chapter 5, suggests that Harvey's grand passion for Philip Sidney originated in his liver, making it sexual. It is precisely this passage that Nashe later quotes verbatim in *Have with You to Saffron Walden* (1596) and describes as Harvey's attempt to turn Sidney into a Ganymede. Thus, Harvey's unfortunate description of himself as all liver in *Gratulationes Valdinenses* was included in *Pedantius* and so attracted the attention of Cambridge wits a good fifteen years before Nashe used Harvey's address to Sidney to ridicule him.²⁹ In addition to the Cambridge audience, we know that Harington, who complimented Spenser in his *Metamorphosis of Ajax*, and Essex, who later offered him patronage, attended the performance of *Pedantius*.

In addition to the Cambridge reaction, in 1581, some time between 1 January and 14 February William Withie of Christ Church, Oxford, responded to *Familiar Letters* by addressing a verse satire to Harvey entitled 'Vppon Haruyes vile arrogant English versyfyinge' in a notebook originally intended for chemical notes and translations.[30] He is irritated with Harvey for positioning himself as the supreme authority on versifying and on rhetoric. Warren B. Austin suggests that he is 'satirizing E.K.'s presentation of the *Shepheardes Calender* to Harvey as "the most excellent and learned both Orator and Poete, Mayster Gabriell Harvey"' (300). According to Austin:

> By his reference to page 8 (i.e., to the close and postscript of Spenser's letter) here and in the phrase below, 'youre ffrend Meriton tibj' and by the significant juxtaposition of the injunction, 'Nosti magnum & stylum', Withie seems to be hinting his suspicion that Harvey wrote himself or, at least edited, the Spenser letter.[31]

Spenser's contemporaries, as the evidence of Withie, the authors of *Pedantius*, Lyly, and Nashe suggests, thought that Harvey was responsible for the publication of *Familiar Letters* and, discounted the suggestion that Spenser was his collaborator.

Harvey's Career and *Foure Letters* (1592)

Twelve years later when Harvey published *Foure Letters* (1592), his principal concern was to vindicate himself. In 1580, he never mentions his campaign to be named University Orator at Cambridge, but in 1592, we are told:

> I was supposed not vnmeet for the Oratorship of the vniuersity, which in that springe of mine age, for my Exercise, and credite I earnestly affected: but mine owne modest petition, my friends diligent labour, our high Chauncelors [Burghley] most-honourable and extraordinarye commendation, were all pettingly defeated, by a slye practise of the olde Fox [Andrew Perne]. (C2r)

In 1592 we hear nothing about Immerito copying out the correspondence before a friend of Well-Willer's gives it to Harvey's printer; now the events leading to the publication are described as a 'sinister hap' (C2v).

Somehow these 'infortunate Letters' manage to fall into the 'left handes' of 'malicious enemies' or 'vndiscreete friends' (C2v). After papering over the issue of how his correspondence with Spenser came to be published, he offers one neat antithesis after another to summarize events. Someone – a malicious enemy or indiscreet friend – 'aduenture[s] to imprint in earnest, that was scribbled in iest' (C2v). He cannot resist adding yet another antithesis to point out that those responsible for the publication 'requited their priuate pleasure with my publike displeasure' (C2v). In the passages immediately following this explanation of how *Familiar Letters* came to be published, Harvey, characteristically, claims that he has written no fewer than 'forty Academicall Exercises and sundry other politique Discourses' as an apology to Cambridge (C3r).

We know that Harvey got into trouble over publishing *Familiar Letters* because, twelve years later in *Foure Letters*, he defends himself against the charge that he was put into prison for libels against the Earl of Oxford and Sir James Croft. According to Harvey himself, his contributions to *Familiar Letters* caused offence to a number of people. Harvey's *Speculum Tuscanismi* (I.3, E2v), a poem in English hexameters ridiculing an Italianate Englishman, was viewed as an attack on the Edward de Vere, Earl of Oxford. John Lyly, a client of Oxford's, alludes to Harvey's imprisonment over this libel in *Pappe with an Hatchet* (1589) and describes the publication as a 'familiar Epistle':

> And one we coniure vp, that writing a familiar Epistle about the naturall causes of an Earthquake, fell into the bowells of libelling, which made his eares quake for feare of clipping, he shall tickle you with taunts; all his works bound close, are at least six sheetes in quarto, and he calls them the first tome of his familiar Epistle: he is full of Latin ends and worth tenne of those that crie in London, *haie ye anie gold ends to sell* ... and such a one who cares as little for writing without wit, as *Martin* doth for writing without honestie.[32]

In *Foure Letters* (1592) Harvey dismisses Lyly's charge that Oxford took offence at his satire and instead uses the incident as a pretext for claiming an intimacy with the Earl at Cambridge, where De Vere gave him angels (gold coins worth 10 shillings each), and for reminding his readers that he had been the client of Sir Thomas Smith and his son and alluding to the son's position:

> [Lyly] would needs forsooth verye courtly perswade the Earle of Oxforde, that ... the Mirrour of Tuscanismo, was palpably intended against him: whose noble Lordeship I protest, I neuer meante to dishonour with the least preiudicial word of my Tongue, or pen ... since in the prime of his gallantest youth, hee bestowed Angels vpon mee in Christes Colledge in Cambridge, and otherwise voutsafed me many gratious fauours at the affectionate commendation of my Cosen, M. Thomas Smith, the sonne of Sir Thomas, shortly after Colonel of the Ardes in Ireland. (C4r)

In this instance, even Harvey's sympathetic biographer Virginia Stern has questioned his candour. She points out that in his *Letter-Book* (51v–52v) he offers a discourse entitled 'a dialogue in Cambridge between Master GH and his companye at a midsummer Comencement, togither with certayne delicate sonnets and epigrammes in Inglish verse of his makinge' (Stern, *Harvey*, 65–6). One of the gentlemen in the company quotes the first twenty-three lines of what Harvey later published as 'Speculum Tuscanismi' and says, 'tell me ... if this be not a noble verse and politique lesson ... in effecte conteyning the argumente of [Master GH's] curragious and warly[ke] apostrophe to my lorde of Oxenforde in his fourth booke of Gratulationum Valdinensium'.

According to Harvey, at the instigation of Lyly or some other unnamed enemy, Sir James Croft, the Comptroller of Elizabeth's household, was led to believe that Harvey's reference to Spenser's 'olde Controller' in the earthquake letter (*Familiar Letters* I.2) was an attack on him. The passage in question, Harvey's 1580 attack on Perne in *Familiar Letters*, reads as follows:

> And wil you needes haue my Testimoniall of youre [Immerito's, i.e., Spenser's] olde Controllers new behauior? A busy and dizy heade, a brazen forehead: a ledden braine ... a founder of nouelties: a confounder of his owne, and his friends good gifts: a morning bookeworm, an afternoone maltworm: a right Juggler, as ful of his sleights, wyles, fetches, casts of Legerdemaine, toyes to mocke Apes withal, odde shiftes, and knauish practizes, as his skin can holde. He often telleth me, he looueth me as himselfe, but out lyar out, thou lyest abhominably in thy throate. (I.2, D3r–v)[33]

In *Foure Letters* Harvey acknowledges that he intended the reference to Spenser's 'olde Controller' as an allusion to Andrew Perne, indicating also that he believed it was Perne who had engineered the defeat of his campaign to become University Orator.

Almost sixteen years after Harvey's embarrassment occurred, Nashe revived this story in his satiric portrait of Harvey's life and works in *Have with You to Saffron Walden, or Gabriell Harvey's hunt is up. Containing a full Answere to the eldest sonne of the Halter-maker* (1596). To oversee and judge his contest with Harvey, Nashe invents a tribunal of characters, who put him on trial for delaying his reply to Harvey. Senior Importuno upbraids Nashe for failing to reply to Harvey's libels and warns him not to comfort himself by reflecting on the poor sales of Harvey's books because a personal copy may be found in his desk or the printer may bequeath copies to his heirs. Nashe then feigns the discovery of Harvey's latest letters – 'here's a packet of Epistling' (3: 33) – and accuses him of including his name in the title, *Piers his Supererogation, or Nashes Saint* to make it sell well.

> For hauing found that no worke of his, absolute vnder hys owne name, would passe, he vsed heretofore to drawe *Sir Philip Sydney, Master Spencer,* and other men of highest credit, into euerie pild pamphlet he set foorth; ... (from which I have vtterly chac'd him in my *Foure Letters intercepted,*). (3: 35)

In 1596, Nashe couples Spenser with Sidney and describes them both as 'men of highest credit'. In a specific reference to *Familiar Letters*, Nashe quotes directly from the third letter in the first set of *Familiar Letters*, Harvey's lecture on prosody, and then offers a picture of Harvey, not in the 'pantofles of his prosperitie as he was when he libeld against my Lord of *Oxford*, ... but readie to beray himselfe, vpon the newes of the going in hand of my book' (3: 38). After that, he turns to Harvey's diction, which he describes as 'finicall flaunting phrases, and termagant inkhorne tearmes' and labels 'Pedantisme' in an allusion to the Cambridge play *Pedantius*. In his portrait of Harvey as a 'would be' courtier who is found to be unworthy of promotion, he pictures him as a tall, over-dressed fop with 'a paire of moustachies like a black horse tayle tyde vp in a knot, with two tuffts sticking out on each side' and offers details of his rejection (3: 79).

Spenser had no need to defend himself: His contemporaries at Cambridge took care of that in *Pedantius* (1581). The date of entry into the Stationers' Register of *Familiar Letters*, 30 June 1580, makes it unlikely that Spenser was involved in preparing this edition for the press. We know that Grey's appointment was decided by May 1580 when Sidney wrote to Edward Denny admonishing him to be loyal to Grey. In June and July 1580, even if Spenser was in England, he would have been occupied with arrangements for the expedition to Ireland and unlikely to have had the time – or any motivation – to collaborate with Harvey on the publication of *Familiar Letters*. Harvey, on the other hand, was eager to establish his credentials as a rhetorician worthy of appointment as University Orator at Cambridge. He was not finally defeated by Anthony Wingfield until 16 March 1581, over a month after the production of the Cambridge *Pedantius* on 6 February 1581.

In 1580, Harvey portrays Spenser as his admiring disciple. In 1592, he depicts Spenser as his lifelong friend, attributes to him a sonnet dated 1586 supposedly praising Harvey's aloofness, and prints yet another sonnet in which he claims that Spenser has compared him with Homer. It is unlikely that contemporaries would have credited either the 1580 portrait of Spenser as adoring disciple or the 1592 portrait of Spenser as Harvey's fan. Probably borrowing from Spenser, Nashe refers to Harvey as a 'vaine Braggadochio'. It seems reasonable to conclude that, just as Sidney did not react publicly to the homosexual suggestions in Harvey's address to him in *Gratulationes Valdinenses*, Spenser saw fit to ignore Harvey's portrait of him in *Familiar Letters*.[34] Spenser could assume that his contemporaries would dismiss Harvey's insinuations much as Nashe does:

> Immortall *Spencer*, no frailtie hath thy fame, but the imputation of this Idiots friendship: vpon an vnspotted *Pegasus* should thy gorgeous attired *Fayrie Queene* ride triumphant through all reports dominions, but that ... this bile on the browe of the Vnitiversitie, this bladder of pride newe blowne, challengeth some interest in her prosperities. (Nashe, 1: 282)

It is well to keep in mind that Spenser completely ignored Harvey's description of the *Faerie Queene* as 'Hobgoblin runne away with the Garland from Apollo' (I.3, F1v). Harvey's sage advice did not dissuade Spenser from spending the rest of his life working on a poem dismissed by Mr G.H.

Notes

1 In Harvey's *Letter-Book*, ed. Scott, he addresses Spenser as 'my yunge Italianate Seignior and French Monsieur' (fol. 38, p. 65).
2 Harvey's *Letter-Book*, ed. Scott, 101.
3 Jon A. Quitslund, 'Questionable Evidence in the *Letters* of 1580 between Gabriel Harvey and Edmund Spenser', in *Spenser's Life and the Subject of Biography*, ed. Judith H. Anderson, Donald Cheney, and David Richardson (Amherst: University of Massachusetts Press, 1996), 81–98, esp. 87.
4 Hadfield, *Life*, 151.
5 *STC*, 23095, II: 357.
6 Nashe is convinced that Harvey orchestrated the publication of *Familiar Letters*, and William Withie, discussed below, concurs and hints that Harvey invented sections of Spenser's letters.
7 Jon Quitslund seems to interpret Nashe's description of the 'onely writer' in this passage as Nashe's charge that Harvey invented all of Spenser's letters. It seems more likely that Nashe is accusing Harvey of writing Well-Willer's Preface and so praising himself.
8 This particular description of unpublished works occurs in Harvey's 1598 letter to Cecil in which he begs him to stay the election at Trinity Hall and to secure a letter from the Queen appointing him Master of Trinity Hall. Cited from Gabriel Harvey, *Works*, ed. Grosart, I: xxv–xxviii. See Stern, *Harvey*, 124–5.
9 The text of *Familiar Letters* should be subjected to computerized studies of style, such as TACT, and other more advanced stylometric techniques.

10 Harvey's *Letter-Book*, vi.
11 Harvey's Letter-Book, fol. 48v and paged as 89 in Scott's edition.
12 Henry Woudhuysen, 'Letters, Spenser's and Harvey's', *Spenser Encyclopedia*, 434–5. It should be noted that Woudhuysen's unpublished dissertation was on 'Leicester's Literary Patronage'.
13 State Papers, Ireland, 63/70/7, 6 November 1579. Walsingham to Nicholas Malby.
14 State Papers, Ireland, 63/70/, fol. 91, 28 November 1579. William Pelham to Burghley,
15 Raymond Jenkins, 'Spenser with Lord Grey in Ireland', *Publications of the Modern Language Association*, 52 (1937), 338–53, esp. 341.
16 Nicholas Canny, *Making Ireland British: 1580-1650* (Oxford: Oxford University Press, 2001), 109. Canny's discovery deserves further attention.
17 State Papers, Ireland, 63/72/, fol. 100, 7 April 1580. Grey to Leicester certifying that he is to prepare himself for Ireland and complaining about the Queen's indecision.
18 *The Correspondence of Sir Philip Sidney*, ed. Roger Kuin, 2 vols (Oxford: Oxford University Press, 2012), 2: 980.
19 Denny later commented in a letter to Walsingham on 8 September 1580 that the service in Ireland took place in 'boggs, glinnes and woods, as in my opinion it might better fit mastives than brave gentlemen that desire to win honour' and adds that he will stay on only because of his 'love' for Lord Grey (State Papers, Ireland, 63/76/18).
20 On the circulation of Sidney's correspondence, see Duncan-Jones, *Life*, 170–4.
21 James M. Osborn, *Young Philip Sidney, 1572-1577* (New Haven: Yale University Press, 1972), appendix 5, pp. 535–40, p. 537. Duncan-Jones, *Life*, 172.
22 *Eleventh Report of the Deputy Keeper of the Public Records in Ireland*, 18 March 1879 (Dublin: Her Majesty's Stationery Office, 1879), 174. Listed as 3969, but an earlier classification 3220 is also listed parenthetically.
23 British Library, Lansdowne MS 28, fol. 83. Cited from Harvey, *Marginalia*, 32–9.
24 British Library, Lansdowne MS 30, fol. 57; Cited from Harvey, *Marginalia*, 37.
25 Moore Smith wants to change the dates of Harvey's correspondence with Burghley because he thinks that *Familiar Letters* was written in chagrin after Harvey was rejected and that his disappointment led him to attack the intellectual atmosphere at Cambridge and launch an invective against Andrew Perne (Harvey, *Marginalia*, 38).
26 A printed version of *Pedantius* was licensed in the Stationers' Register on 9 February 1631 and printed in 1631. There are two manuscripts: Caius MS 62, written in a beautiful hand; Trinity College MS R.17, which includes the play, copied from the Caius MS 62. I have used Dana Sutton's on-line hypertext edition and translation of *Pedantius* available from the Philological Museum at the University of Birmingham: www.philological.bham.ac.uk/forsett.
27 Edward Forsett, *Pedantius, A Latin Comedy Formerly Acted in Trinity College, Cambridge*, ed. G. C. Moore Smith. In *Materialien zur Kunde des alteren englischen Dramas* (1905; rpt Vaduz: Kraus Reprint, 1963), 8: viii–xi. For evidence that the satire is aimed at Harvey, see xliv–xlix. See, also, H.S. Wilson, 'The Cambridge Comedy "Pedantius" and Gabriel Harvey's "Ciceronianus"', *Studies in Philology*,

45 (1948), 578–91, who emphasizes that Harvey also satirized Ciceronian affectation.
28 Cited from *Pedantius*. ed. G. C. Moore Smith, 8: xi, xxxi. Harington, *A Brief Apology for Poetrie* (1591), Book 14: 'how full of harmeles myrth is our Cambridge *Pedantius*'.
29 Nashe, *Works*, 3: 92.
30 British Library, Sloane MS 300, 54r, cited in Warren B. Austin, 'William Withie's Notebook: Lampoons on John Lyly and Gabriel Harvey', *Review of English Studies*, 23 (1947), 297–309, esp. 301.
31 Warren B. Austin, 'William Withie's Notebook: Lampoons on John Lyly and Gabriel Harvey', *Review of English Studies*, 23 (1947), 297–309, esp. 301. He also points out that among the many allusions to the Harvey–Nashe controversy in *Love's Labour's Lost* Biron says of Armado's letter (IV.i.98): I am much deceived, but *I remember the style*'.
32 John Lyly, *Pappe with an Hatchet. Alias, A figge for my God sonne. Or Cracke me this nut* (London: John Anoke, and John Astile [i.e. T. Orwin], 1589). sig. B3r, B3v. STC 17463. RB 62468. Huntington Library, San Marino, CA.
33 The *OED* lists 'severe critic' as another meaning for 'controller', but, rather than pleading a linguistic confusion or misunderstanding, Harvey acknowledges that he attacked Perne. Harvey's phrase, 'youre [Spenser's] olde Controllers new behavior' seems to implicate Spenser in Harvey's resentment of Perne, but I have found no source for this.
34 In addition to the homosexual references in Harvey's address to Sidney in *Gratulationes Valdinenses*, it should be noted that there are homosexual undertones to the Harvey–Spenser relationship as it is presented in *Familiar Letters*, particularly, in Spenser's Latin poem.

10

Ireland and the preferment of Edmund Spenser (1580)

Two intertwined threads connect the sixteenth-century England and Ireland of Edmund Spenser: one involved studies of Roman colonization, very learned Latin debates on how colonization should proceed, and the other was complaints about the barbarity of the Irish and their 'savage soyle'. The latter is frequently misconstrued and probably was not universally understood even in the sixteenth century. In a watershed article contextualizing Spenser's *View of the Present State of Ireland*, Debora Shuger explains that, to many Elizabethans, Ireland represented their own medieval past, a feudal world in which there was no middle class. Aristocratic noblemen held sway over their vassals, most of whom lacked the self-reliance of the English yeoman, merchant, or guildsman.[1] To cite only characteristically medieval events which occurred: rival leaders conclude that battles will be determined by their own single combat; avowed enemies become sworn brothers because they each kept their word.[2] Shuger's formulation explains why descriptions of events in Ireland in Henry Sidney's *Memoirs* sometimes read like passages out of Malory's *Knights of King Arthur*. The early modern chivalric code, largely an honour code, bound both Irish and English military servitors, like 'Black Tom', Thomas Butler, tenth Earl of Ormond; Hugh O'Neill, second Earl of Tyrone; Sir Henry Sidney, and Sir Walter Ralegh,

The learned Latin debates on Roman colonization seem to concern Harvey more than Spenser, who would have heard from Harvey about efforts to colonize south Antrim and east Down in Ireland. Harvey's marginalia report that he was invited to witness debates focusing on colonial policy from Sir Thomas Smith, his patron. Smith himself greatly admired the Romans and credited them with having brought law and civilization to England. Smith's philological comments suggest his admiration for Roman colonialism. He acknowledges that a 'Colonel' in French is the leader of footmen, as a marshal is of horsemen.

> Here it betokeneth a leader forth of men to inhabit and till waste and desolate places, who in ancient times were *Deductores Coloniarum* and the action was called deducere coloniam. It is no name either of high honour or authority, yet wherewithal we are best content because it sheweth the nature of our actions.[3]

As Smith's approach to titles suggests, he thought of himself and his followers as successors to those Roman soldiers who had established colonies to extend the Roman empire. Among the organizational details of the colony, Smith specifies that the Irish 'churles, that will plow the grounde and beare no kind of weapons nor armoure, shalbe gentlye entertained' (p. 548). This gentle entertainment, however, seems not to have extended to the right to purchase land, to be bound as apprentices, or to hold public office.

Smith, who had moved from the university to the court, used his protégé Harvey as a facilitator in the Latin classics in a series of debates in which Latin texts were used to hammer out policy for Smith's projects in Ireland. Between 1570 and 1573, Harvey described occasions in his marginalia in which formal readings took place on Livy's *Decades* with Thomas Smith the younger, who, Harvey, characteristically, emphasizes, bore the title of 'Royal Deputy in the Irish Ardes'. Harvey was also acquainted with Sir Humphrey Gilbert, Ralegh's half-brother and a military servitor in Ireland. Harvey recounts witnessing a debate on colonial policy between Gilbert and Captain Smith the younger (conquest by force) and Sir Thomas Smith and Walter Haddon (reasoned colonial strategy). Although there is no evidence that Spenser himself actively participated in any of these debates, he is likely to have heard Harvey's descriptions of them. Connecting the dots of these various strategies aimed at using lessons from Roman history to work out plans for establishing colonies in Ireland, Lisa Jardine, ably assisted by Willy Maley, has suggestively reconstructed possible connections between the colonizing ventures of the Smiths and the formation of Edmund Spenser's colonial outlook.[4]

In accord with his Roman model, Smith planned to have his colonists construct a central capital, *Elizabetha*.[5] To gain colonists, he advertised the colonies as a solution to overpopulation, particularly the problem of younger sons who, because of primogeniture, were disinherited in the English inheritance system; this same selling point was later used to advertise the plantations of Munster and Ulster. By a propaganda campaign that included the publication *A Letter sent by I.B.* (1572), Sir Thomas and his son assembled between seven and eight hundred adventurers at Liverpool by May 1572. After a number of delays, which eroded the strength of his colonial force, Captain Smith finally set out on 30 August, but his force had dwindled to only one hundred men. The expedition managed to hold on for over a year, but Captain Thomas Smith met a dramatic, but untimely end. He was murdered on 20 October 1573. It was reported that he was attacked by his Irishmen, 'whom he overmuch trusted' who boiled him and then fed his carcass to the dogs.[6] It was also rumoured that he had been fed alive to the dogs. Providence was reaffirmed by reports that his servants in retribution were devoured by wolves. The Smiths' family estate was located near Cambridge, and Spenser was in his fourth year at Pembroke when these events occurred, and the lurid circumstances of Smith's unhappy demise ensured that these events were talked about in Cambridge and probably court circles.

Ireland: economic advantages and the medieval past

For Spenser, Ralegh, and perhaps others, Ireland was attractive because it was associated with an aristocratic past, the world in which the English War of the Roses took place. Whatever challenges a man encountered in Ireland, he was less likely to be brought down by slander and envy than at the fiercely competitive Elizabethan court. In the 1580s and 1590s, Ireland also had little of the middle-class commercial culture of London, fewer guilds to restrict business, fewer inns to shelter travellers. Ireland offered clear advantages to 'new' men without inherited estates. It is true that sixteenth-century Englishmen complained that Ireland was wild and inhospitable, but these complaints have to be juxtaposed with their demonstrable willingness, even eagerness, to find employment – and above all property – in Ireland. John Donne, for example, unsuccessfully attempted to become a secretary in both Ireland and Virginia before taking holy orders.[7]

Class mattered less in Dublin than in London, but land, unquestionably, was far more easily obtained across the sea. In Ireland and the New World, the government did not finance colonization – at least directly. Plantations were granted to 'undertakers' who had the economic means to 'undertake', i.e., finance colonization. Likewise, the privateers who preyed on Spanish shipping were 'undertakers' who sold shares of their prospective spoils to investors. Capitalist enterprises, such as piracy and colonization, had to turn profits, but both promised handsome rewards

By the machinations of the English government or by accident, or both, land became available in Elizabethan Ireland. Each of the sixteenth-century rebellions by the Anglo-Norman or Old English earls resulted in the confiscation of vast tracts of land from the rebels. From the vantage point of the English government, the lands of these 'traitors' were then forfeit to the Crown. The land was then awarded to powerful members of the Privy Council, such as Sir Christopher Hatton, to wealthy English and Irish landowners, such as the English Sir John Popham, the English Sir William Herbert, and the Irish Thomas Butler, Earl of Ormond, and sometimes to well-connected military servitors, such as Sir Walter Ralegh, Sir Edward Denny, and Sir Thomas Norris.[8] An English profiteer, such as Richard Boyle, could metamorphose into the Earl of Cork in one lifetime; likewise, George Carew, military servitor and then colonial official, became the Earl of Totnes.

Ireland and religious toleration

It is not self-evident that Spenser would have enjoyed dealing with the requisite compromises required to make a career as a clergyman in Whitgift's England. Sixteenth-century Ireland could be a more congenial place for an independent thinker than England, and there is evidence that difficult intellectuals, particularly those with 'Puritan leanings', were sent to Ireland to protect them from officials in the Church of England. We know as well that a number of Elizabethan poets who were involved with the court and its patronage system died while relatively young in 1590s England. Christopher Marlowe, a government agent, died in 1593 before he was thirty. Thomas Nashe, employed even by churchmen, died or disappeared in 1601 before he was thirty-five. Spenser himself died, not in fierce and savage Ireland, but in Westminster early in 1599 at forty-five years of age. The advent of James I allowed for more social mobility. The poet Samuel Daniel received a court appointment. Daniel, however, was frightened for his life during his imprisonment over *Philotas* – so much so that he, the only would-be laureate who succeeded in winning a position at the court, abandoned his courtly career. Ben Jonson was imprisoned for his writing, but was perhaps just distant enough from court circles to avoid getting caught up in the intrigues in which pawns, however gifted, were ruthlessly sacrificed.

During Spenser's time, Dublin offered far more religious toleration than Elizabethan London. Thomas Cartwright was not a religious fanatic, though the Puritan label he was given in the sixteenth century has continued to colour his reputation. In 1564, during the Queen's visit to Cambridge, he debated philosophy with Thomas Preston, who later became master of Trinity College. In Ireland, Cartwright served as a chaplain in the household of Adam Loftus, Archbishop of Armagh. Adam Loftus was a liberal cleric, who, when he moved from Armagh to Dublin as archbishop, wrote to Burghley to nominate Cartwright to succeed him as Archbishop of Armagh. This was the same Adam Loftus whom Spenser was later to serve in his position as register or clerk in the chancery for faculties. Loftus, as Archbishop of Dublin, was charged with approving or disapproving ecclesiastical dispensations, formerly processed by Rome, but now by archbishops in the Church of England. Only in sixteenth-century Ireland could an intellectual dissident, such as Cartwright, be nominated to serve as an archbishop in the established church!

The earlier account of events at Cambridge has implications for religious toleration in Ireland. In 1569, the very year that Spenser matriculated at Pembroke College, Cambridge, Thomas Cartwright was appointed Lady Margaret Professor of Divinity. By December 1570, Whitgift had succeeded in depriving him of that position. With the assistance of Andrew Perne, Whitgift succeeded in revising the statutes so that they were less liberal than they had been under Catholic Mary Tudor. By September 1571, Thomas Cartwright had been deprived of his fellowship. A movement to make him professor of Hebrew in 1572 came to nothing. As an undergraduate, Spenser witnessed Whitgift succeed in hounding Cartwright, by all reports an excellent scholar, out of Cambridge.

Cartwright was not an isolated example of the relocation of English intellectuals to Ireland to evade persecution in England. Walter Travers, who belonged to a family reported to have had connections with Spenser's sister, Sarah, affords us another striking instance of an intellectual who found asylum in Ireland.[9] Travers matriculated at Christ's College but transferred to Trinity where he distinguished himself intellectually. He was selected to give the formal address to Queen Elizabeth when she visited Cambridge in 1564. Whitgift, as master of the college, however, instituted so many disciplinary procedures against Travers that he gave up his fellowship and left Cambridge in 1570. After spending some time on the continent, Travers was offered in 1580 a position at St Andrews University, but elected instead to become the chaplain to Lord Burghley and tutor to his son Robert. In 1581, sponsored by Lord Burghley, he became deputy to Richard Alvey at the Temple, where services were offered to those attending the Middle and Inner Temples and the other Inns of Court.

After Whitgift was appointed Archbishop in succession to Grindal, in 1584 he promoted Fifteen Articles which were designed to weed out nonconformists. Burghley thought that the entire procedure smacked too much of the Spanish Inquisition. Leicester insisted upon a debate between Whitgift and the opposition. The two-day conference was attended by Leicester, Walsingham, Burghley, and Lord Grey. We should take note that Spenser's early patron, Lord Grey, was also the patron of Thomas Sparke, the Puritan-leaning cleric to whom Grey presented the rectory of Bletchley, Buckinghamshire. At the conference, Travers and Sparke represented the opposition to Whitgift.

Although Burghley supported Travers, Richard Hooker was named as Alvey's successor. It is easy to imagine the intellectual excitement of hearing Travers at midday and then Hooker in the evening and so listening to two different perspectives on the Protestant Reformation. Whitgift, however, wrote to the Queen that Travers could not be trusted:

> Travers hath been and is one of the chief and principal authors of dissension in this church, a contemner of the Book of Prayers, and of other orders by authority established; an earnest seeker of innovation; and either in no degree of the ministry at all, or else ordered beyond the seas.[10]

In March 1586, Whitgift silenced Travers and successfully blocked Burghley's efforts to assist him in his attempt to pursue his profession – though the Lord Treasurer seems to have managed to keep Travers out of prison. We next find Travers in Ireland, where he was inaugurated on 5 June 1594 as the Provost of Trinity College, Dublin.

If Burghley, Lord Treasurer of England, arguably the most influential figure in the English government, could not establish Travers in England and shielded a promising intellectual by 'banishing' him to Ireland, then we may want to reconsider what banishment entailed. It is a matter of record that the Dublin of Edmund Spenser was more tolerant of dissidents, such as Thomas Cartwright and Walter Travers, than was London, where both the left and the right were persecuted. John Penry was executed for being a Presbyterian; and John Donne's Catholic younger brother contracted a fever and died in prison for harbouring a priest; the very gifted Catholic Thomas Campion was tortured and then executed in 1581, a year before Spenser decided to remain in Ireland.

Spenser's preferment

There remains an unfortunate sense that no one would have willingy chosen Ireland over Elizabethan London and the Elizabethan court.[11] Karl Marx's view of Spenser as Elizabeth's 'arse-kissing poet' is more than a ghost that occasionally haunts Spenser studies, the view of Spenser as the disappointed would-be court poet is an ever-present shade casting doubt on the early Spenser's success in winning preferment.

Spenser's appointment as secretary to Arthur, fourteenth Lord Grey of Wilton, however, was a preferment. Almost twenty years later, William Camden brings up Grey's appointment in his obituary notice of Spenser and alludes to it because it was an extraordinary preferment for a twenty-five-year-old poet, certainly a brilliant student, but without demonstrable experience. It was not until 1910, and during political struggles between Ireland and England, that this appointment became suspect. In 1910, Edwin Greenlaw launched his still influential theory that Leicester hustled Spenser off to Ireland because of his having written a politically insensitive poem. Greenlaw's proof was another poem by Spenser, 'Virgils Gnat', an imitation of an apocryphal Vergilian apology, published in *Complaints* (1591).[12]

Over thirty-five years later, writing the biography appearing with the *Spenser Variorum*, Alexander Judson rejected Greenlaw's theory. Judson predictably thought that Spenser would have preferred a position in England, but that none was forthcoming and so he went to Ireland.[13] In spite of Judson's rejection of the banishment theory, doubts have persisted. In an article on patronage, authored by Barbara Lewalski, in the *Spenser Encyclopedia* (1990), we are told that 'in 1580, his [Spenser's] hoped-for advancement at court was blocked, in large part because his *Mother Hubberds Tale* satirized Burghley and the Queen's proposed French marriage, and he was forced to make his subsequent career in Ireland' (535).[14] In a recent and more sophisticated approach, Andrew Hadfield, in his *Edmund Spenser, A Life* (2012), concludes: 'We will probably never know whether this was a great opportunity for the newly married poet in need of gainful employment or an effective banishment as a result of offending too many people in his early work, most significantly Leicester rather than the usual suspect, Burghley' (155).[15]

As has been demonstrated above, particularly in Chapters 4 and 7, Spenser's *Shepheardes Calender* is not a work likely to have offended anyone; it is a very politic poem, as subtle as the first three books of the *Faerie Queene*, which may have earned Spenser both a pension and the patent to Kilcolman.[16] *Mother Hubberds Tale* was printed in 1591 and the 1591 version contains unmistakable topical satire on Lord Burghley and his son Robert Cecil, but there is *no* evidence that manuscripts of any version of this poem circulated in 1579–80.[17] The known facts concerning reactions to *Mother Hubberds Tale* are succinctly summarized by William Oram in his introduction to Spenser's early poems.[18] After its publication in the *Complaints* (1591), copies of *Mother Hubberds Tale* were made from the printed text, and this contemporary reaction in the 1590s has been ably contextualized by Richard Peterson.[19]

Spenser's appointment as Grey's secretary has also been misunderstood: he did not become a quasi-civil-servant and join a governmental secretariat in 1580. Spenser served Grey as Henry Wotton was later to serve the Earl of Essex. The notion that Spenser occupied the same position as Timothy Reynolds and was a civil servant employed by the government has obscured how significant it was for Grey to select the twenty-five-year-old poet as his personal secretary. This appointment allows us to make inferences about the personality of the early Spenser that are not obvious from the letters which Harvey selected to include in *Familiar Letters* (1580).

A lord deputy of Ireland needed someone loyal and remarkably astute to manage affairs in Dublin when he was away on campaigns. He also needed someone with administrative talent to administer the budget with captains in the field and to employ and manage spies. Sir Henry Sidney's memoir describing his experiences as Lord Deputy of Ireland makes clear the many challenges encountered in serving as lord deputy of Ireland. Loyalty and tact would have been among the foremost characteristics which Grey would have required, but intelligence and judgement would also have been a plus. Grey had a distinguished military background and a strong sense of honour. At the very least, Grey must have been persuaded that Spenser was a man of honour who could be trusted with confidential information and astute enough not to be manipulated by the opposition to Grey's leadership. Grey must also have thought that Spenser would not regard the appointment as a sinecure, that he would be both competent and hard-working.[20] From this appointment we can infer that Spenser's personal presence commanded respect and that his character favourably impressed an experienced military leader accustomed to leading and directing young men. Spenser, like Henry Wotton, who later served as Essex's secretary, was recognized as a man of quality and promise in 1580.

Notes

1 For a compelling study of the Elizabethan context for Spenser's *View of the Present State of Ireland*, see Debora Shuger, 'Irishmen, Aristocrats, and Other White Barbarians', *Renaissance Quarterly*, 50 (1997), 494–525.
2 For Ormond's proposed single combat, see *The First and Second Volumes of Chronicles, comprising 1. The description and historie of England, 2. The description and historie of Ireland, … Now newlie augmented … to the yeare 1568.* by John Hooker aliàs Vowell, Gent. … (At London: Iohn Harison, George Bishop, Rafe Newberie, Henrie Denham and Thomas Woodcocke, 2 vols: Printed [by Henry Denham], 1587, 1:173. RB 497126. The Huntington Library, San Marino, CA. See also Thomas Churchyard, *A Generall Rehearsall of Warres, called Churchyardes Choise* (London: J. Kingston for E. White, 1579), M1r-v; Q1r-R4r. RB 56403. The Huntington Library, San Marino, CA.
3 31 July 1574, Carte MS 56, fol. 218. Cited in David Beers Quinn, 'Sir Thomas Smith (1513–1577) and the Beginnings of English Colonial Theory', *Proceedings of the American Philosophical Society*, 89, No. 4 (December 1945), 543–60.
4 Lisa Jardine, 'Encountering Ireland: Gabriel Harvey, Edmund Spenser, and English Colonial Ventures', in *Representing Ireland: Literature and the Origins of Conflict, 1534–1660*, ed. Brendan Bradshaw, Andrew Hadfield, and Willy Maley (Cambridge: Cambridge University Press, 1993), 60–75.
5 On Smith, see Hiram Morgan, 'The Colonial Adventure of Sir Thomas Smith in Ulster', *Historical Journal*, 28 (1985), 261–78; see also Quinn, 'Sir Thomas Smith', and Nicholas Canny, *The Elizabethan Conquest of Ireland* (Hassocks: The Harvester Press, 1976), 85–8.
6 TNA: PRO, SP 62/42, No. 58.
7 R.C. Bald, *John Donne, A Life* (Oxford: Oxford University Press, 1970), 160–2, 240, 340, 538.
8 Michael MacCarthy-Morrogh, *The Munster Plantation: English Migration to Southern Ireland, 1583–1641* (Oxford: Clarendon Press, 1986), pp. 55–6.
9 The genealogical connection is reported in George Lillie Craik, *Poetical Works of Edmund Spenser* (1845), 251, but this Sarah Spenser is described as the grandmother of Walter Travers and so is not likely to have been the sister of Edmund Spenser (1554–99).
10 Alan Ford, 'Walter Travers', *ODNB* (2008).
11 A later version of this chapter was printed as 'Spenser's "Home"', *Spenser Studies*, 31/32 (2018), 439–58. See also the earliest version, '"All his minde on honour fixed": The Preferment of Edmund Spenser', in *Spenser's Life and the Subject of Biography*, ed. Judith H. Anderson, Donald Cheney, and David A. Richardson (Amherst: University of Massachusetts Press, 1996), 45–64. I want to acknowledge Judith Anderson's editorial assistance in completing this essay and the warmth of her collegiality at a difficult time.
12 Edwin Greenlaw, 'Spenser and the Earl of Leicester', *Publications of the Modern Language Association*, 26 (1910), 535–61.
13 Judson, *Life*, 69–72, esp. 72.
14 Barbara Lewalski, 'Patronage', *Spenser Encyclopedia*, 534–5.

15 For instances in which Spenser may have antagonized the powerful, Hadfield turns to *Familiar Letters*, claiming that the 'key to the origins of Spenser's career in Ireland can be found in the *Letters* and that his relationship to Leicester is the key' (128).

16 I would not rule out topical satire of Burghley in *Februarie* or of Lettice, Countess of Leicester, in *March*, but neither of these topical hints moves from gossip to libel.

17 Peter Beal's Catalogue of English Literary Manuscripts (CELM) now identifies eight manuscripts of *Mother Hubberds Tale*. Of these, using Beal's notation, I have examined *SpE 15*, British Library, Add. MS 34064, fols 33v–35r, collated in P.M. Buck, Jr, 'Add. MS 34064 and Spenser's *Ruins of Time* and *Mother Hubberd's Tale*', *Modern Language Notes*, 22 (1907), 41–6; *SpE 17*, Harvard, MS Eng 266, fols 38r–58r, a neatly written transcript of the *Complaints*; *SpE 18*, British Library, Add. MS 68942. The latter manuscript of Spenser, dated 5 June 1607 and once owned by Grosart, is collated in his edition.

18 *Yale Edition of the Shorter Poems of Edmund Spenser*, ed. William A. Oram, Einar Bjorvand, Ronald Bond, Thomas H. Cain, Alexander Dunlop, and Richard Schell (New Haven: Yale University Press, 1989), 327–33.

19 See Richard Peterson, '"Laurel Crown and Ape's Tail": New Light on Spenser's Career from Thomas Tresham', *Spenser Studies*, 12 (1988), 153–68. Prior to this publication, Richard Peterson kindly confirmed to me that the Tresham materials related only to the 1591 printed text.

20 See the recent collection of letters relating to the Grey administration, many of them penned by Edmund Spenser, demonstrating that his appointment was not a sinecure, *Selected Letters and Other Papers*, ed. Christopher Burlinson and Andrew Zurcher (Oxford: Oxford University Press, 2009).

Conclusion

Edmund Spenser was born in 1554. The numerological structure of the *Amoretti* and the *Epithalamion* suggests that he was born in 1554, a date confirmed by the dates of his matriculation at and graduation from Pembroke College. We do not know who his father was. R.B. Knowles and Alexander Grosart guessed that Edmund was the son of a journeyman merchant tailor named John Spenser to account for his having attended Merchant Taylors' School and because the last name worked. Spenser's name, in fact, does not appear in the Admission Records for Merchant Taylors' School. We know only from Manchester, Chetham Library, MS A.6.50 ('Nowell Account Book') that he attended that school because of bequests he received. This account book details grants to professors, students, and teachers from the estate of Robert Nowell, Attorney of the Queen's Court of Wards. Robert Nowell, in addition to being Spenser's benefactor, was the brother of Alexander Nowell, author of Nowell's *Catechism* and Dean of St Paul's. One of the entries mentioning grants to Spenser from the 'Nowell Account Book' is in Alexander Nowell's hand.

Spenser was the protégé of a circle of clergymen who included Alexander Nowell; Thomas Watts, Archdeacon of Middlesex; Edmund Grindal, then Bishop of London and later Archbishop of Canterbury. It is likely that these clergymen expected Spenser to take holy orders and that he, in fact, considered combining his literary aspirations with a career in the church. As noted previously, his willingness to stay on at Pembroke College and work towards the M.A., after completing the B.A. in 1573, suggests that he was considering taking holy orders. Ninety per cent of those completing the M.A. took holy orders, but he was one of the ten per cent who did not. That Spenser considered a career in the church with some seriousness is suggested by his early association with apocalyptic verse in Jan van der Noot's *Theatre for Worldlings* and, even more so, by his later devoting the first book of the *Faerie Queene* to holiness.

Between 1574, when he left Cambridge, and 1578, it is likely that he was employed by John Young in London, where he met Machabyas Chylde, whom he is presumed to have married on 27 October 1579 at St Margaret's, Westminster. We cannot be sure what prompted Spenser to question his religious vocation and decide against taking holy orders. His reluctance to embark on a career in the church may have begun at Cambridge when he watched John Whitgift and Andrew Perne revise the University Statutes in order to drive Thomas Cartwright, then Lady Margaret Professor of Divinity, from Cambridge. In London, he watched the fall from grace of Edmund Grindal, then Archbishop of Canterbury. In 1578, we know that he was employed by John Young because Gabriel Harvey describes him as Young's 'secretary' in the book which Spenser gave him as a Christmas gift.

In the *Shepheardes Calender*, Spenser describes himself as the 'Southerne shepheardes boye' (*Aprill*, 21) and later Hobbinol remarks, 'Colin Clout I wene be his selfe boye' (*September*, 176), perhaps suggesting his interest in the church, but certainly indicating his warm regard for John Young, Master of Pembroke and then Bishop of Rochester. This biographical study supports the view that the *Shepheardes Calender* records Spenser's vocational shift from shepherd-priest to shepherd-poet. By 5 December 1579, when this poem was entered in the Stationers' Register, Spenser had decided against a career in the church. The *Shepheardes Calender* not only treats Edmund Grindal sympathetically, but also attacks John Aylmer (Elmer, Elmore as Morrill), then Bishop of London.

We know that Spenser's next patron was Arthur, Lord Grey of Wilton, a military man who had previously acted as the patron of George Gascoigne, but we do not know when their relationship began. In this study of the early Spenser, the text of *Familiar Letters* is used to suggest that Lord Grey was Spenser's patron by October 1579. Having received this preferment, Spenser was then in a position to marry on 27 October 1579 and a month or so later to enter the *Shepheardes Calender* in the Stationers' Register, thus ending any possibility of making a career in the church.

Because of the residual medieval lustre of knightly chivalry, poetry and military service seemed compatible to men like Spenser in the early modern period. The poet, and later preacher, John Donne accompanied Essex and Ralegh on the expeditions to Cadiz and the Islands Voyage. Likewise, the poet Sir John Harington joined the expedition to Ireland where he was knighted by Essex. Ralegh and Essex both wrote poetry, and Ralegh's lyrics are impressive. These literary men, like the somewhat earlier Elizabethan poets Thomas Churchyard, George Whetstone, and George Gascoigne, felt no incompatibility between writing poetry and taking up arms. Spenser's attraction to chivalric ideals and his admiration for the soldier-knight, represented by Philip Sidney, were also in keeping with his decision to accompany Grey to Ireland.

Philip or Sir Henry Sidney is likely to have introduced Spenser to Lord Grey. We have no letter documenting the intimacy of Spenser and the Sidneys, and the one letter that may connect them is ambiguous. In Chapter 6, I summarize the circumstantial evidence connecting Spenser with Philip Sidney. The relationship between the Sidneys and Bryskett is particularly significant in explaining Spenser's willingness to trade London for Dublin in 1580. Lodowick Bryskett, who was later a friend and literary colleague of Spenser's in Ireland, was resident in London from June 1579 to February 1581. Bryskett owed his position in Ireland to Sir Henry Sidney whom he credits with changing him from a scholar to a 'servant'.[1] Bryskett's personal description of his debt to Sir Henry Sidney is confirmed by a reference to 'one Bryskett' being left by Sir Edward Molyneux, then Clerk of the Council, as substitute in April 1571; the letter specifically describes Bryskett as 'a yonge gentleman of my L Deputys'.[2] The next year Sir Henry arranged for Bryskett to accompany Philip on his grand tour beginning in May 1572.[3] Since Bryskett was intimate with the Sidneys and later a close friend to Spenser in Ireland, this connection constitutes a very suggestive link between Spenser and the Sidneys.

In contrast, we have no evidence – circumstantial or otherwise – that Spenser ever held the position of secretary to Robert Dudley, Earl of Leicester.[4] The only evidence connecting Spenser to Leicester, other than laudatory passages in his poems, is a reference to the location 'Leicester House' in the 5 October 1579 letter to Harvey in *Familiar Letters* (II.1, H3r). Leicester's status, as a Dudley, a grand peer, and the Queen's favourite, would have made him less accessible than the Sidneys to a twenty-five-year-old of Spenser's class.

Harvey

It is important to keep in mind that in June 1580, when *Familiar Letters* was entered in the Stationers' Register, Harvey could not see into the future and realize that he would fail to become University Orator in 1581 and that in ten years Spenser would return from Ireland to publish the *Faerie Queene* (1590). In June 1580, Harvey thought of himself, not Spenser, as Leicester's client. He thought that Leicester or the Queen would send him to Italy – 'de vultu Itali [he already looked Italian]'. He seems persuaded that this assignment will soon be forthcoming. In response to Spenser's Latin poem, he writes:

> Youre Latine Farewell is a goodly braue yonkerly peece of work, and Goddilge yee, I am always maruellously beholding vnto you, for your bountifull Titles: I hope by that time I haue been resident a yeare or twoo in *Italy*, I shall be better qualifyed in this kind, and more able to requite your lauishe, and magnificent liberalitie that way. (II.2, J1r)

In marginalia written in his Sacrobosco, Harvey echoes Sidney's letter to Edward Denny, and the connecting link is likely to have been Edmund Spenser.

One particular passage in *Familiar Letters* is suited only to Lord Grey's circumstances in October 1579. In their discussions of travel, Harvey, in his letter dated 23 October 1579, says that he is preparing a lecture for Spenser's 'lord' on Homer's *Odyssey* and Vergil's *Aeneid*:

> Wherof I haue the stronger hope he muste needes proue a most capable and apt subiecte ... hauing the selfe same ... *Minerua* and ... *Venus*: that is (as one Doctor expoundeth it) the pollitique head, and wise gouernement of the one: and the amiable behauiour, and gratious courtesie of the other: the two verye principall, and most singular Companions, of a right Trauailer. (II.2, J2r)

These allusions to Homer and Vergil are appropriate to Grey because as Lord Deputy of Ireland he will need the 'politique head and wise gouernement' of Minerva and the 'gracious courtesie' of Venus (J2r) to succeed. In October 1579, Leicester, the usual candidate for Spenser's 'lord', was not in particular favour with Elizabeth, who was actively negotiating a match with the Duke of Anjou. It was not until 1585 that Leicester led an expeditionary force to the Netherlands in support of the Dutch war for independence from Spain. These allusions to Grey as Spenser's patron in a letter written on 23 October 1579 also give credence to the likelihood of Spenser's being secure enough professionally to marry Machabyas Chylde on 27 October 1579.

Harvey waged a campaign to promote and advertise his talents in a manner that sometimes appears obsessive. There are many possible scenarios that might explain why he included Spenser in *Familiar Letters*. Perhaps, he felt betrayed by Spenser's having edited his commentary on the eclogues in the *Shepheardes Calender* (E.K.'s Gloss). We should not rule out the possibility that Harvey thought that he was doing Spenser a great favour by advertising their association. We know that Harvey was untroubled by misgivings about the price paid by those who sought courtly favour. Anthony Grafton and Lisa Jardine have labelled Harvey a 'practical humanist' and concluded that he pursued the *'ars disserendi'* principally as a route to high government office, without being overly troubled about becoming a *'vir bonus'*.[5] As we also know from the design of the *Faerie Queene*, Spenser, in contrast, was preoccupied with defining, characterizing, and shaping through poetry a *'vir bonus'* or 'noble person'.

There is some evidence that Spenser was as aware as others such as Thomas Nashe of the flaws in Harvey's personality, particularly of his tendency to take himself too seriously. In Christmas 1578, prior to the internal dates of correspondence in *Familiar Letters*, Spenser, in addition to giving Harvey an Italian travel book, made a wager with his friend, which reveals his personal assessment of Harvey. As gifts, he gave Harvey four books in the vernacular that would have to be classified as light reading: Howleglas, Scoggin, Skelton, and Lazarillo. The gift of Skelton is particularly suggestive because Spenser borrows the name 'Colin Clout' from Skelton's poem of the same name.[6] These books (including 'Skelton') are jestbooks and picaresque adventure stories. Spenser gave them to Harvey on the condition that he must read them all by 1 January or else forfeit to Spenser his four-volume edition of the Greek author Lucian. Although Spenser's wager suggests that he would have liked to own Harvey's edition of Lucian, it also demonstrates that he understood that his ambitious friend should relax, take himself less seriously, and, generally, 'lighten up'.

If we look briefly into the future, Spenser, in contrast to Harvey, was able to deal with challenging superiors. Lord Grey, a military man, would not have tolerated insubordination on the part of a young secretary. And, although Spenser, like Milton, seems to have been uncomfortable with the patronage system, he did become the client of Sir Walter Ralegh, and, possibly Ralegh's friend. Ralegh, though not necessarily an irascible man, is reputed to have fought several duels when not accorded adequate deference from contemporaries. Essex also became a patron of Spenser's, and he is not regarded as having been easy-going – he was jealous of his honour and seems to have even drawn his sword during an audience with the Queen. Further, it tells us something about Spenser's subtlety and diplomacy that his various patrons did not get along with each other: Grey resented Ralegh for undercutting him with the Privy Council. Ralegh and Essex were frequently at odds. Spenser, it must be concluded, had as much tact as wit.

The academic discourses in *Familiar Letters*, as Harvey later confided in *Foure Letters* (1592), had to do with his campaign to be named University Orator at Cambridge. As Well-Willer observes, the subject matter of *Familiar Letters*, the science of earthquakes and the subtleties of quantitative verse, would not have recommended themselves to courtiers or diplomats, when the Anjou match and the harsh punishment meted out to Stubbs for writing the *Gaping Gulf* were issues of principal concern. *Pedantius* was produced at Cambridge on 6 February 1581 in reaction to the publication of *Familiar Letters*, but, since all of Harvey's Latin works were satirised, more was at stake than Harvey's diatribe on Andrew Perne or his disparaging remarks on the lamentable state of learning at Cambridge. We know from Harvey's *Letter-Book* that he had interpersonal difficulties with his peers. Even though his struggle to get the M.A. awarded is presented from his point of view, it seems clear that he had antagonized the Fellows at Pembroke College. They were united in opposing his receipt of the Master of Arts. The story does not end there. Even after John Young intervened and insisted that he be awarded the M.A. degree, there seems to have been a residual sense that he had manipulated Young. In 1581, in spite of his success in mastering Latin rhetoric and oratory, his application to be University Orator was rejected. When he later studied Civil Law at Cambridge, his degree had to be awarded at Oxford rather than Cambridge, perhaps because resentment lingered concerning his machinations to obtain the M.A. In response to *Familiar Letters*, Cambridge intellectuals produced *Pedantius* (1581) and used phrases from his own works to turn Harvey into a figure of fun. Nashe, more than a decade later, picked up on the humorous digs at Harvey in *Pedantius* and portrayed Harvey as a buffoon, a hanger-on who dropped the names of Edmund Spenser and Philip Sidney to enhance his own importance.

In 1580, Spenser chose to trade England for Ireland because he recognized that more opportunities existed for him in Ireland than in England. He left for Ireland with the conviction that he had been honoured by an appointment which would ensure his future: the world was all before him. The *Shepheardes Calender* (1579) announces that the shepherd-priest, who had intended to become a clergyman, will become a shepherd-poet and that he will make 'winges' of his 'aspyring wit' and attempt a 'famous flight'. Recently married, and fully committed to writing a Renaissance epic that would 'over-go Ariosto' and that might even establish him as an early modern Vergil, Spenser had reached a high point in his life. At twenty-five, he concluded the *Shepheardes Calender* with the bold claim that it was a '*Calender* for euery yeare' and the fervent hope that his pastoral would outwear 'steele in strength' and 'continewe till the worlds dissolution'. The aspiration in these lines testifies to the idealism that inspired the early Spenser and that prompted him to envision a life in Ireland where he might succeed in fashioning an epic that would become a 'pillour of Eternity'.

Notes

1 Lodowick Bryskett, *A Discourse of Civill Life*, ed. Thomas E. Wright, San Fernando Valley State College Renaissance Editions (Northridge, CA: San Fernando State College, 1970), 15.
2 For Bryskett's life, see Henry R. Plomer and Tom Peete Cross, *The Life and Correspondence of Lodowick Bryskett*. Modern Philology Monographs. (Chicago: University of Chicago Press, 1927), 4–6.
3 Bryskett was paid a salary, but Sidney refers to him as 'my friend Bryskett'. See the excellent edition, *The Correspondence of Sir Philip Sidney*, ed. Roger Kuin, 2 vols (Oxford: Oxford University Press, 2012), 1: 233.
4 See Simon Adams, *Household Accounts and Disbursement Books of Robert Dudley, Earl of Leicester, 1558–1561, 1584–1586* (Cambridge: Cambridge University Press, 1995), and H.R. Woudhuysen, 'Leicester's Literary Patronage: A Study of the English Court, 1578–1582', D.Phil. thesis, University of Oxford, 1981.
5 Anthony Grafton and Lisa Jardine, *From Humanism to Humanities: Education and the Liberal Arts in Fifteenth and Sixteenth Century Europe* (Cambridge, MA: Harvard University Press, 1986), 184–96.
6 Robert S. Kinsman, 'John Skelton', *Spenser Encyclopedia*, 660–1. See also Paul E. McLane, 'Skelton's *Colyn Cloute* and Spenser's *Shepheardes Calender*', *Studies in Philology*, 70 (1973), 141–59.

Bibliography of works cited

Manuscripts

British Library
    Add. MS 23089, D.1. MS collections by Mr George Vertue
    Add. MS 34064, 'Mother Hubberds Tale', fols 33v–35r
    Add. MS 68942, 'Mother Hubberds Tale'. Dated 5 June 1607
    Sloane MS 93, Harvey's 'Letter-Book'
Cambridge
    'Pembroke College Account Books'
Harvard
    Harvard, MS Eng 266, fols 38r–58r. A neatly written transcript of the *Complaints*
Kansas
    Kenneth Spencer Research Library, MS 240A:1024. Receipt for Quit Rent. Kirtling, Cambridgeshire. 24 November 1587. In Spenser's hand
London National Archives
    PRO, SP 12, 159, Sir Henry Sidney's Memoir of his Government of Ireland, 1583
    PRO, SP 63/70/7, 6 November 1579. Walsingham to Malby
    PRO, SP 63/70/, fols. 91, 28 November 1579. William Pelham to Burghley
    PRO SP 63/72/36, fol. 100, 7 April 1580. Grey to Leicester
Manchester
    Manchester, Chetham's Library, A.6.49. Theological commonplace book consisting of 42 folios
    Manchester, Chetham's Library, MS A.6.50. 'Accounts of the Executors of Robert Nowell', Attorney of the Queen's Court of Wards [Nowell Account Book]

Early printed books

A Summary of the Life of Mr. Edmond Spenser', in *Works of Mr. Edmond Spenser* (London: Henry Hills for Jonathan Edwin, 1679). RB 106944. The Huntington Library, San Marino, CA.

Buckeridge, 'Sermon Preached at the Funeral of ... Lancelot late Lord Bishop of Winchester ... On Saturday being the XI. Of November, A.D. MDCXXVI', included in the 1629 edition of *XCVI Sermons*, ed. Archbishop Laud and John Buckeridge (London: George Miller for Richard Badger, 1629). RB 43440. The Huntington Library, San Marino, CA.

Camden, William, *Tomus alter idem: or, The historie of the life and reigne of that famous princess, Elizabeth* ... Trans. Thomas Browne. Fourth part of Camden's *Annales rerum ... covering the years 1589-1603* (London: Printed by Tho. Harper for William Web, 1629). RB 600237. The Huntington Library, San Marino, CA.

Camden, William, *The Historie of the Most Renowned and Victorious Princesse Elizabeth ... Composed by Way of Annals* (London: Printed for Benjamin Fisher, 1630). RB 60054. The Huntington Library, San Marino, CA.

Churchyard, Thomas, *A General Rehearsall of Warres, called Churchyardes Choise* (London: J. Kingston for E. White, 1579). RB 56403. The Huntington Library, San Marino, CA.

Harvey, Gabriel, *Foure Letters, and certaine sonnets; especially touching Robert Greene, and other parties by him abused* (London: John Wolfe, 1592). RB 61305. The Huntington Library, San Marino, CA.

Gabrielis Harueij Gratulationum Valdinensium Libri Quatuor (Londini: Henrici Binnemani, 1578). RB 59268. The Huntington Library, San Marino, CA.

Gabrielis Harueii Valdinatis: Smithus; vel Musarum Lachrymae. RB 35263. The Huntington Library, San Marino, CA.

Harvey, Gabriel, *Three Proper and wittie, familiar Letters.: lately passed betwene two Universitie men: touching the Earthquake in Aprill last, and our English refourmed Versifying. With the Preface of a wellwiller to them both. Two Other very commendable Letters of the same mens writing: both touching the foresaid Artificiall Versifying, and certain other Particulars: More lately delivered unto the Printer* (London: H. Bynnneman, 1580). This copy is missing F2–F3. EEBO reproduces this defective text. RB 69544. The Huntington Library, San Marino, CA.

Harvey, Richard, *Astrological Discourse* (London: Henrie Bynneman, 1583). RB 17109. The Huntington Library, San Marino, CA.

Holinshed, Raphael, *The First and Second Volumes of Chronicles, comprising 1. The description and historie of England, 2. The description and historie of Ireland, ... Now newlie augmented ... to the yeare 1568*. by John Hooker aliàs Vowell, Gent. ... (At London: Iohn, Harison, George Bishop, Rafe Newberie, Henrie

Denham and Thomas Woodcocke, 2 vols: Printed [by Henry Denham], 1587, 1:173). RB 497126. The Huntington Library, San Marino, CA.
Hoole, Charles, *A New Discovery of the Old Art of Teaching Schoole, in four small treatises. 1. Concerning A Petty-schoole. 2. The ushers duty 3. The masters method 4. Scholastick discipline in a grammar schoole. Written about twenty-three yeares ago* (London: printed by J[ohn] T[wyn] for Andrew Crook, 1660). RB 384529. The Huntington Library, San Marino, CA.
Letters and Memorials of State, ed. Arthur Collins. 2 vols (London: Printed for T. Osborne, 1746). RB 601620. The Huntington Library, San Marino, CA.
Lyly, John, *Pappe with a Hatchet. Alias, A figge for my God sonne. Or, Cracke me this nut* (London: John Anoke, and John Astile, i.e. T. Orwin, 1589). RB 62468. The Huntington library, San Marino, CA.
Norden, John, *The Mirror of Honor* (London: by the widowe Orwin for Thomas Man, 1597). RB 59383. The Huntington Library, San Marino, CA.
Wase, Christopher, *Considerations Concerning Free Schools as Settled in England* (London: Mr Simon Millers, 1678). RB 349367. The Huntington Library, San Marino, CA.
Whetstone, George, *Sir Phillip Sidney, his honorable life, his valiant death, and true virtues* (London: [By T. Orwin] for Thomas Cadman, 1587). RB 14643. The Huntington Library, San Marino, Ca.

Modern books, editions and articles

Acts of the Privy Council of England, New Series, ed. John Roche Dasent (London: Eyre and Spottiswoode, 1895).
Adams, Simon, 'Favourites and Factions at the Elizabethan Court', in *The Tudor Monarchy*, ed. John Guy (London and New York: Arnold and St Martin's Press, 1997), 253–74.
Adams, Simon, *Household Accounts and Disbursement Books of Robert Dudley, Earl of Leicester, 1558–1561, 1584–1586* (Cambridge: Cambridge University Press, 1995).
Alumni Cantabrigienses: A Biographical List of All Known Students, Graduates and Holders of Office at the University of Cambridge from the Earliest Times to 1900, compiled by John Venn and J.A. Venn (Cambridge: Cambridge University Press, 1922).
Anderson, Judith, *Reading the Allegorical Intertext: Chaucer, Spenser, Shakespeare, Milton* (New York: Fordham University Press, 2008).
Ascham, Roger, *The Schoolmaster* (1570), ed. Lawrence V. Ryan (Ithaca, NY: Published for the Folger Shakespeare Library by Cornell University Press, 1967).
Attwater, Aubrey, *A Short History of Pembroke College* (1936; rpt Cambridge: Cambridge University Press, 1973).

Austen, Gillian, *The Literary Career of George Gascoigne: Studies in Self Presentation* (Woodbridge: D.S. Brewer, 2008).
Austin, Warren B., 'William Withie's Notebook: Lampoons on John Lyly and Gabriel Harvey', *Review of English Studies*, 23 (1947), 297–309.
Bacon, Sir Francis, *The Letters and Life of Francis Bacon*, ed. J. Spedding. 14 vols (London, 1868).
Baker-Smith, Dominic, 'Sidney's Death and the Poets', in *Sir Philip Sidney 1586 and the Creation of a Legend*, ed. Jan van Dorsten, Dominic Baker-Smith, and Arthur Kinney (Leiden: E.J. Brill and Leiden University Press for the Sir Thomas Browne Institute, 1986), 83–103.
Bald, R.C., *John Donne, A Life* (Oxford: Oxford University Press, 1970).
Baldwin, T.W., *William Shakespeare's Petty School* (Urbana: University of Illinois Press, 1943).
Barker, William, ed., Richard Mulcaster, *Positions Concerning the Training Up of Children* (Toronto: University of Toronto Press, 1994).
Bates, Catherine, *The Rhetoric of Courtship in Elizabethan Language and Literature* (Cambridge: Cambridge University Press, 1992).
Bennett, Josephine, 'Spenser and Gabriel Harvey's "Letter-Book"', *Modern Philology*, 29 (1931), 163–86.
Bjorklund, Nancy Basler, '"A Godly Wyfe is a Helper": Matthew Parker and the Defense of Clerical Marriage', *Sixteenth Century Journal*, 34 (2003), 347–65.
Bowker, Margaret, 'Thomas Cooper', *ODNB* (2008).
Brady, Ciaran, *A Viceroy's Vindication? Sir Henry Sidney's Memoir of Service in Ireland, 1556–1578* (Cork: Cork University Press, 2002).
Brink, Jean R., '"All his minde on honour fixed": The Preferment of Edmund Spenser', in *Spenser's Life and the Subject of Biography*, ed. Judith H. Anderson, Donald Cheney, and David A. Richardson (Amherst: University of Massachusetts Press, 1996), 45–64.
Brink, Jean R., 'Literacy and Education', in *A Companion to English Renaissance Literature and Culture*, ed. Michael Hattaway (Oxford: Blackwell Publishers, 2000), 95–105.
Brink, Jean R., 'Manuscript Culture Revisited', *Sidney Journal*, 17 (1999), 19–30.
Brink, Jean R., *Michael Drayton Revisited* (Boston: G.K. Hall, 1990).
Brink, Jean R., 'Revising Edmund Spenser's Birth Date to 1554', *Notes and Queries*, NewSeries, 56, No. 4 (2009), 523–8.
Brink, Jean R., 'Sidney's *Letter to Queen Elizabeth*: Text and Context', *Sidney Journal*, 32 (2014), 1–16.
Brink, Jean R., 'Spenser's "Home"', *Spenser Studies*, 31/32 (2018), 439–58.
Brink, Jean R., 'Spenser's Romances: From "Lying Shepherd's Tongues" to Wedded Love', *Sidney Journal*, 26, No. 2 (2008), 101–10.
Brink, Jean R., 'Who Fashioned Edmund Spenser? The Textual History of the *Complaints*', *Studies in Philology*, 88 (1991), 153–68.
Brook, V.J.K., *Whitgift and the English Church* (London: The English Universities Press Ltd, 1957).

Bryskett, Lodowick, *A Discourse of Civill Life*, ed. Thomas E. Wright, San Fernando Valley State College Renaissance Editions (Northridge, CA: San Fernando State College, 1970).
Buck, P.M., Jr, 'Add. MS 34064 and Spenser's *Ruins of Time* and *Mother Hubberd's Tale*', *Modern Language Notes*, 22 (1907), 41–6.
Byrom, HJ., 'Edmund Spenser's First Printer, Hugh Singleton', *The Library*, 4th Series, 14 (1933), 121–56.
Calendar of State Papers, Domestic, 1619–23, ed. Mary Anne Everett Green (London: HMSO, 1858).
Calendar of State Papers, Spanish, 1569–79, ed. Martin A. S. Hume (London: HMSO, 1894).
Calendar of State Papers, Venetian, 1558–1580, ed. Rawdon Brown and G. Cavendish Bentinck (London: HMSO, 1890).
Calendar of the Manuscripts of the Marquis of Salisbury: The Cecil Papers, 1572–83, ed. M.S. Giuseppi. (London: HMSO, 1883).
Cambridge University Transactions During the Puritan Controversies, ed. James Heywood and Thomas Wright, 2 vols (London: Henry G. Bohn, 1854).
Canny, Nicholas, *The Elizabethan Conquest of Ireland* (Hassocks: The Harvester Press, 1976).
Canny, Nicholas, *Making Ireland British: 1580–1650* (Oxford: Oxford University Press, 2001).
Carlson, Eric Josef, *Marriage and the English Reformation* (Cambridge, MA: Blackwell, 1994).
Carlson, Eric Josef, 'Clerical Marriage and the English Reformation', *Journal of British Studies*, 31 (1992), 1–31.
Carroll, D. Allen, 'The Meaning of E.K', *Spenser Studies*, 20 (2005), 169–82.
Chaplains in Early Modern England: Patronage, Literature and Religion, ed. Hugh Adlington, Tom Lockwood, Gillian Wright (Manchester: Manchester University Press, 2013).
Cheney, Patrick, *Spenser's Famous Flight: A Renaissance Idea of a Literary Career* (Toronto: University of Toronto Press, 1993).
Churton, Ralph, *The Life of Alexander Nowell, Dean of St. Paul's* (Oxford: Oxford University Press, 1809).
Clegg, Cyndia, *Press Censorship in Elizabethan England* (Cambridge: Cambridge University Press, 1997).
Collection of Statutes for the University and the Colleges of Cambridge, ed. James Heywood (London: William Clowes & Sons, 1840).
Collinson, Patrick, 'Andrew Perne and His Times', in *Andrew Perne: Quartercentenary Studies: Patrick Collinson, David McKitterick, Elisabeth Leedham Green*, ed. David McKitterick. Cambridge Bibliographical Monograph Series 11 (Cambridge: Printed for Cambridge Bibliographical Society by Cambridge University Press, 1991).
Coren, Pamela, 'Edmund Spenser, Mary Sidney, and the Doleful Lay', *Studies in English Literature, 1500–1900*, 42 (2002), 25–41.

Cressy, David, *Literacy and the Social Order: Reading and Writing in Tudor and Stuart England* (Cambridge: Cambridge University Press, 1980).
Curtis, Mark H., *Oxford and Cambridge in Transition, 1558–1642* (Oxford: Clarendon Press, 1959).
Dawley, Powel Mills, *John Whitgift and the English Reformation* (New York: Charles Scribner's Sons, 1954).
Dees, Jerome, 'Homiletics', *Spenser Encyclopedia* (Toronto: University of Toronto Press, 1990), 376–7.
DeMolen, Richard., *Richard Mulcaster and Educational Reform in the Renaissance* (Nieukoop: De Graaf Publishers, 1991).
Documents Relating to the Office of the Revels in the Time of Queen Elizabeth, ed. Albert Feuillerat (Reprinted Louvain: A. Uystpruyst, 1963).
Doran, Susan, *Monarchy and Matrimony* (London: Routledge, 1996).
Dovey, Zillah, *An Elizabethan Progress: The Queen's Journey into East Anglia, 1578* (Stroud: Alan Sutton and Madison, Teaneck: Fairleigh Dickinson Press, 1996).
Duncan-Jones, Katherine, *Sir Philip Sidney, Courtier Poet* (New Haven: Yale University Press, 1991).
Eccles, Mark, 'Spenser's First Marriage', *Times Literary Supplement*, 31 December 1931, 1053.
Eccles, Mark, 'Elizabethan Edmund Spensers', *Modern Language Quarterly*, 5 (1944), 413–27.
Edmund Spenser: New and Renewed Directions, ed. J.B. Lethbridge *(Madison and Teaneck: Fairleigh Dickinson University Press, 2006).*
Eleventh Report of the Deputy Keeper of the Public Records in Ireland, 18 March 1879 (Dublin: HMSO, 1879).
Elizabethan Critical Essays, ed., G. Gregory Smith, 2 vols (Oxford: Clarendon Press, 1904).
Esler, Anthony, *The Aspiring Mind of the Elizabethan Younger Generation* (Durham, NC: Duke University Press, 1966).
Finch, Mary E., *The Wealth of Five Northamptonshire Families, 1540–1640*. Northamptonshire Record Society 19 (Oxford: Charles Batey at the University Press, 1956).
Ford, Alan, 'Walter Travers', *ODNB* (2008).
Forsett, Edward, *Pedantius, A Latin Comedy Formerly Acted in Trinity College, Cambridge*, ed. G.C. Moore Smith, Vol. 8, in *Materialen zur Kunde des älteren Englishchen Dramas* (Louvain, Leipzig, and London: A. Uystpruyst 1905).
Forster, Leonard, 'The Translator of the "Theatre for Worldlings"', *English Studies*, 48 (1967), 27–34.
Foxe's Book of Martyrs, ed. G.A. Williamson (Boston and Toronto: Little, Brown and Company, 1965).
Fry, Frederick M., Master of the Company for 1895–6, *A Historical Catalogue of the Pictures, Herse-Cloths & Tapestry at Merchant Taylors' Hall* (London: Chapman and Hall, Ltd, 1907).

Gellar, Sherri, 'You Can't Tell a Book by Its Contents: (Mis)Interpretation in/ of Spenser's *The Shepheardes Calender*', *Spenser Studies*, 13 (1999), 21–55.
Gless, Daryl J., *Interpretation and Theology in Spenser* (Cambridge: Cambridge University Press, 1994).
Goldberg, Jonathan, 'Colin to Hobbinol: Spenser's *Familiar Letters*', *South Atlantic Quarterly*, 88 (1989), 107–26.
Goldberg, Jonathan, *Sodometries: Renaissance Texts, Modern Sexualities* (Stanford: Stanford University Press, 1992).
Grace Book Delta Containing the Records of the University of Cambridge for the Years 1542–1589, ed. John Venn (Cambridge: Cambridge University Press, 1910).
Grafton, Anthony and Lisa Jardine, *From Humanism to Humanities: Education and the Liberal Arts in Fifteenth and Sixteenth Century Europe* (Cambridge, MA: Harvard University Press, 1986).
Greenlaw, Edwin, 'Spenser and the Earl of Leicester', *Publications of the Modern Language Association*, 26 (1910): 535–61.
Gregerson, Linda, *The Reformation of the Subject: Spenser, Milton and the English Protestant Epic* (Cambridge: Cambridge University Press, 1995).
Greville, Fulke, *The Prose Works of Fulke Greville, Lord Brooke*, ed. John Gouws (Oxford: Clarendon Press, 1986).
Grey, Arthur Lord Grey of Wilton, *A Commentary of the services and Charges of William Lord Grey of Wilton, K.G.*, ed. Sir Philip de Malpas Grey Egerton, Vol. 40 (London: Printed for the Camden Society by J.B. Nichols and Son, 1847).
Grosart, Alexander B., *The Townley Manuscript: Spending of the Money of Robert Nowell* (Manchester: Charles E. Simms, 1877).
Guazzo, Stephano, *The Civile Conversation*, trans., George Pettie and ed. Charles Whibley. 2 vols. The Tudor Translations (New York: AMS Press, 1967).
Hackett, Helen, *Virgin Mother, Maiden Queen: Elizabeth I and the Cult of the Virgin Mary* (New York: St Martin's Press, 1995).
Hackett, M.B., *The Original Statutes of Cambridge University: The Text and Its History* (Cambridge: Cambridge University Press, 1970).
Hadfield, Andrew, *Edmund Spenser, A Life* (Oxford: Oxford University Press, 2012).
Hadfield, Andrew, 'Edmund Spenser (1552?–1599)', *ODNB* (2008).
Hadfield, Andrew, 'Spenser's Rosalind', *Modern Language Review*, 104 (2009), 935–46.
Haller, William, *The Elect Nation: The Meaning and Relevance of Foxe's Book of Martyrs* (New York: Harper & Row, 1963).
Hamer, Douglas, 'Spenser's Marriage', *Review of English Studies*, 7 (1931), 271–90.
Hamer, Douglas, 'Edmund Spenser's Gown and Shilling', *Review of English Studies*, 23 (1947), 218–25.
Hammer, Paul E.J., 'The Earl of Essex, Fulke Greville and the Employment of Scholars', *Studies in Philology*, 91 (1994), 167–80.
Hammer, Paul E.J., 'Robert Devereux, 2nd Earl of Essex', *ODNB* (2008).
Hammer, Paul E.J., 'The Uses of Scholarship: The Secretariat of Robert Devereux, c. 1585–1601', *English Historical Review*, 109 (1994), 26–51.

Hannay, Margaret, *Philip's Phoenix* (Oxford: Oxford University Press, 1990).
Harington, Sir John, *A New Discourse of a Stale Subject, Called the Metamorphosis of Ajax*, ed. Elizabeth Story Donno (London: Routledge & Kegan Paul, 1962).
Harrison, William, *The Description of England* (1587) by William Harrison, ed. Georges Edelen. Folger Shakespeare Library (Ithaca, NY: Cornell University Press, 1968).
Harvey, Gabriel, *Ciceronianus*, ed. and trans. Harold S. Wilson and Clarence A. Forbes (Lincoln: University of Nebraska Studies, 1945).
Harvey, Gabriel, *Works of Gabriel Harvey*, ed. Alexander Grosart, 3 vols, Huth Library (London: Hazell, Watson & Viney, Ltd, 1884–85).
Harvey, Gabriel, *Four Letters and Certain Sonnets, especially touching Robert Greene, and other parties by him abused*. A New Edition (London: Longman, Hurst, Rees, Orme, and Brown. Printed by T. Davison, 1814).
Harvey, Gabriel. *The Letter-Book of Gabriel Harvey, A.D. 1573–1580, edited from the original ms. Sloane 93 in the British Library*, ed. Edward John Long Scott, Camden Society New Series, 33 (Westminster: Nichols and Sons, 1884).
Hay, M.V., *The Life of Robert Sidney, Earl of Leicester, 1563–1626* (Washington, DC: Folger Books, 1984).
Heaton, Gabriel, *Writing and Reading Royal Entertainments* (Oxford: Oxford University Press, 2010).
Heffner, Ray, 'Edmund Spenser's Family', *Huntington Library Quarterly*, 2 (1938–39), 79–85.
Helgerson, Richard, *Self-Crowned Laureates: Spenser, Jonson, Milton and the Literary System* (Berkeley: University of California Press, 1983).
Heninger, S.K, 'The Implications of Form for *The Shepheardes Calender*', *Studies in the Renaissance*, 8 (1962), 309–21.
Heninger, S.K., *Sidney and Spenser: The Poet as Maker* (University Park and London: Pennsylvania State University Press, 1989).
Heninger, S.K., 'The Typographical Layout of Spenser's *Shepheardes Calender*', in *Word and Visual Imagination*, ed. Karl Josef Holtgen and Peter M. Daly (Erlangen: University of Erlangen Press, 1988), 33–71.
Herron, Thomas, 'Complex Spenser: New Directions in Recent Research', *Renaissance Quarterly*, 68, No. 3 (Fall 2015), 957–69.
Hieatt, A. Kent, *Short Time's Endless Monument: The Symbolism of Numbers in Edmund Spenser's 'Epithalamion'* (New York: Columbia University Press, 1960).
Higginson, James Jackson, *Spenser's Shepheardes Calender in Relation to Contemporary Affairs* (New York: Columbia University Press, 1912).
Hoole, Charles, *A New Discovery of the Old Art of Teaching School; in four small treatises*, ed. E.T. Campagnac (Liverpool: Liverpool University Press, 1913).
Hulbert, Viola, 'Diggon Davie', *Journal of English and Germanic Philology*, 42 (1942), 349–67.
Hume, Anthea, *Edmund Spenser: Protestant Poet* (Cambridge: Cambridge University Press, 1984).

James, Mervyn, 'English Politics and the Concept of Honour, 1485–1642', in *Society, Politics and Culture: Studies in Early Modern England* (Cambridge: Cambridge University Press, 1986), 308–415.

Jameson, Thomas Hugh, 'The "Machiavellianism" of Gabriel Harvey', *Publications of the Modern Language Association*, 56 (1941): 647–8.

Jardine, Lisa, 'Encountering Ireland: Gabriel Harvey, Edmund Spenser, and English Colonial Ventures', in *Representing Ireland: Literature and the Origins of Conflict, 1534–1660*, ed. Brendan Bradshaw, Andrew Hadfield, and Willy Maley (Cambridge: Cambridge University Press, 1993), 60–75.

Jardine, Lisa and Anthony Grafton, '"Studied for Action": How Gabriel Harvey Read His Livy', *Past & Present*, 129 (1990), 30–78.

Jenkins, Raymond, 'Spenser with Lord Grey in Ireland', *Publications of the Modern Language Association*, 52 (1937), 338–53.

Johnson, Francis R., 'The First Edition of Gabriel Harvey's *Foure Letters*', *The Library*, Series 4, 15 (1934–35), 212–23.

Johnson, Francis R., 'Gabriel Harvey's *Three Letters*: A First Issue of His *Foure Letters*', *The Library*, Fifth Series, 1 (1946), 134–6.

Johnson, Lynn Staley, *The Shepheardes Calender: An Introduction* (University Park: The Pennsylvania State University, 1990).

Jonson, Ben, *Works*, ed. C.H. Herford and Percy Simpson, 11 vols (Oxford: Clarendon Press, 1925).

Judson, Alexander C., *A Biographical Sketch of John Young, Bishop of Rochester, with Emphasis on His Relations with Edmund Spenser* (Bloomington: Indiana University Studies, 1934).

Judson, Alexander C., *The Life of Edmund Spenser* (Baltimore: Johns Hopkins University Press, 1945).

Kane, Brendan, *The Politics and Culture of Honour in Britain and Ireland, 1541–1641* (Cambridge: Cambridge University Press, 2010).

Kaske, Carol V., *Spenser and Biblical Poetics* (Ithaca: Cornell University Press, 1999).

Kaske, Carol V., 'Spenser's *Amoretti and Epithalamion* of 1595: Structure Genre and Numerology', *English Literary Renaissance*, 8 (1978), 271–95.

Kennedy, William J., *Authorizing Petrarch* (Ithaca: Cornell University Press, 1994).

King, John, 'Reformation', *Spenser Encyclopedia* (Toronto: University of Toronto Press, 1990), 593–5.

King, John, *Spenser's Poetry and the Reformation Tradition* (Princeton: Princeton University Press, 1990).

King, John, 'Was Spenser a Puritan?', *Spenser Studies*, 6 (1986), 1–31.

Kinsman, Robert S., 'John Skelton', *Spenser Encyclopedia* (Toronto: University of Toronto Press, 1990), 660–1.

Knapp, Jeffrey, 'Spenser the Priest', *Representations*, 81 (2003), 61–78.

Knowles, R.B., ed., *Fourth Report of the Royal Commission of Historical Manuscripts* (London: George Edward Eyre and William Spottiswoode, 1874).

Lamb, Mary Ellen, *Gender and Authorship in the Sidney Circle* (Madison: University of Wisconsin Press, 1990).

Lane, Robert, *Shepheards Devises: Edmund Spenser's* Shepheardes Calender *and the Institutions of Elizabethan Society* (Athens: University of Georgia Press, 1993).

Leader, Damian Riehl, *A History of the University of Cambridge* (Cambridge: Cambridge University Press, 1988).

Leicester's Commonwealth: The Copy of a Letter written by a Master of Art of Cambridge (1584) and Related Documents, ed. D.C. Peck (Athens: Ohio University Press, 1985).

Levy, F.J., 'Spenser and Court Humanism', in *Spenser's Life and the Subject of Biography*, ed. Judith H. Anderson, Donald Cheney, and David A. Richardson (Amherst: University of Massachusetts Press, 1996), 65–80.

Lewalski, Barbara Kiefer, 'Patronage', *Spenser Encyclopedia* (Toronto: University of Toronto Press, 1990).

Lewis, C.S., *English Literature in the Sixteenth Century Excluding Drama* (Oxford: Clarendon Press, 1954).

Lodge, Edmund, *Illustrations of British History, Biography, and Manners*, 2 vols (London, 1838).

Long, Percy W., 'Spenser and the Bishop of Rochester', *Publications of the Modern Language Association*, 31 (1916), 713–35.

Lossky, Nicholas, *Lancelot Andrewes, The Preacher (1555–1626)*, trans. Andrew Louth (Oxford: Clarendon Press, 1991).

Luborsky, Ruth Samson, 'The Allusive Presentation of *The Shepheardes Calender*', *Spenser Studies*, 1 (1980), 29–67.

Lucas, Scott, 'Diggon Davie and Davy Dicar: Edmund Spenser, Thomas Churchyard, and the Poetics of Public Protest', *Spenser Studies*, 16 (2002), 151–65.

Lynn, Richard E., 'Ewe/Who? Recreating Spenser's *March* Eclogue', *Spenser Studies*, 26 (2011), 153–78.

MacCarthy-Morrogh, Michael, *The Munster Plantation: English Migration to Southern Ireland, 1583–1641* (Oxford: Clarendon Press, 1986).

Mack, Peter, *Elizabethan Rhetoric: Theory and Practice* (Cambridge: Cambridge University Press, 2002).

Mallette, Richard, *Spenser and the Discourses of Reformation England* (Lincoln: Nebraska University Press, 1997).

Maley, Willy, 'Spenser's Life', in *The Oxford Handbook of Edmund Spenser*, ed. Richard A. McCabe (Oxford: Oxford University Press, 2010), 13–29.

Maley, Willy, 'Bibliography: Spenser and Ireland', *Spenser Studies*, 9 (1991), 227–42.

The Marprelate Tracts: A Modernized and Annotated Edition, ed. Joseph L. Black (Cambridge: Cambridge University Press, 2008).

May, Steven W., 'Sir Philip Sidney and Queen Elizabeth', *English Manuscript Studies, 1100–1700*, Vol 2, ed. Peter Beal and A.S.G. Edwards (Oxford: Blackwell, 1990), 257–68.

May, Steven W., 'Tudor Aristocrats and the Mythical Stigma of Print', *Renaissance Papers*, 10 (1980), 11-18.
McCabe, Richard, '"Little booke: thy selfe present": The Politics of Presentation in *The Shepheardes Calender*', in H. Erskine-Hill and R.A. McCabe, eds, *Presenting Poetry: Composition, Publication, Reception* (Cambridge: Cambridge University Press, 1995), 15-40.
McCanles, Michael, 'The *Shepheardes Calender* as Document and Monument', *Studies in English Literature*, 22 (1982), 5-19.
McCoy, Richard C., *The Rites of Knight Hood: The Literature and Politics of Elizabethan Chivalry* (Berkeley: University of California Press, 1989).
McLane, Paul E., 'Skelton's *Colyn Cloute* and Spenser's *Shepheardes Calender*', *Studies in Philology*, 70 (1973), 141-59.
McLane, Paul E., *Spenser's Shepheardes Calender: A Study in Elizabethan Allegory* (Notre Dame: University of Notre Dame Press, 1961).
Mears, Natalie, 'Courts, Courtiers, and Culture in Tudor England', *The Historical Journal*, 46 (2003), 703-22.
Merchant Taylors' School. *A Register of the Scholars Admitted into Merchant Taylors' School, from A.D. 1562 to 1874*, ed. Rev. Charles J. Robinson, 2 vols (London: Lewes Farncombe & Co., 1882).
Merchant Taylors' School Register 1561-1934, ed. E. P. Hart 2 vols (London: Merchant Taylors' Company, 1936).
Mildmay, Sir Walter, *The Statutes of Sir Walter Mildmay, Kt, Chancellor of the Exchequer and one of Her Majesty's Privy Councillors; authorized by him for the government of Emmanuel College founded by him*, ed and trans. Frank Stubbings (Cambridge: Cambridge University Press, 1983).
Miller, David L., 'Spenser's Vocation, Spenser's Career', *English Literary History*, 50 (1983), 197-231.
Mohl, Ruth. 'Edmund Spenser', *The Spenser Encyclopedia*. (Toronto: University of Toronto Press, 1990), 668-71.
Montrose, Louis Adrian, '"Eliza, Queene of shepheardes," and the Pastoral of Power', *English Literary Renaissance*, 10 (1980), 153-82.
Montrose, Louis Adrian, 'The Elizabethan Subject and the Spenserian Text', in *Literary Theory / Renaissance Texts*, ed. Patricia Parker and David Quint (Baltimore: Johns Hopkins University Press, 1986), 907-46.
Montrose, Louis Adrian, 'The "perfecte paterne of a Poete": The Poetics of Courtship in *The Shepheardes Calender*', *Texas Studies in Literature and Language*, 21, No. 1 (Spring 1979), 34-67.
More, Sir Thomas, *The Life of Sir Thomas More* in *Two Early Tudor Lives*, ed. Richard S. Sylvester and Davis P. Harding (New Haven: Yale University Press, 1962).
Morgan, Hiram, 'The Colonial Adventure of Sir Thomas Smith in Ulster', *Historical Journal*, 28 (1985), 261-78.
Mounts, Charles E., 'Spenser and the Countess of Leicester', in *That Souveraine Light: Essays in Honor of Edmund Spenser, 1552-1952*, ed. William Mueller

and Don Cameron Allen (Baltimore: Johns Hopkins University Press, 1952), 111–22.

Mulcaster's Elementarie, ed. E.T. Campagnac (Oxford: Clarendon Press, 1925).

Nashe, Thomas, *The Works of Thomas Nashe*, ed. R.B. McKerrow, 5 vols (Oxford: Blackwell, 1958).

Nelson, Allen H., *Monstrous Adversary: The Life of Edward de Vere, 17th Earl of Oxford* (Liverpool: Liverpool University Press, 2003).

Nichols, John, *Progresses, and Public Processions of Queen Elizabeth*, 3 vols (London: Society of Antiquaries, 1788).

Nichols, John, *The Progresses and Public Processions of Queen Elizabeth I: A New Edition of the Early Modern Sources*, ed. Elizabeth Goldring, Faith Eales, Elizabeth Clarke, and Jayne Elisabeth Archer, 5 vols (Oxford: Oxford University Press, 2014).

Norbrook, David, *Poetry and Politics in the English Renaissance* (1984; rev. ed. Oxford: Oxford University Press, 2002).

O'Neill, Maria, 'Forgotten Figure on the Bridge: Richard Mulcaster', *Sederi*, VII (1996), 93–7.

Oram, William, 'Introduction: Spenser's Paratexts', vii–xviii in *The 1590 Faerie Queene: Paratexts and Publishing*, ed, Wayne Erickson, SLI: *Studies in the Literary Imagination*, 38 (2005).

Osborn, James M., *Young Philip Sidney, 1572–1577* (New Haven: Yale University Press, 1972).

Parks, George Bruner, *Richard Hakluyt and the English Voyages*, ed. James A. Williamson, Geographical Society Serial Publication No. 10 (Lancaster, PA: Lancaster Press, 1928).

Patterson, Annabel, *Pastoral and Ideology: Virgil to Valery* (Berkeley: University of California Press, 1987).

Peterson, Richard, 'Laurel Crown and Ape's Tail: New Light on Spenser's Career from Thomas Tresham', *Spenser Studies*, 12 (1988), 153–68.

Phillips, James E., 'Spenser's Syncretistic Religious Imagery', *English Literary History*, 36 (1969), 110–30.

Pienaar, W.J.B., 'Edmund Spenser and Jonker Jan van der Noot', *English Studies*, 8 (1926), 33–44 and 67–76.

Plomer, Henry R. and Tom Peete Cross, *The Life and Correspondence of Lodowick Bryskett*, Modern Philology Monographs (Chicago: University of Chicago Press, 1927).

Porter, H.C. *Reformation and Reaction in Tudor Cambridge* (Cambridge: Cambridge University Press, 1958).

Prescott, Anne Lake, *French Poets and the English Renaissance: Studies in Fame and Transformation* (New Haven: Yale University Press, 1978).

Prouty, C.T., *George Gascoigne: Elizabethan Courtier, Soldier, and Poet* (New York: Columbia University Press, 1942).

The Quenes Maiesties Passage through the Citie of London To Westminster the Day before her Coronacion (London: Richard Tottel, 1559). Reprinted by

John Nichols, *The Progresses and Public Processions of Queen Elizabeth*, 2 vols (1788–1805; rpt New York: Burt Franklin, 1966).

The Quenes Maiesties Passage through the Citie of London To Westminster the Day before her Coronacion (London: Richard Tottel, 1559). Reprinted by Arthur F. Kinney, ed., *Elizabethan Backgrounds* (Hamden, CT: Archon Books, 1975).

Quinn, David Beers, 'Sir Thomas Smith (1513–1577) and the Beginnings of English Colonial Theory', *Proceedings of the American Philosophical Society*, 89, No. 4 (December 1945), 543–60.

Quitslund, Jon A., 'Questionable Evidence in the *Letters* of 1580 between Gabriel Harvey and Edmund Spenser', in *Spenser's Life and the Subject of Biography*, ed. Judith H. Anderson, Donald Cheney, and David A. Richardson (Amherst: University of Massachusetts Press, 1996).

Rambuss, Richard, *Spenser's Secret Career* (Cambridge: Cambridge University Press, 1993).

Remains of Archbishop Grindal (Cambridge: Cambridge University Press, 1843).

The Renaissance in England: Nondramatic Prose and Verse of the Sixteenth Century, ed. Hyder E. Rollins and Herschel Baker. (Lexington, MA: D.C. Heath & Co., 1954).

Ringler, William A, Jr 'Spenser, Shakespeare, Honor, and Worship', *Renaissance News*, 14 (1961), 159–61.

Rosenberg, Eleanor, *Leicester: Patron of Letters* (New York: Columbia University Press, 1955).

Ruutz-Rees, Caroline, 'Some Notes of Gabriel Harvey's in Hoby's Translation of Castiglione's *Courtier* (1561)', *Publications of the Modern Language Association*, 25 (1910), 608–39.

Satterwaite, Alfred W., *Spenser, Ronsard, and Du Bellay: A Renaissance Comparison* (Princeton: Princeton University Press, 1960).

Schleiner, Louise, 'Spenser's "E.K." as Edmund Kent (Kenned / of Kent): Kyth (Couth), Kissed, and Kunning-Conning', *English Literary Renaissance*, 20 (1990), 374–407.

Scott-Warren, Jason, 'Gabriel Harvey', *ODNB* (2008).

Sheils, William Joseph, 'John Whitgift', *ODNB* (2008).

Shirley, Evelyn Philip, ed., *Original Letters and Papers in Illustration of the History of the Church in Ireland* (London: Francis and John Rivington, 1851).

Shore, David R., 'E.K.', *Spenser Encyclopedia* (Toronto: University of Toronto Press, 1990).

Shuger, Debora, 'Irishmen, Aristocrats, and Other White Barbarians', *Renaissance Quarterly*, 50 (1997), 494–525.

A Sidney Chronology, 1554–1654, ed. Michael G. Brennan and Noel J. Kinnamon (New York: Palgrave Macmillan, 2003).

Sidney, Sir Henry, 'Sir Henry Sidney's Memoir of His Government of Ireland, 1583', transcribed and edited by Herbert Hoare, *Ulster Journal of Archaeology*, First Series, 3 (1855), 33–52, 85–109, 336–57.

Sidney, Sir Henry, *A Viceroy's Vindication? Sir Henry Sidney's Memoir of Service in Ireland, 1556–1578*, ed. Ciaran Brady (Cork: Cork University Press, 2002).
Sidney, Sir Philip, *The Correspondence of Sir Philip Sidney*, ed. Roger Kuin, 2 vols (Oxford: Oxford University Press, 2012).
Sidney, Sir Philip, *Miscellaneous Prose of Sir Philip Sidney*, ed. Katherine Duncan-Jones and Jan Van Dorsten (Oxford: Clarendon Press, 1973).
Smith, Bruce R., *Homosexual Desire in Shakespeare's England* (Chicago: University of Chicago Press, 1991, rev. ed. 1994).
Spenser Allusions in the Sixteenth and Seventeenth Centuries, compiled by Ray Heffner, Dorothy E. Mason, Frederic M. Padelford, ed., William Wells, *Studies in Philology*, 68, Texts and Studies (Chapel Hill: University of North Carolina Press, 1973).
Spenser, Edmund, *Complaints*, ed. W.L. Renwick (London: Scholartis Press, 1928).
Spenser, Edmund, *The Complete Works of Verse and Prose of Edmund Spenser, edited with a New Life*, ed. Rev. Alexander Grosart, 9 vols (London and Aylesbury: Hazell, Watson, and Viney, Ltd, 1882–84).
Spenser, Edmund, *Daphnaida and Other Poems*, ed. W.L. Renwick (Cambridge: Cambridge University Press, 1929).
Spenser, Edmund, *The Faerie Queene*, ed. A.C. Hamilton, Text ed. Hiroshi Yamashita and Toshiyuki Suzuki (London: Longman, 2001).
Spenser, Edmund, *Poetical Works of Edmund Spenser*, ed. George Lillie Craik (London, 1845).
Spenser, Edmund, *Selected Letters and Other Papers*, ed. Christopher Burlinson and Andrew Zurcher (Oxford: Oxford University Press, 2009).
Spenser, Edmund, *The Shorter Poems*, ed. Richard A. McCabe (London: Penguin, 1999).
Spenser, Edmund, *A View of the Present State of Ireland*, ed. W.L. Renwick (Scholartis Press, 1934; modernized and reprinted, Oxford: Clarendon Press, 1979).
Spenser, Edmund, *A View of the Present State of Ireland*, ed. Rudolf Gottfried, in *Spenser's Prose Works*, vol. 10 in *Works of Edmund Spenser: A Variorum Edition*, ed. Edwin Greenlaw, Charles Grosvenor Osgood, Frederick Morgan Padelford, Ray Heffner, 11 vols (Baltimore: Johns Hopkins University Press, 1932–45).
Spenser, Edmund, *Works of the Famous English Poet, Mr. Edmond Spenser* (London: Henry Hills for J. Edwin, 1679).
Spenser, Edmund. *The Works of Edmund Spenser: A Variorum Edition*, ed. Edwin Greenlaw, Charles Grosvenor Osgood, Frederick Morgan Padelford, and Ray Heffner, 10 vols (Baltimore: The Johns Hopkins Press, 1949).
Spenser, Edmund. *Yale Edition of the Shorter Poems of Edmund Spenser*, ed. William A. Oram, Einar Bjorvand, Ronald Bond, Thomas H. Cain, Alexander Dunlop, and Richard Schell (New Haven: Yale University Press, 1989).

Spenser's Life and the Subject of Biography, ed. Judith Anderson, Donald Cheney, and David A. Richardson (Amherst: University of Massachusetts Press, 1996).
Spenser: The Critical Heritage, ed. R.M. Cummings (London: Routledge & Kegan Paul, 1971).
Stern, Virginia, *Gabriel Harvey: His Life, Marginalia, and Library* (Oxford: Clarendon Press, 1979).
Stewart, Alan, *Philip Sidney: A Double Life* (New York: St Martin's / Dunne, 2000).
Stillinger, Jack, 'A Note on the Printing of E.K.'s Glosses', *Studies in Bibliography*, 14 (1961), 203–5.
Stone, Lawrence, 'The Educational Revolution in England, 1560–1640', *Past and Present*, 28 (1964), 41–80.
Stopes, Mrs C. C., *William Hunnis and the Revels of the Chapel Royal* (Louvain and London: A. Uystpruyst and David Nutt, 1910).
Strong, Roy, *Gloriana: The Portraits of Queen Elizabeth I* (Wisbech: Thames and Hudson, 1987).
Stubbs, John, *John Stubbs's Gaping Gulf with Letters and Other Relevant Documents*, ed. Lloyd E. Berry (Charlottesville: Folger Shakespeare Library by University of Virginia Press, 1968).
Taylor, E.G.R. Taylor, *Late Tudor and Early Stuart Geography, 1583–1650* (London: Methuen & Co. Ltd, 1934).
A Transcript of the Registers of the Company of Stationers of London, ed. Edward Arber (1875, rpt Gloucester, MA: Peter Smith, 1967).
Tribble, Evelyn, 'Glozing the Gap: Authority, Glossing Traditions and *The Shepheardes Calender*', *Criticism*, 34 (1992), 155–72.
Trim, David J.B., 'The Art of War: Martial Poetics from Henry Howard to Philip Sidney', in *Oxford Handbook of Tudor Literature, 1485–1603*, ed. Mike Pincome and Cathy Shraunk (Oxford: Oxford University Press, 2009), 587–605.
Trombley, F.B., 'Lodowick Bryskett's Elegies on Sidney in Spenser's *Astrophel* Volume', *Review of English Studies*, New Series, 37 (1986), 384–8.
Tudeau-Clayton, Margaret, *Jonson, Shakespeare and Early Modern Virgil* (Cambridge: Cambridge University Press, 2006).
Usher, Brett, 'Queen Elizabeth and Mrs Bishop', in *The Myth of Elizabeth*, ed. Susan Doran and Thomas S. Freeman (New York: Palgrave Macmillan, 2003), 200–20.
Usher, Brett, 'John Aylmer', *ODNB* (2008).
Ussher, Brett, 'John Young', *ODNB* (2008).
Van Dorsten, Jan, *The Radical Arts: First Decade of an Elizabethan Renaissance* (Leiden: Sir Thomas Browne Institute, 1970).
Venn, John, ed., *Grace Book Delta Containing the Records of the University of Cambridge for the Years 1542–1589* (Cambridge: Cambridge University Press, 1910).
Watkins, John, *The Specter of Dido: Spenser and Virgilian Epic* (New Haven: Yale University Press, 1995).

Watson, Foster, *The English Grammar Schools to 1660: Their Curriculum and Practice* (1908; rpt New York: Augustus M. Kelley, 1970).
Weatherby, Harold L., *Mirrors of Celestial Grace: Patristic Theology in Spenser's Allegory* (Toronto: Toronto University Press, 1994).
Weisheipl, J.A., 'The Structure of the Arts Faculty in the Medieval University', *British Journal of Educational Studies*, 19 (1971), 263–71.
Welsby, Paul A., *Lancelot Andrewes, The Preacher, 1555–1626* (London: SPCK, 1958).
Whitelocke, James, *Liber Famelicus of Sir James Whitelocke*, ed. John Bruce, Camden Society, No. 70 (Westminster: J.B. Nichols and Sons, 1858).
Wilson, Rev. H.B., *History of Merchant-Taylors' School* (London: Marchant and Galabin, 1814).
Wilson, H.S., 'The Cambridge Comedy "Pedantius" and Gabriel Harvey's "Ciceronianus"', *Studies in Philology*, 45 (1948), 578–91.
Wilson-Okamura, David, 'Problems in the Virgilian Career', *Spenser Studies*, 26 (2011), 1–30.
Worden, Blair, *The Sound of Virtue: Philip Sidney's* Arcadia *and Elizabethan Politics* (New Haven: Yale University Press, 1996).
Woudhuysen, H.R., 'Letters, Spenser's and Harvey's', *Spenser Encyclopedia* (Toronto: University of Toronto Press, 1990), 434–5.
Yates, Frances A., 'Queen Elizabeth as Astraea', *Journal of the Warburg and Courtauld Institute*, 10 (1947), 69–70.

Unpublished material

Jameson, Thomas Hugh, 'The *Gratulationes Valdinenses* of Gabriel Harvey', unpublished PhD dissertation, Yale University, 1938.
Woudhuysen, H.R., 'Leicester's Literary Patronage: A Study of the English Court, 1578–1582', unpublished DPhil thesis, University of Oxford, 1982.

Online resources

Forsett, Edward, *Pedantius*, ed. and trans. Dana F. Sutton, www.philological.bham.ac.uk/forsett/contents.html.
ODNB, *Oxford Dictionary of National Biography*, ed. H.C.G. Matthew and Brian Harrison, 60 vols (Oxford, 2004). I have updated my citations from the 2004 printed edition to the 2008 version cited online as per September 2018.
Spenser and the Tradition: English Poetry, 1579–1830, compiled by David Hill Radcliffe. http://Spenserians.cath.vt.edu.
World Spenser Bibliography, ed. Donald Stump. http://bibs.slu.edu/Spenser.

Index

active / contemplative life 120, 128–9
Adams, Simon 151, 214, 217
aegrotat payments 53–4
allegory / typology 1, 37–8, 143–4
Anderson, Judith ix, 86, 106, 131, 195, 206, 217–18, 224, 227–8
Andrewes, Lancelot 25–7, 30, 43–4, 53–4, 224, 230
Anjou and Alençon, François Duc de 79, 100, 103, 105, 115, 117, 125, 133–5, 137, 141, 148, 150–2, 183, 213
Ascham, Roger, author of the *Schoolmaster* 39, 41, 43, 48, 59, 69, 120, 124, 132, 217
Attwater, Aubrey, Librarian, Pembroke College 53, 67–9, 217
Aylmer, John, Bishop of London 75, 78, 80–3, 86, 93–4, 161, 209, 229

Bacon, Sir Francis 35, 40, 47, 218
Barker, William ix, xiii, 27, 30, 48, 218
Bates, Catherine 28, 152, 218
Bennett, Josephine Waters 218
Berry, Lloyd E. 151, 229
Black, Joseph L. 86, 224
Boyle, Elizabeth 9, 28, 66, 118, 168
Boyle, Richard, first Earl of Cork 201
Bridgewater, Richard 95, 188
Brink, Jean R. 27–8, 46–8, 84, 131–2, 169, 218
Browne, Lancelot 57, 63
 addresses Harvey to show that he has not received the MA 65

Bryskett, Lodowick (biography) 2, 5, 110, 115, 117–22, 131–2, 184–5, 210, 214, 226
Bryskett, Lodowick (works) 131–2, 214, 219
 A Discourse of Civill Life 126–7, 218, 229
 elegies on Sidney 118, 131, 229
 Spenser's *Amoretti* alludes to Bryskett 118–19
Burghley, Lord *see* Cecil, William
Bynneman, Henry 44, 91–2, 107, 173, 175–6, 181, 216

Camden, William 1, 6, 10, 27, 40, 47, 63, 136–7, 151, 204, 216
Canny, Nicholas 184–5, 196, 206, 219
Carroll, D. Allen 168, 219
Cartwright, Thomas 54–7, 66, 74, 136, 202–3, 209
Cecil, Robert 115, 179, 195, 205, 219
Cecil, William, Lord Burghley, Lord Treasurer of England 7, 32, 51, 56, 68, 76, 94–7, 108, 114–17, 121–3, 135, 160, 191, 196, 202–7, 215
 Harvey's letter to Burghley asking his support to be appointed University Orator at Cambridge 188–9
celibacy 66–8, 73, 78–80
Chapman, George ix
Chaucer 1, 34, 69, 77–8, 108, 158–9
Church of England 61, 64, 73–4, 78, 80, 84, 201–2
Churchyard, Thomas 86, 99, 124, 132, 171, 206, 210, 216, 224

232   Index

Collinson, Patrick 86, 219
Cooper, Thomas, Bishop of Lincoln, 1571; translated to Winchester on 12 March 1581 82, 86, 161, 218
Court Humanism 119–23, 126, 131, 224
  Sir Thomas Smith as ideal 121
  see also Levy F. J.
Croft, Sir James 192–3

Daniel, Samuel 8–9, 201
Dees, Jerome 74, 85, 220
Denny, Edward 90, 120, 122, 185–7, 194, 201, 211
  Letter to Walsingham on Grey and Ireland 196
De Vere, Edward, seventeenth Earl of Oxford 32, 46, 52, 58, 96, 125, 172, 187, 192, 226
Devereux, Robert, second Earl of Essex 107, 116, 122, 131, 186, 191, 205, 210, 212–13, 221
Devereux, William, first Earl of Essex 25, 81, 100, 111, 133–4
Drant, Thomas 172
Drayton, Michael 8–9, 27, 32, 46, 218
Dudley, Lettice (born Knollys). Widow of William Devereux, first Earl of Essex 25, 100–11, 133–4, 182, 207
  Topical allusions in Spenser's *March* eclogue 80–1
Dudley, Robert, first Earl of Leicester 72–3, 76, 81, 85–6, 94–109 *passim*, 119–20, 122, 125–8, 129, 135, 150, 168–9, 172, 182–3, 185, 196, 203, 206–7, 210–11, 214–15, 217–18, 221–2, 224, 230
  Leicester House 25, 109–11, 114, 116, 118, 129, 135, 157
  Leicester's Commonwealth 33, 46, 127, 157
  Shepheardes Calender first dedicatee 160–2
Duellum 125–8
Duncan-Jones, Katherine xiii, 103–4, 107, 109, 111, 119, 130–2, 134, 151, 169, 196, 220
Dyer, Edward 23, 160, 168–9

E. K. 77, 80–3, 95, 99, 139, 141–52 *passim*, 153–60, 162, 165, 168–9, 173, 176, 178–9, 191, 212, 227, 229
  'fine addition' of a Gloss 157
  Harvey as collaborator 154–60

Early Modern Chivalric Code 4, 110, 119–23, 126–7, 129, 198
  Henry Sidney 123–5
  idealized knightly service 121–2
  see also James, Mervyn; Kane, Brendan; McCoy, Richard; Trim, David
Eccles, Mark 6, 18, 29, 169, 220
Elizabeth I 3–5, 9, 15, 35, 41, 44, 69, 79, 96–100, 103–4, 113–14, 119, 122, 125–6, 133–52 *passim*, 168, 182–3, 202, 220, 224, 229–30
  cult of Elizabeth 139–42
  Dutch independence 104, 106
England
  international political situations in 1579 132–8
Erasmus 166
Essex, first Earl of *see* Devereux, William
Essex, second Earl of *see* Devereux, Robert

Fitzmaurice, James [ODNB James Fitz Maurice Fitzgerald] 115, 133–4
Fletcher, Giles 26, 95
Fletcher, John 22–3
Forsett, Edward 189–91, 196, 230

Galen 104
Gascoigne, George 42, 48, 95, 108, 162, 181, 209–10, 218, 226
Gellar, Sherri 169, 221
Gless, Daryl J. 74, 85, 221
Goldberg, Jonathan 169, 221
Grafton, Anthony 69, 90, 107, 130, 212, 214, 221, 223
Greenlaw, Edwin xiv, 107, 204–6, 221, 228
Gregerson, Linda 74, 85, 221
Greville, Fulke (later Lord Brooke) 107, 110, 120–2, 131–2, 184, 221
  admirer of Sir Henry Sidney 115–17
  boat trip on River Shannon estuary with Bryskett and possibly Spenser 184–5
  witnessed Sidney's tennis court quarrel with the Earl of Oxford 125–6
Grey, Lord Arthur 2, 4, 48, 73–4, 85, 118, 126, 194, 196, 203–5, 221, 223
  appointment as Lord Deputy 181–8
  patron of Gascoigne 209–10

Index

Grindal, Edmund, Archbishop of Canterbury 8, 19–20, 25, 49–51, 56, 68, 74–6, 78, 84, 86, 203, 208–10, 227
Grindal as Spenser's Algrind 81–3
Grosart, Alexander B. 52–4, 68, 71, 84, 168, 207
  biographer of middle-class Spenser xiii, 11–13, 16–17, 228
  editor, Harvey, *Works* xi, 88, 93, 106, 109, 170–1, 223
  transcription of 'Nowell Account Book' as *Spending of the Money of Robert Nowell* xiv, 18–30 *passim*, 221

Hackett, Helen 141, 146, 151–2, 221
Hadfield, Andrew viii, 1–2, 4, 6n.4, 11–17 *passim* 27–8, 86–7, 106, 174, 195, 204, 206–7, 221, 223
  lost years 84n.5
  Machabyas Chylde as Rosalind 168–9
  portrays Spenser as annoying Leicester 86n.28, 168n.9, 207n.15
  Spenser as would-be secretary 85n.11
Hamer, Douglas 22, 30, 221
  on Spenser's wife 167, 169
Hammer, Paul 90, 107, 122, 131, 221
Harington, Sir John 28, 82, 197, 210, 222
  attended performance of *Pedantius* with Essex 190–1
  lineage and Spencers of Althorp 15–16
Harvey, Gabriel (biographical) 5, 88–109 *passim*, 153–60
  ambition to be University Orator 5, 93, 160, 173–4, 181, 188–9, 191, 194, 211, 213
  controversy over M.A. degree with Pembroke fellows 58–65
  Harvey and Spenser 60, 88–109 *passim*, 187
  Harvey as court humanist 119–23
  interest in Ramism 59
  lost works 178–9
  not Spenser's tutor 5, 57
  quarrel with Perne at funeral of Sir Thomas Smith 92–3, 154–5
Harvey, Gabriel (works)
  Anticosmopolita 94, 178
  Ciceronianus, Rhetor 91, 175, 230
  Familiar Letters or Three proper and wittie, familiar letters 170–97
  audience of *Familiar Letters* 174–5

Harvey's agency 174
Letter-Book and *Familiar Letters* 157–8, 179–81
Nashe on authorship 176
Part I: three letters dated 2–23 April 1580 171
  attack on Andrew Perne 92–3, 171, 188–9
  discussion of prosody 171
  earthquake letter 171–3, 178, 192–3
  Speculum Tuscanismi 172, 190, 192–3
Part II: two letters dated 5–23 October 1579 172
  Spenser's Latin poem addressed to Harvey 172
  Well-Willer's Preface 171–8
Foure Letters x, 29, 58, 69, 89, 107–8, 173, 176, 192–4, 213, 216
  revisits submission of *Familiar Letters* to the press 188–9
Gratulationes Valdinenses 95–106
  de Oscula 96–8, 138, 156
  de Vultu Iali (Bk 2) 97, 99, 156, 211
  no poem of Spenser's included 97
  sum iecur (Bk. 4) 138, 104–5, 190
Letter-Book 16, 60, 62, 69, 89–90, 92, 97, 107–9, 157–8, 168, 173, 176, 193, 213
Letter-Book and *Familiar Letters* 176, 179–81
Marginalia 107, 111, 123, 131, 157, 187, 190, 196, 199, 211
Smithus; vel Musarum Lachrymae 67, 92, 97, 100, 154, 175, 190, 216
Harvey, Richard 93–4, 107, 216
Astrological Discourse dedicated to Bishop Aylmer 94
Hatton, Sir Christopher 96, 103, 126, 135–6, 201
Heninger, S. K. 130, 151, 168, 222
  credits Harvey with design of *Shepheardes Calender* 158
Herbert, Lady Mary (born Sidney) 8, 113, 117, 135
Baynard's Castle, the Pembroke's London house 117–18, 134–5, 151
Herron, Thomas ix, 6, 222
Hieatt, A. Kent 11, 28, 222
Higginson, James Jackson 86, 222
Holinshed, Raphael 47, 206, 216
Hume, Anthea 85, 222

Ireland
  feudal world of medieval past 198, 200–1
  religious toleration 201–4

James, Mervyn 131, 223
Jameson, Thomas Hugh 100, 105, 108, 223, 230
Jardine, Lisa 69, 90, 130, 199, 206, 212, 214, 221, 223
Jenkins, Harold 196, 223
Johnson, Francis R. 107, 223
Johnson, Lyn Staley 152, 223
Jones, Norman viii
Judson, Alexander viii, xiii, 28–9, 72, 84, 204, 206, 223
  aristocratic Spenser 11–16

Kane, Brendan 131, 223
Kaske, Carol 11, 28, 74, 85, 223
King, John 85, 223
Knowles, R. B. xiii, 12, 19, 28–9, 208, 223
  Spenser not the son of John Spenser merchant tailor 17
Kuin, Roger xiii, 131, 196, 214, 228

Lane, Robert 146, 152, 224
Langherne, Richard (Langher and Langhorne) 52–5, 61–2, 69
Leicester, Countess of see Dudley, Lettice
Leicester, first Earl of see Dudley, Robert
Levy, F. J. 119–23, 131, 224
literacy 31, 35–6, 46–7, 218, 220
Lodge, Thomas 10, 42
Loftus, Adam (Archbishop of Armagh in 1563; translated to Dublin in 1567) 55, 68, 202
Long, Percy 53, 82, 85, 224
Lucas, Scott 86, 224
Lyly, John 6, 107, 191–3, 197, 217–18
Lyly, William 38, 46
Lynn, Richard E. 81, 86, 224

McCabe, Richard viii, xiv, 6, 27–8, 46, 81, 84, 86, 149, 152, 169, 224–5, 228
McCanles, Michael 168, 225
MacCarthy-Morrogh, Michael 206, 224
McCoy, Richard 131, 225
Machiavelli 100–3, 105, 108, 138
  in debate on Machiavellian issue: should a prince be feared or loved 95–6

McLane, Paul E. 86–7, 148–9, 152, 214, 225
Mallette, Richard 74, 85, 224
Marlowe, Christopher 1, 6, 201
Marprelate tracts 55, 76, 82, 86, 224–5
May, Steven ix, 131, 161, 169, 224
Mears, Natalie 151, 225
Merchant Taylors' School 5, 7, 9–10, 12, 16–23, 31–48 passim, 53, 75, 100, 120, 208–9, 225, 230
Miller, David 6, 225
Milton, John 37, 41, 55, 212
Montrose, Louis 142, 146, 151–2, 225
Morgan, Hiram 206, 225
Moul, Virginia 106, 108–9
Mounts, Charles E. 81, 86, 225
Mulcaster, Richard (biographical) 20, 24, 35–6, 40–4, 46–8, 120, 129, 131, 218, 220, 225, 226
  Buckeridge's funeral sermon 26, 30
  'Nowell Account Book' 18–27 passim
Mulcaster, Richard (works)
  First Part of the Elementary, which entreateth Chiefly of the Right Writing of our English Tongue 40–1, 44, 47–8, 226
  Positions Concerning the Training up of Children 27, 30, 41, 47–8, 218, 220
Mulryan, John ix, 108

Nashe, Thomas xii, 5–6, 10, 48, 58, 60–1, 88–9, 96, 103–5, 107, 154–6, 169, 170–97 passim, 201, 212–13, 226
Nelson, Allen 46, 132, 226
Neville, Alexander 61
Neville, Thomas 61–5, 75
  leader of opposition to Harvey at Pembroke College 61–4
Nichols, John xii, 47–8, 96, 98, 106, 108, 226
Norbrook, David 6, 85, 152, 226
Norreys, Sir John 131
Norreys, Sir Thomas 126
Nowell Account Book 5, 12, 17, 18–30 passim, 52, 54, 73, 208, 215
  entries related to Spenser 21, 22, 52
Nowell, Alexander 18–21, 29, 70, 208, 209
Nowell's Catechism 37
Nowell, Robert 5, 18–21, 208, 221

Index

Oram, William ix-x, 46, 130, 205, 207, 226, 229
Osborn, James 186-7, 196, 226
Oxford, seventeenth Earl of *see* De Vere, Edward

Parker, Matthew (Archbishop of Canterbury) 51, 61, 69, 74, 218
Patterson, Annabel 149, 152, 226
Pedantius 5, 91, 169, 194, 196-7, 213, 220, 230
  Ridicule of Harvey 189-91
Pelham, William (Lord Justice of Ireland) 134, 184, 196, 215
Pembroke College 49-69 *passim*
Pembroke College Account Books 4, 52, 65, 70, 215
Pembroke, Countess of *see* Herbert, Lady Mary (born Sidney)
Perne, Andrew 55, 74-7, 86, 89, 154-5, 171, 196-7, 202, 209, 213, 214
  Harvey's nemesis 92-3, 188, 191, 193
Peterson, Richard 205, 207, 226
Phillips, James E. 142-5, 152, 226
Ponsonby, William 28, 45
Prescott, Anne ix, 48, 168, 226
progress of 1578 95-109 *passim*
Puritan 49, 54-9, 61-4, 68, 73-6, 79-82, 84-6, 92, 136, 138, 201-3, 219, 223
Puttenham, George 163

Quitslund, Jon 106, 169, 174, 195, 227

Ralegh, Sir Walter 3, 5, 10, 113, 119, 126, 149, 198-203 *passim*, 210-13
Ramus, Peter 59, 62
Ringler, William ix, 160, 169, 227
Rosenberg, Eleanor 85, 108, 227

Schleiner, Louise 168, 227
Shakespeare, William 1, 6, 8-9, 27, 32, 36, 41, 65
  anti-court sentiment 129
  'carpet knight' 122
Shore, David R. 154, 168, 227
Shuger, Debora 198, 206, 227
Sidney, Lady Mary (born Dudley) 116-17, 122
Sidney, Sir Henry 2, 75, 114-18, 123-5, 184, 198, 205, 210, 215, 218

Sidney, Sir Philip (biography) 1, 3, 4-5, 7, 8, 10, 33, 46, 90-2, 96, 104, 107, 110-15, 117-22, 126, 129-32, 135, 148-9, 160-1, 169, 210, 213-14, 217, 220, 224, 226-30
  early modern chivalric code 119-23
  letter to Edward Denny regarding Lord Grey, May 1580 185-8
  tennis court quarrel with Oxford 125-8
Sidney, Sir Philip (works)
  Arcadia 162
  Astrophil and Stella 8-9
  Defence of Leicester 33, 46, 125-8, 132
  Defence of Poesy 161-2, 169, 187
Singleton, Hugh 79, 136-8, 151, 173, 176, 219
Skelton, John 8, 168, 212, 214, 223, 225
  Boke of Colin Clout (1530) 158
  skeltonics in Harvey's *Letter-Book* 158-9
Smith, G. C. Moore xii, 107, 196-7, 220, 227
  editor of *Pedantius* 190
Smith, Sir Thomas 58, 89-2, 94, 154-5, 175, 181, 190, 192, 206, 225, 227
  as exemplar of court humanist 120-1
  colonial investments 198-9
  patron of Gabriel Harvey 52, 90
  Smithus, vel Musarum Lachrymae 92, 100, 155, 175, 190
Smith, Thomas the younger or Captain Smith 199-200
Spencers of Althorp 7, 13-16, 26, 28
  Edward 13, 52
Spenser, Edmund (biography)
  anonymity of Spenser 74, 83, 161-2, 187
  biographical methodology 2, 5
  biographies 11-18
  birth date 9-11
  meetings with Queen Elizabeth 3-4
  rental receipt in Spenser's hand 71-2
  Shepheardes Calender as high point in Spenser's early life 214
  Spenser and Harvey 88-109 *passim*
  Spenser and Sidney 110-32 *passim*
Spenser, Edmund (works)
  Astrophel 117-18, 131, 229
  Colin Clouts Come Home Againe 3-4, 15, 119, 168

236 Index

Complaints 13, 45, 48, 117, 130, 178–9, 198, 200, 204–5, 207, 215, 218, 228
  Mother Hubbeds Tale, or Prosopopoia 94, 112, 123, 127, 130, 138, 151, 187, 204–5, 207, 215
  Ruines of Time 112, 121
  Virgils Gnat 204
Faerie Queene 13, 15, 21, 32–4, 37, 44–6, 66, 69, 74, 83, 110, 112–14, 117–20, 128–30, 137–9, 142–3, 146, 162, 168, 185, 187, 195, 204, 209, 211–12, 226, 228
Shepheardes Calender 4, 7, 20, 77, 86
  dedicated first to Leicester and then to Sidney 110, 112–14, 133, 160
  Januarie and homosexuality 154, 158, 164–6
  March and topicality 80–2
  Aprill 133–52 passim
    critique of cult of Elizabeth 140–2
    function of Niobe 145–6
    omission of Astraea from Aprill 141, 147–8
    polyvalent symbolism 142–8
  Maye and dialogical structure 76–80
  Julye and topicality 81–4
  October and courtly panegyric 138–9
  November and crosscurrents with Aprill 3, 147–50
    links between Elizabeth and Dido 147–8
  December and Spenser's youth 16, 50, 99
Theatre for Worldlings 44–6, 48, 179, 209, 220
View of the present state of Ireland 6, 198
  execution of Murrough O'Brien 2–3
Stern, Virginia xii, 69, 84, 89, 105, 107–9, 129, 173, 186, 193, 195, 229
Still, John 24–5, 93, 110
Stillinger, Jack 168, 229
Stone, Lawrence 35, 47, 229
Stubbs, John 79, 151, 213, 229
  author of Gaping Gulf, attack on French match 135–8

Travers, Walter 85, 202–3, 206, 220
Tribble, Evelyn 168, 229

Trim, David J. B. 131, 229
Tyndall, Humphrey 58, 60, 63–4
  chaplain to Leicester 25, 111

Usher, Brett 67, 69, 73, 81, 86, 229

Van der Noot, Jan 44–6, 48, 209, 226
Van Dorsten, Jan xiii, 48, 130, 132, 169, 218, 228, 229
Venn, J. A. 4, 6, 68–9, 217, 221, 229

Walsingham, Sir Francis (Queen Elizabeth's principal secretary) 86, 115, 121, 135–6, 184–5, 196, 203, 213, 215
Watkins, John 3, 6, 86, 229
Watts, Thomas, Archdeacon of Middlesex 20, 23–5, 46, 53, 208
Weatherby, Harold 74, 85, 230
Webbe, William author of Discourse of English Poetrie (1586)
  praise of Harvey 163–4
Whetstone, George 169, 210, 217
  mistaken attribution of Shepheardes Calender to Sidney 163
  Sidney not a 'carpet knight' 162
Whitelock, Sir Thomas 42–3, 48, 230
Whitgift, John (Archbishop of Canterbury) 50, 61, 66, 68, 85–6, 92–3, 202, 209, 218–19, 227
  Elizabethan Settlement 74–6, 83
  Fifteen Articles debate with Travers and Sparke 203
  Henry Sidney's deputy when Bishop of Worcester 117, 184
  revises Cambridge statutes 54–8
Wilson-Okamura, David 169, 230
Withie, William 191, 195, 197, 218
Worden, Blair 130, 151, 230
Woudhuysen, Henry 130, 196, 214, 230

Yates, Frances A. 139, 151, 230
Young, John (Master of Pembroke College, 1567–78; Bishop of Rochester, 1578–1605) 4, 24–5, 34, 46, 50–1, 53, 58, 60–5, 68, 80–7, 93, 105, 111–12, 161, 168, 171, 189, 209–10, 213, 223, 229
  anonymity of Roffy's boy 74, 161–2
  married Watts' widow 20
  Spenser's patron 50–1, 70–4

EU authorised representative for GPSR:
Easy Access System Europe, Mustamäe tee 50,
10621 Tallinn, Estonia
gpsr.requests@easproject.com

www.ingramcontent.com/pod-product-compliance
Lightning Source LLC
Chambersburg PA
CBHW070237240426
43673CB00044B/1824